W9-CBQ-625

ALSO BY TOM CHRISTOPHER

In Search of Lost Roses
Water-Wise Gardening

ALSO BY MARTY ASHER

Shelter
57 Reasons Not to Have a Nuclear War

ALSO BY TOM CHRISTOPHER
AND MARTY ASHER

Compost This Book!

THE 20-MINUTE GARDENER

The Garden of Your Dreams
Without Giving Up Your Life,
Your Job, or Your Sanity

Illustrations by Steven D. Guarnaccia

RANDOM HOUSE • NEW YORK

The 20-MINUTE GARDENER

Tom Christopher and Marty Asher

To Joe, for bringing us together.
We'll never forgive him.

Copyright © 1997 by Marty Asher and Tom Christopher
Illustrations copyright © 1997 by Steven D. Guarnaccia

All rights reserved under International and Pan-American Copyright
Conventions. Published in the United States by Random House, Inc.,
New York, and simultaneously in Canada by Random House
of Canada Limited, Toronto.

Library of Congress Cataloging-in-Publication Data is available

ISBN 0-679-44814-4

Random House website address: http://www.randomhouse.com/

Printed in the United States of America on acid-free paper

4689753

Book design by Carole Lowenstein

Contents

Introduction

"That's it," snarled Marty. "I can't deal with this @#$%&* garden anymore."

And so was born the 20-minute gardener.

Marty, a recent émigré from city to suburb, had called his literary collaborator, Tom—who also happens to be a professional horticulturist—for a consultation. As he generally is when he contemplates his garden, Marty was hysterical.

"Calm down," said Tom. He had been through Marty's semi-nervous breakdown over compost a few years earlier.*

"Calm down? Calm down? Just look around you." Marty gestured wildly from his seat by the teak patio table. "It's mid-June. My roses are spontaneously generating Japanese beetles. My lawn is knee-high; the mower cracked a blade when I strayed into the focal point—the pile of rocks that high-priced landscaper put right in the middle of the front yard. The meadow in a can that was supposed to take care of the backyard has produced two daisies and two hundred thousand weeds. The native shrubs I planted in April are taking over—they're threatening to start a casino.

"I'm an editor, so I bought a bunch of gardening books to help me out, and they all read like encyclopedias. How the hell do I know what my drainage is? Do I have to call a plumber to plant my flowers? My neighbors won't speak to me because they're trying to flee and no one will buy their homes when they see what's next door. There's only one solution."

"Marty, no—"

"Yes, the cement truck arrives tomorrow. I'm going to pave the whole thing over. I'm going home, Tom; I should never have left the city."

---

* Marty's hysteria over compost and Tom's response resulted in *Compost This Book!* (Sierra Club, 1994).

"Marty, you don't want to do that. You've forgotten. You like to garden."

"You're right, I did. But that was before I actually started doing it. I thought it was going to be *fun* and healthy exercise. You know, digging around in the dirt for an hour, watering something, then waking up the next morning and going, 'Wow, tomatoes.' But this is worse than work. At least I get paid at work. At least I get a lunch hour at work. In the garden, I can pull weeds for an entire day, then it rains for an hour and it's like all I did was provoke them."

"But it *is* fun," Tom insisted (weakly).

"Why can't you just garden for a little while every day and keep it under control? If growing plants was really that difficult wouldn't the world have turned into one vast desert centuries ago? Tom, why is gardening so damned complicated? Isn't there a better way?"

"Of course not," Tom replied, in horror. He's a Serious Professional Horticulturist. He has spent many years studying the gardening literature, secretly marveling over the countless ways men and women have found to complicate this relatively simple activity. In what other profession do they still speak Latin? No, Tom knows that complication is the basic commodity of his craft, for it is what stuns the amateurs and forces them to call for professional help (like his).

Still, Tom did feel sorry for Marty. Besides, Tom's knees were still aching from last weekend's weeding marathon in the herbaceous borders, and he knew that double-digging the new radicchio bed this weekend was going to inflame the compressed disk in his lower back. (Tom maintains that no one is a true gardener until he or she has developed at least one compressed disk.) Yes, secretly Tom, too, was longing for an easier way. But it would never do to admit that to a civilian. Hypocrisy seemed like the best policy. Tom raised his right hand.

"As God is my witness, Marty—"

Suddenly there was a blinding flash of light and a deafening boom.

"Hey look at that!" Crawling out from under the patio table, Tom pointed to the smoke rising from its fashionably weathered top.

"Wow. Close call," said Marty. "Almost hit by lightning."

"But look at it," said Tom. "There are letters burned into it."

They looked together and this is what they saw:

The Ten Commandments
of 20-Minute Gardening

1. There shall be no weeds—you don't have time for them.

2. You shall never buy more than three of any plant—four is the beginning of monotony and smacks of the unimaginative excess that makes traditional gardening such hard work.

3. You shall not spray any plant more than once a season, or more than two years running. If it requires more, it should be in a nursing home, not in your garden.

4. Nursery catalogs, while a great pleasure to read, have no relevance to gardening, unless used as mulch. The magnificent plants described in and pictured on their pages have never actually appeared on this planet.

5. The soil and the weather in your garden are unlike those of any other in the world—including those of your neighbors on either side. The 20-minute gardener sometimes has to wing it.

6. Bugs are the gardener's equivalent of Vietnam—they cannot be defeated by sheer firepower. They know the country better than you do. But you can outsmart them.

7. Honor thy lawn mower and keep it in good repair.

8. It always rains right after you water, but that's life, and it doesn't change the fact that your hose is your most important gardening tool. The 20-minute gardener uses it to create a garden that will be virtually weed-, bug-, and disease-free and that will flourish with minimal maintenance.

9. When in doubt, do nothing. The problem will either get worse (in which case it will become obvious what you have to do) or it will go away.

10. Compost happens.

And, because HE always gives good weight, an extra commandment, the last and the most important:

11. You shall spend no more than twenty minutes a day working in your garden, and your tasks will be only those that you enjoy.

THE 20-MINUTE GARDENER

Chapter I

What's Wrong with This Picture?

Both Tom and Marty were sobered by this close encounter with the primordial force, but unfortunately, neither one was especially enlightened. Marty fretted about his contract with Country Casuals Concrete and how to remove the burns from his designer table. Tom could not imagine how they were going to create and maintain a garden in just 20 minutes a day—and if they did, what would that do to his reputation in the horticultural world?

Then Marty took charge. In his masterful way, he volunteered to suspend all activity. He would do nothing to his yard, he would wait. Meanwhile, it would be Tom's job to figure out where gardening had gone wrong. Only when they understood this, Marty said, could they interpret the new scripture that he would be sanding off his table. So Tom must search back through the canon of gardening literature (all those composted white males!). He must go back to the beginning, Marty said. Back to the very first garden.

Tom's Report

In the beginning there were weeds. But no one minded. In fact, our ancestors loved weeds. As primitive hunter-gatherers, they depended on weeds for everything from salads to clothing and laxatives. Identifying the virtues of each plant had, of course, involved a good deal of hardship. Can you imagine the time your progenitor went in to the clinic with a complaint about dry, flaky skin and the shaman said, hey, what the heck, this ivy-like number here with the three shiny leaflets looks soothing? But despite the casualties along the way, humans preserved a touching, Father Flanagan–like faith in the basic goodness of plants, and persisted.

No doubt man (and we do mean man) persisted because of the sheer convenience of the situation. Whenever the family wanted something, you grabbed your hat, whistled up the dog, and went out for a walk. You just took whatever you wanted. A truly stress-free life. It couldn't last.

The end of this idyll came toward the end of the New Stone Age, sometime around nine thousand years ago. Paleontologists theorize that it was the end of the last ice age that upset the apple cart, for as the glaciers retreated the climate changed, and local populations of plants and animals also changed, drastically. This, of course, threatened to put hunter-gatherers back at square one as far as weed research went. So when some genius suggested building a mud dam to trap snow and rain runoff and thus ensure the preservation of a favorite weed patch, the hunter-gatherers listened.

[Could this explain Commandment 8? Tom and Marty were later to draw from this a whole system of garden maintenance, as outlined in the chapters on pests and weeds, chapters 8 and 9.]

That marked the end of man's golden age. For interfering with nature in this way not only demanded hard work but also created an opportunity for experts and consultants. Suddenly, you had to make all sorts of decisions. Which weed patches did you foster, and which ones did you let die? Which were the *good* weeds, and which were the *bad* ones? What besides building dams should we be doing to encourage the growth of good weeds? Maybe we could even make good weeds grow where the bad ones are growing now? This kind of judgmental thinking was the beginning of gardening.

The practice of this new craft had obvious benefits. It made men (and again, we do mean men) far more productive. Whereas previously they had always had an excuse to wander off on what they claimed were important errands, now they had to spend the bulk of every day laboring in the weed patches, where the responsible members of society (we bet you can guess their sex) could keep an eye on them and make sure that they really were working. Hard.

[Oddly enough, this issue of sexual differentiation among gardeners was not addressed in the Commandments. Tom and Marty did explore it, however, and included their results in chapter 3.]

The invention of gardening not only meant less free time, it also meant settling down in one place; this is what archaeologists call the "effective village stage of development" (a big improvement over the ineffectual village stage). Settling down and really putting your back into growing weeds assured a far more reliable food supply, but it brought with it a host of worries. Gardeners (male and female) found that they now had to worry about the weather. They worried about the bad weeds, and why they kept coming back despite all the gardeners did to discourage them. Gardeners had to begin worrying about bugs, too. Previously, insects had just been an alternative form of protein. Now, they might eat your good weeds—and why did bugs always seem to prefer good weeds to bad ones?

[The antiquity of this problem underscores the importance of Commandment 6—Tom and Marty have devoted a whole chapter, chapter 9, to the resolution of this issue.]

What did the first gardens look like? To be honest, we don't really know. The only information we have about that comes from the Bible, which makes them sound pretty good, a bit like a cross between an arboretum and Club Med. But as you may recall, that first essay in gardening ended with the expulsion of the human residents and with an injunction to eat bread in the sweat of your face. That, unfortunately, set the tone for gardening for a long time to come.

For although gardening continued to grow in popularity, somehow gardeners became proud of doing things the hard way. What had begun as a convenience (keeping the weeds accessible) soon developed into a kind of penance.

No doubt all of this occurred because politicians got in on the act. Or maybe it was the other way around: the politicians became fascinated by gardening because it was punitive and inefficient. Whatever the reason, gardening soon became the sport of kings, queens, and megalomaniacs.

One of the first great kingdoms, and the site of the first famous garden, was the Assyrian empire that sprang up in the Middle East when a tough, aggressive group of people (the Assyrians) figured out that they would never have to wipe sweat off their bread again if they simply announced that everyone in the effective villages was working for them—and backed up this announcement with appropriate threats. The Assyrians began doing this sometime around 3000 B.C., and by 800 B.C. they owned all of what is now Iraq, Syria, Jordan, Israel, Egypt, and parts of Saudi Arabia as well.

[Alas, threats are no longer adequate as motivation for the workforce. Tom and Marty explain what is in chapter 3.]

With all those villagers at their disposal, the Assyrian kings and queens could really cut loose with the landscaping. In fact, this was when Queen Semiramis invented a style of gardening that remains popular to this very day and that has been Tom's professional nemesis. He calls it "tour de force gardening." This is the school of gardening that takes a perverse pride in flying in the face of nature and forcing plants to grow in areas where they have no business growing. Tour de force gardeners grow subtropical shrubs in the North and cool-loving rhododendrons in the South. Queen Semiramis set the example for all of this by making the clearly idiotic decision to plant an alpine garden in her capital, Babylon.

[Tour de force gardening is implicitly prohibited by Commandment 3; Tom and Marty assault this gardening style head on in their chapters about selecting garden plants, chapters 6 and 7.]

Babylon was a hot and humid city in the middle of a lowland plain—hardly the place to cultivate mountain plants. But Semiramis dealt with this difficulty by ignoring it. She ordered up a herd of effective villagers and had them build a ziggurat, a sort of step-sided pyramid made of bricks. On top of each step was a terrace, and these the queen had covered with soil and filled with mountain plants.

Ostensibly, the goal was to provide the queen with a refreshing escape from the sticky reality of Babylon. But Tom has worked for enough rich clients to know what the real motive was: Semiramis wanted to prove that she could make the underlings sweat and that she could afford anything she wanted—that she was rich enough to defy even nature. The gardeners who were hauling buckets of water up the steps to revive the withered, homesick plants could have provided another perspective on this garden, but they never did. Which is not surprising, given that bas-reliefs surviving from this period indicate that Assyrian monarchs liked to festoon their gardens with the heads of their enemies.

The most pitiful part of this story is that Semiramis's tasteless monstrosity really wowed the tourists. Indeed, her "hanging gardens" were declared one of the Seven Wonders of the Ancient World. Tom believes this marks the historical beginning of gardening's long decline.

He managed to trace the Assyrian influence right down to the modern day. Sure, subsequent generations created many other kinds of landscapes, but the essential elements—a labor-intensive, impractical design and a childish desire to cheat nature—remained central to virtually all. There were changes along the way: the end of slavery in western Europe meant that garden owners had to draft a lot of serfs instead, and the freeing of the serfs meant that garden owners had to turn to technology and nonunion workers to do the dull, repetitive work. But the trend from the hanging gardens right through Versailles was always toward larger, more expensive, and more impractical landscapes.

[For a penetrating analysis of the modern suburban labor force, see chapter 3.]

Over the millennia, the garden owners' motive also remained the same: pharaohs, caesars, archdukes, and CEOs always wanted to amaze the rubes. What depresses Tom the most about all of this is that the effective villagers, the ones on whose backs the "wonder" gardens were built, almost always went home at the end of the day to re-create something similar—on a meager scale—around their own hovels. So even on the rare day off, the gardeners had to struggle with their own stunted tour de force.

[This, of course, flies in the face of Commandment 11. Tom and Marty lead gardening back onto a spiritually purer path in the next chapter, chapter 2.]

Actually, Tom did uncover one very different approach to gardening. He found it in his own backyard, too. For the very best school of horticulture Tom encountered in all his reading was that practiced in the New World, before the introduction of liability insurance, motor vehicle departments, and all the other accoutrements of civilization. The practitioners of this primitive but brilliant gardening—the peoples we call "Native Americans" in honor of a self-promoting fifteenth-century Italian navigator (Amerigo Vespucci) who never actually visited North America—were not aware, of course, that their world was new. Nor were they familiar with the great gardening traditions of Europe. That, and their unsophisticated technology, were their salvation.

Sad to say, the Native Americans never wrote any garden guides, so for information on their gardens we have to rely on the accounts of early European visitors. From Captain John Smith's *Description of Virginia*, an account published in 1612 of this pioneer's travels up and down the Atlantic Coast of North America, we learn that the natives of the James River region of Virginia not only planted useful species—mulberry trees, grapevines, and sunflowers—around their villages, they also grew roses and wildflowers. In many cases, of course, the garden plants weren't transplanted to the site, but instead were survivors of the native vegetation that the Indians had preserved when clearing the area. Trees, for example, were left standing here and there so that they might provide shade not only for human residents but also for other plant crops.

The emphasis was on doing things the easy way. You chose a spot close to water and game, and selected the trees you wanted to keep. Then you killed the rest by hacking a ring of bark off their trunks. When the dead wood had dried, you set fire to it to clear the land. You poked holes in the ash-covered earth, and planted.

Tall plants such as corn were used as living trellises for climbers such as beans, which, because they can absorb nitrogen directly from the atmosphere, fertilized the soil as they grew. Squash was grown underneath taller plantings so that its broad leaves might serve as a living mulch. In this way plants were intermingled, and large plantings of a single species (what scientists call a monoculture, a type of planting that makes a big, attractive target for pests) were avoided.

[As is called for in Commandment 2. Tom and Marty adapt this attitude for modern use in chapter 9.]

Anyway, pest control, though not as simple as in the Stone Age Middle East, was still simple: when larger animals found a way in through the brushwood piled around the garden, you ate them, and when bugs moved in, you got the shaman to curse them. You kept your house simple—a structure of bent saplings and bark that could be built in an afternoon—so that moving was painless. And move you did, as soon as pests became entrenched or the soil gave signs of wearing out.

Life was easy, especially since the natives were this continent's first democrats; later on, the newly formed United States would model its government on that of the Iroquois. The Native Americans didn't generally give chiefs the authority to put their fellows to work pulling weeds or hauling water.

[Our hats are off to these instinctive respecters of Commandment 8.]

Unfortunately, since there were no beasts of burden, most of the hard work had to be done by the women. According to John Smith, the men "bestowed their times in man-like exercises" such as fishing and hunting, and probably telling lies, maybe going down to the neighborhood tavern, "which is the cause that the women be very painefull, and the men often idle."

But according to an account written by Arthur Caswell Parker, a twentieth-century archaeologist descended from Seneca Indians, his female ancestors got the better part of the deal, for they had the gardening admirably organized. A respected woman in each community was chosen as field matron. She paced the work, announcing breaks as necessary; and during these breaks stories were told, games were played, and songs were sung.

European colonists never learned to sing and play as they gardened (we hope to change that), but otherwise they adopted the native routines virtually intact. They learned to grow native crops in a native fashion, and though they didn't move into bark-covered long houses, their log cabins were almost as easy to erect and abandoned with no more regret when the time came to move on. For many frontiersmen, that time came as soon as there were no longer trees close enough to the cabin that when felled, the firewood dropped right by the door. Why work harder than you had to?

Alas, that blissful innocence couldn't last. Americans began exporting their beautiful native plants to Europe; unfortunately, the traffic went both ways. Within a few generations, European horticulturists—especially English horticulturists—were arriving by the boatload to poison the minds of the more prosperous class of Americans. Get yourself a pair of shears, a lawn mower, and flunkies to operate them, advised the horticultural immigrants—they're all laughing at you back home.

The immigrant gardener's native-born pupils took this a step farther: sprucing up wasn't enough for them. This second generation invented a new profession, that of the "landscape architect," whose premise was that all geographical distinction between Old World and New could be erased, if only the customer would budget enough money. Get the Irish out of Central Park, promised the greatest of these landscape architects, Frederick Law Olmsted, and I'll make it look like a suburb of Liverpool. That's what he did, too.

❀

This was a particularly unfortunate time to take England as a model, because by 1841 that country was already in the depths of the Victorian Age. This era had arrived with the coronation of Queen Victoria four years earlier. An admirable woman in many ways, Her Majesty, however, had no sense of humor. Her mission (and it became a national preoccupation for some sixty years) was to make sure that no one anywhere had a good time. The Victorians certainly succeeded in taking any remaining vestiges of fun out of gardening.

Tom shared with Marty the writings of Gertrude Jekyll (that's GEE-kull, you boob). This woman is widely regarded as the greatest horticultural genius to emerge from Victorian England, and her work as a designer continues to dominate English gardening to this very day. Marty was staggered.

In the photograph on the frontispiece of her book, Marty saw what appeared to be Winston Churchill in drag. Plunging into the text, he was blindsided by passages such as this:

> The good gardener knows with absolute certainty that if he does his part, if he gives the labour, the love and every aid that his knowledge of his craft, his experience of the conditions of his place, and exercise of his personal wit can work together to suggest, that so surely will God give the increase. Then with the honestly-earned success comes the consciousness of encouragement to renewed effort, and, as it were, an echo of the gracious words, "Well done, good and faithful servant."

Note the emphasis on "servant." Jekyll could afford to take a rather philosophical view of gardening because, like most people of her class, she didn't have to do any more of the dirty work than pleased her. Sure, she'd stump around the garden all day in her hobnail boots, and she'd take charge of the glory jobs, like transplanting the phlox or birthing the hedgehogs. But the really unpleasant tasks—pinching all the thousands of wilted blossoms off the rhododendrons, for example—were done by refugees from the poorhouse, whom Miss Jekyll could hire in for pennies a day.

The great woman's cardinal rule was never to settle for one plant when you could shoehorn three or five or even seven into the same spot. She called this planting in "drifts."

[Tom and Marty call this a direct violation of Commandment 2.]

Jekyll was also a great proponent of what the English call "wild gardening," which ostensibly encourages garden plants to flourish in a natural sort of arrangement.

But the truth is that her selections of plants had little to do with what would grow naturally on the site. Instead, they tended to reflect the progress of Britain's colonial wars. As country after country was added to the empire, their floras became *its* flora, so that to fill a "wild garden" in Surrey with Canadian conifers,

Himalayan rhododendrons, and Chinese lilies became the natural thing to do.

It's easy to understand how Gertrude Jekyll could seize control of a nation raised by nannies—her bullying was just a continuation of the same experience. But why did American gardeners also fall under her spell? And why do American gardeners still revere her and follow the rules she laid down some one hundred years ago?

Beats us. But the fact is that Americans are still planting up Kansas City and Seattle as if they were Wapping or East Grinstead. We still garden as if we had all inherited incomes and a staff. Except that now the gardener's boy is us.

So we go on planting Jekyllian "herbaceous borders" of perennial flowers a hundred yards long, filling them with delphiniums, summer phloxes, Russell lupines, and other English-bred perennials that generally behave like annuals in North America. What's more, we have stepped right into the imperialist tradition of plant collecting.

We plant gardens full of alpine plants in the humid suburbs of New York while filling Denver with lowland shrubs and grasses. We put rivers in pipes so that we can spread lawn over the southern California desert, and we wrap fig trees in a hobo's overcoat of newspaper to nurse them through northern winters. It all takes a lot of effort, and it doesn't work very well. Certainly it's no fun. Even when we succeed, the English tell us gently that, well, it's not bad, and not to take it too hard, but we just can't match their climate. To which any reasonable North American must reply: thank goodness.

I Like Ike

By this time, Tom had reluctantly concluded that log cabins were not an option (where to get the trees?), nor were bark houses (the family had all sorts of practical objections). He wondered if maybe he could turn the clock back at least to the paradise of his youth, the Eisenhower administration. Those were the days. He remembered the simple gardens of lawn, foundation planting, and white-washed tractor tire filled with petunias. How easy gardening was then! Run around with the push mower, water the lawn once in a while, lie in the hammock and listen to a baseball game on the portable radio. Wake up late Sunday afternoon. Throw a few burgers on the grill, lay back a few Buds. Happiness. Truth. Justice. The American Way.

Tom realized that his task was to combine the simplicity, innocence, and ease of the '50s with the new, harder realities of the '90s. He had to revive real American gardening, but he could do that only by adapting it to a decade in which everyone worked, in which most gardeners had only forty minutes at home between the day and night jobs. And while he simplified, he also had to satisfy the tastes of a generation that grew up on Russian vodka, Swedish cars, and mesquite-grilled salmon but was now totally stressed out from the demands of multiple children, multiple houses, multiple orgasms, and multiple gardening chores.

The Answer

It seemed impossible. Tom had invited Marty over for a tasting of his homegrown, homemade hard cider, but he was finding no answers in the elixir. He pried the bottle from Marty's hand and poured himself another tankardful. It still seemed impossible. And anyway, why 20 minutes a day?

Even as he voiced this question, Tom was struck by the futility of directing it at Marty. Tom knew that Marty hadn't a clue about how to plan, install, and maintain a real garden. But what Tom hadn't realized was that this was Marty's greatest strength.

"Why 20 minutes a day? That's pretty obvious," said Marty. "That's as much time as anyone I know has to devote to anything besides work. Besides, if *Seinfeld* can fit a whole episode (excluding the commercials) into 20 minutes, then that ought to be enough time to maintain a garden."

"What does *Seinfeld* have to do with it?"

"If we figure out this gardening stuff right," Marty said, "then I'll have time to watch *Seinfeld* or do whatever else I want to do in the meager leisure time I have left."

"Heavy," said Tom, downing the dregs of the cider. "So the challenge is to devise a method of gardening where 20 minutes a day really is all the time you need."

"Ask not what you can do for your garden, ask what your garden can do for you," Marty solemnly contributed.

Tom continued to muse over the sheer outrageousness of the concept. If he could get it to work, he would be a hero to amateur gardeners around the world forever. Of course, he would also be ostracized and ridiculed by the horticultural community and would be unemployed and unemployable for life. But buoyed on the fizz of the cider, Tom again rose to the challenge.

"The answer," Tom proudly announced, "is to reframe the question."

"Brilliant," rejoined Marty. "Only what does that mean?"

"It means," said Tom cockily, "that you stop asking 'How can I possibly maintain the garden of my dreams in the amount of time I can devote to it?' You just can't increase your time and energy to match that dream. So adjust the dream. You say, 'Okay, I've got only so much to give, so how can I use the amount of time that I do have to create a garden that's fun and satisfying, and that can exist in the real world?'

"In other words," he continued, "your garden should reflect *your* lifestyle, not that of the Duke and Duchess of Windsor. The garden lives for you—you don't live for the garden."

"If you can't be with the one you love, love the one you're with," said Marty.

"What does that have to do with it?" asked Tom.

"Great song," said Marty.

THE FIRST 2🕐-MINUTE PROJECT

A 20-Minute Nocturne

Marty had sworn off gardening until all the conceptual work for the new 20-minute method was completed. But Tom couldn't wait. He's a compulsive gardener. Anyway, he doesn't own a television set. He couldn't fill his leisure time with *Seinfeld*.

Not that Tom had had much time to fill lately. He had run into an exceptionally busy period at work. In fact, he was spending so many hours at the word processor that he hardly ever emerged into sunlight; by the time he signed off for the day, the sun had already set. At the moment, 20 minutes seemed like a stretch. The only time when he had an interval of freedom that long was right after dinner, just before he collapsed into bed.

That was not a good time of day to work at the kind of horticulture he had always practiced. Indeed, by then Tom's garden had gone to sleep. The darker-hued foliage and flowers were virtually invisible in the darkness, and the butterflies and birds had gone to roost. Most of the flowers Tom was growing were those like roses or daylilies whose blossoms open in the morning—by nightfall, the blossoms were spent. Some of the flowers, such as those of his water lilies, actually closed up at sunset, so that Tom no longer got to enjoy them at all.

Tom vowed to cultivate healthier work habits; but because he is a realist he also began plotting a kind of gardening better suited to his wretched schedule. It had to be quick, and the result had to be a planting that stayed up late. What was the sense, after all, of creating a garden that the average working person could enjoy only on weekends?

Tom envisioned his new garden as a horticultural nocturne—a short composition designed, like a Chopin piece, to be enjoyed during the hours of darkness. To turn this vision into reality, though, he first had to assemble the players. That is, he had to find flowers that bloom at night.

For help with this, Tom turned to the same source of information that he has relied on ever since his days as a horticultural student. He paid a visit to the library of the New York Botanical Garden. When he had explained his errand, the librarian, with the aplomb of a Houdini, plunged her hand into a drawer and pulled out a fat file of clippings all about night-blooming plants.

From those clippings Tom learned that what he wanted were flowers that had adapted to pollination by moths. Apparently, there are a lot of them, though among the names Tom didn't recognize any he had actually seen growing in gardens. The reason for that quickly became clear as he read the descriptions: these are not flowers that are particularly attractive by day. They are pale; most, indeed, are white. White, after all, is the hue that shows up best by moonlight. Nor are these blossoms long-lasting as a rule. After opening in the evening, most of them wither the next morning as soon as they are struck by the sun.

One special attraction of the night bloomers is their fragrance. Most of the flowers are strongly perfumed; they have to be, for on moonless nights even white flowers become invisible and moths can find the blossoms only by following their noses. Indeed, Tom found that most of the night-blooming flowers are described as "overpoweringly sweet."

This makes night bloomers ideal for a 20-minute garden, because one plant can do the job of ten. Anyway, a handful of plants was plenty for Tom's nocturne. He wasn't planning this garden for strolling; he might break his neck stumbling around in the dark. No, what he planned was a little planting he could arrange around the cracked concrete patio where he sits with his evening glass of cider.

Tom ordered seeds of five plants: flowering tobacco and four o'clocks to grow in the bed beside the patio, and bottle gourd and cucuzzi (an edible gourd from Italy) to train over the arbor under which Tom has placed his chair. He also ordered seeds of moonflower (*Ipomoea alba*), another climber.

He chose flowering tobacco (*Nicotiana alata*) because he liked the trashy name of the cultivar—'Only the Lonely'— and because Tom's part of Connecticut used to be tobacco-growing country. He figured the nicotiana would flourish.

He was confident that the four o'clocks (*Mirabilis jalapa*) would thrive too, since they are one of those heirloom plants that have been passed down from grandmother to grandmother from time immemorial. (See page 124 to learn more about that.) Those grandmothers don't waste their time on inferior plants. Besides, the four o'clocks (as their name suggests) open their flowers in late afternoon. Tom wanted to make sure that if he did develop healthier work habits (anything is possible), he would still have something to enjoy at quitting time.

Tom ordered the bottle gourds and cucuzzi (both of which belong to an African species, *Lagenaria siceraria*) because they offered a double reward: attractive flowers *and* spectacular fruits. Why not get the most that he could for his 20-minute investment? He ordered moonflower because it sounded romantic, and a nocturne needs an element of romance.

On April 1st, he sowed the seeds of the nicotiana and four o'clocks into plastic seedling packs filled with commercial seed-starting mix that he bought at a local garden center. Because the nicotiana seeds were so small—dustlike, really—he mixed them with a handful of clean sand before sprinkling them over the soil-filled pots; adding sand made it possible to distribute the seed more evenly. After sowing the seeds, Tom watered the pots and set them under fluorescent lights. (For tips on this process, see page 114.)

Because he had heard they are fast-growing, Tom waited until the first week of May before sowing the moonflowers and gourds. These he planted in 4-inch pots filled with the same seed-starting mix. A gardening friend had told Tom that most of her moonflower seeds had failed to germinate, and he suspected that the reason was the rock-hard coat that encases the pea-sized seeds. So Tom rubbed his moonflower seeds across a sheet of medium-fine sandpaper a couple of times, to weaken their coats before sowing them.

All of his seeds germinated promptly (even the moonflowers), and by the middle of May the seedlings were ready to plant out into the garden. Tom knew that the last spring frost in his area usually occurred before May 15th; the Cooperative Extension agent had told him this. So on May 15th he planted out a half dozen each of the nicotiana and four o'clock seedlings in the bed beside the patio (this job took him just ten minutes). He waited until the 25th to move the moonflowers, gourds, and cucuzzis outdoors, because he knew these are all tropical plants that need warm weather. He planted one gourd plant and one cucuzzi at opposite sides of the arbor and set three little moonflowers into a big terra-cotta pot right by the chair where he likes to sit, running strings up to the timbers overhead so the vines could climb as they liked.

Tom won't bother to describe the subsequent growth of either the moonflowers or the nicotianas, since he shared these plants with Marty, who will discuss them later. The gourd and cucuzzi grew like kudzu, scrambling up the arbor and vaulting off into adjacent trees, to drape them with white flowers. The bottle gourds Tom harvested and dried, turning them into birdhouses with his son Matthew's help. The long, thin cucuzzi fruits (which looked like oversexed zucchinis) Tom turned into a succession of dinners.

As weird and wonderful as all these plants were, none were as reliable as the four o'clocks. They bloomed and bloomed through one of the hottest, driest summers on record in Tom's part of Connecticut. Tom found very refreshing the fragrance of lemon that wafted from their little trumpet-shaped yellow-and-red flowers. By the time Tom had his fill of that, the other, paler flowers of the night would be opening, their heavier perfumes inviting Tom to join them for an hour of moon worship.

Implicit in this seduction was a sobering reminder: Tom couldn't look at the virginal blossoms without reflecting that by morning they would crumple like a discarded tissue. The nocturnal flowers had to seize the opportunity for fulfillment. And if a writer is smart, it occurred to Tom, he will turn off his computer before the hour gets too late, and he will do the same.

Chapter 2

Of the Virtues of Lawn and Cosmic Onions

Tom and Marty had dreamed the dream. Now came the time to turn it into reality. It was all very well to talk of 20-minute gardens. To actually create one was another matter.

Tom told Marty to sharpen up a mess of pencils.

"Why pencils?" Marty asked.

Tom responded with the good-humored smile that professional gardeners reserve for their conversations with amateurs.

"Because before we can create our new 20-minute gardens, we have to design them."

Marty shuddered. He thought about high school and having to repeat the class in mechanical drawing three times. Color blending, focal points, forcing the perspective—as Tom droned on, Marty poured himself another cup of coffee and turned to the sports pages. This prompted Tom to question Marty's commitment to their cause. Marty responded with the suggestion that Tom take a look at the tie rack in his closet. That should convince anyone that he ought to leave all matters of design strictly alone.

"That's low," said Tom. Marty shrugged. Tom began to polish up a really crushing response, one that had to do with the real source of Marty's "designer" suits, when Marty (typically) changed the subject.

"Why," he demanded, "can't we just go outside and plant things?"

Putting on his professional smirk again, Tom explained that gardens *always* begin with a design. They begin that way because without a proper plan you can't possibly coordinate all the different activity areas within the landscape, texture won't be balanced with color, you can't develop all of the potential of the site. Blah, blah, blah.

"That sounds like a lot of work," Marty said.

"Sure it's lots of work," Tom replied, "but that's what gardening is all about, and—"

"Not our kind of gardening."

"So what are you suggesting?" Tom asked.

"Why don't we forget the design stuff."

Tom started to respond, then stopped—and experienced an overwhelming sense of relief. Could Marty be onto something? Maybe he would never have to fake his way through the design process again! But if they didn't start with a design how would they know what to do?

"Isn't it pretty obvious most of the time?" Marty continued. "When you buy a house there's a lawn and shrubs and trees. And when the grass needs cutting or the leaves need raking, it's clear what you have to do."

"Sure, but we were talking about gardening, and that sort of work isn't really gardening," Tom replied. "That's just landscape maintenance. It's the outdoor equivalent of cleaning the house or changing the oil in the car."

"So what is gardening, then?"

Tom thought long and hard. Gardening, he finally told Marty, is playing duets with nature. It's taking the time to figure out how a shrub wants to grow and then pruning it in such a way as to enhance that process. Gardening is finding the exact opportunity

The Virtues of Lawn and the Ugly Truth About Garden Designers

"God Almighty first planted a garden" wrote Francis Bacon, as the opening line of his famous essay "Of Gardens." Back in his student-gardener days, Tom was always having this essay quoted at him by various teachers of garden design. Eventually he read it and found that the design which the famous Elizabethan wit proposed included some thirty acres of grounds; a list of trees, shrubs, and flowers that ran on for pages; and instructions for constructing everything from aviaries to ornamental molehills.

"In this I have spared no cost" is how Bacon grandly closed the essay. Tom put the book down with the distinct impression that Sir Francis was designing with the Divine Client in mind: only a deity could have managed Bacon's garden and still have found time to rest on the seventh day.

Designers have grown more sophisticated and glib since Bacon's day, but not much more reasonable in their goals. Fundamentally, their aim is to stamp their vision on the world, and to do this they drive their clients to the limits of their strength and finances, and beyond. Designers begin by asking how much money and time you can devote to the landscape and immediately start calculating how to spend all of it. They cannot look at some perfectly good, self-sufficient patch of weeds or brush without imagining how it would look if converted into a high-maintenance nightmare like a perennial border, or a pseudo-Baroque boxwood parterre.

The best example of this is the abhorrence for lawn that is expressed by nearly all contemporary designers. Even to suggest turf as a landscape option these days is to commit the ultimate horticultural sin. You would do better to confess a taste for lawn jockeys.

What's really wrong with lawns? They are an environmental offense, but that's only because *we* make them one. We spray our lawns with chemicals to keep them weedless and insectless and then complain that lawns pollute. But lawns will grow just fine without those chemicals; they won't be flawless, but then neither are we. We gorge the grass with megadoses of fertilizers and then we whine when the fertilizers run off into streams and lakes and cause algal blooms.

We insist on keeping the lawns green all summer, when the grass naturally would be dormant and brown, and then we complain that lawn irrigation depletes the water supply. So don't water. If your lawn has been planted with a grass adapted to your soil and climate, it won't need significant amounts of irrigation. Where grasses can't survive without watering, plant something else.

The real problem with lawns, from the designer's point of view, is that they are 1) déclassé and 2) boring.

Think about it: the neatest lawns you have ever seen were probably in blue-collar neighborhoods where keeping the turf perfect is a labor of love. Do the rich folks down the road want to be shown up by their working-stiff neighbors? No way. So rather than compete, they declare lawns to be uncool. Of course the designers agree—they're in a service industry, and success in a service industry depends on telling the clients what they want to hear.

Are lawns really boring? Sure—but for the 20-minute gardener, that is their greatest virtue. They are easy to maintain, if you don't demand perfect turf. In fact, lawns are almost the only type of greenery that you can with any degree of confidence entrust to unskilled labor—which is the only kind of labor you are liable to find in most American suburbs.*

There are many other justifications for lawns. They cool the air in summertime and cleanse it, too. A lawn surrounds your house with a most effective firebreak, and it is inhospitable to Lyme disease–bearing ticks. Lawns don't mind being walked on or even driven over occasionally—try that on your upscale flowering meadow.

But for the 20-minute gardener, these things are all beside the point. What matters is that lawns are delegable; you can safely entrust their care to the help (paid or unpaid). Which means that the more of your landscape you plant to grass, the more time you will have to do whatever it is that pleases you. Unless you listen to some garden designer.

* For more on this, see the next chapter.

each of your plants needs to flourish. It's pinching a sprig of basil from a plant you raised from seed and thinking about that when you taste the herb in your salad. Gardening is watching the sun come through the ornamental grass and admiring the way it turns the feathered seed spikes into pure gold at sunset. That's gardening.

Applauding wildly, Marty said, "So let's spend our 20 minutes a day doing that."

"But what about all the maintenance?"

"We'll keep that out of our garden—like you said, it's not really gardening, anyway."

"How are we going to do that?"

"By redefining our terms," said Marty, always the editor. "If the job is something we like doing, we define that as gardening. The rest of the stuff, we call that landscape maintenance. We'll turn that over to hired help, the kids, family members, whatever."

"What about the things all over the yard that we can't delegate?"

"If it's something we like doing, we'll make that part of our 20 minutes. If not, we'll get rid of it."

Garden Versus Landscape

Tom knew that to realize the utopia Marty had outlined, he was going to have to work substantial changes on his yard. If he was going to assign jobs to hired help, he had to make them simple, both to keep the cost down and to ensure that the jobs would be done right. (Just try asking the teenager from down the street to weed your perennial border and see where that gets you.) Likewise, if he was going to ask his very busy wife, Suzanne, to help him, Tom had to make his requests reasonable. And that, he knew, would mean changes in the way he had organized the yard.

Thanks to Marty, Tom saw now that he hadn't planned well when he was planting his yard. Like most gardeners, his goal had been to make it picturesque. In pursuit of that, he had often confused garden and landscape.

Take the spring bulbs Tom had planted all through his front lawn in imitation of the "flowering mead" he had seen in a medieval tapestry. The effect was beautiful when all the narcissuses, snowdrops, and species tulips were in bloom. The blossoms looked impossibly fresh set against the emerald green of the spring turf.

But mixing garden (flowers) with landscape (turf) in this fashion had created an enormous maintenance headache. To ensure that the bulbs would return year after year, Tom had to leave their foliage in place long after the flowers had faded, since the foliage was making the food that the bulbs would draw on the following spring to produce that year's crop of flowers.

That meant Tom couldn't cut his front lawn with a mower all spring. Instead, he had to clip it by hand, carefully snipping the grass short around the bulbs' leaves. A week or two later, and he would be down on his hands and knees again doing the same thing—grass grows quickly in springtime.

At $7 per hour, paying a teenager to do this would be a ruinous expense. Anyway, Tom suspected he'd face a mutiny if he even asked. So Tom decided to untangle landscape from garden. While the bulbs were actively blooming and growing in springtime, the part of the yard in which they were planted he would call garden. Then he wouldn't have to cut the grass there, because lawn mowing is a landscape-maintenance chore, and as such not allowed in the garden. After the bulbs went dormant in early summer and the foliage withered, the area would revert to landscape, and then Tom would resume mowing there. In this way, the bulb-planted lawn would either be all garden or all landscape, depending on the season.

Tom began keeping notes about yard work, identifying the more obvious maintenance problems. How many clippings did it take to keep that formal yew hedge trimmed to a line? Tom had already decided not to hire a landscape service, and he knew that no normal teenager could clip a hedge in a way that would satisfy him. Could he settle for a less tailored profile? If so, he could cut the hedge back hard in the spring, feed it, and let it go for the rest of the year. Suzanne said that although she didn't have the time or inclination for monthly clipping, she would enjoy doing this task once a year.

Tom found that his most time-consuming maintenance problems were caused by the way he had configured his lawn. He had used a pencil for that, drafting outlines on sheets of vellum. Yet his actual point of contact with this scheme was the lawn mower. Curves and peninsulas that had been easy to negotiate with a pencil point had proven difficult to follow with his old push mower. As a result, Tom was spending lots of time backing and turning, and having to use his hand shears to clip the areas the mower blades couldn't reach.

Tom resolved to redraw the outlines of the lawn, this time using his mower as a drafting tool. He let the grass grow long and then pushed his mower around all of the lawn's boundaries; his rule was no stopping and no backing. Then he marked the lawn's new, more flowing edge with stakes and extended the flower beds and the sheets of mulch around the shrubbery out to meet the lawn. Any trees, rocks, or other features that interrupted the sheet of grass Tom enclosed with islands of mulch, configuring the islands so that they, too, could be mowed around without stopping or backing.

Of Camus and Onions

While Tom was dealing with his maintenance problems ad hoc, back in Westport Marty was implementing the 20-minute principles in a rational, systematic way. He started (as he usually does) with a literary approach—he turned to his beloved Albert Camus. Marty's familiarity with Camus's moody writings, together with his beret and the pack of Gauloises, had once made Marty the coolest sophomore at Brooklyn College. Now, in his hour of need, he returned to the master, creating something that could only be described as existential horticulture.

According to the rules of this new school, Marty could do whatever he felt like whenever and wherever he felt like it. What did it matter, after all, in this ultimately pointless universe? And when he became bored with whatever he was doing, Marty just dropped tools and walked away.

Unfortunately, his family failed to appreciate the philosophical underpinnings of Marty's work. He hadn't even finished his first 20 minutes before they expressed extreme unwillingness to live in the kind of filthy and hazardous eyesore Marty was creating.

So he came up with another theory, this one based on the ancient Egyptian belief that the universe is a cosmic onion composed of a series of ever-expanding layers. To Tom's amazement, this theory proved brilliantly effective.

What Marty did was to organize his yard in a series of concentric circles, with himself at the center. Where Marty tended to spend his outdoor time, that was where he clustered features that were most ornamental, but which also demanded the most maintenance.

He edged the patio outside the kitchen door, for example, with his "chaos garden" (for a description of that, see page 71). In the sunny spot between the driveway and the porch, Marty arranged his herbs, so that he could sniff their therapeutic aromas on the way to the car in the morning and on the way to his martini in the evening. On hot afternoons, the herb smells enveloped him as he sat and read in the shade of the porch. The handful of annual flowers that Marty's wife, Judy, had time to cultivate, they arranged in window boxes, where the family couldn't fail to see them every time they looked out.

The circle just beyond the ornamental center of his landscape Marty kept green and carefully trimmed. The circle beyond that, he left shaggier—the lawn was still mowed, but the shrubbery was not trimmed, and ferns were allowed to sprout in the shade as they would. The outermost circle, the yard's perimeter, Marty left substantially untouched. Saplings might struggle up among the trees, the shrubs were left wild, and Marty intervened only if the growth became unsightly. To this outermost circle Marty also consigned areas of the yard he found he never visited, such as the shaded passage behind the house. Why waste time grooming that?

Like with Like

Tom admired Marty's circular approach enough to steal the idea for use in his own yard. Only Tom, who sees the world from a horticultural perspective rather than a philosophical one, planned his circles as a hierarchy of plants. He realized that caring for his landscape would be far simpler if he made a point of putting together only plants with similar needs.

For example, drought-tolerant plants should go only with other drought-tolerant plants, so that most of the time he could skip watering that area altogether. Plants that need regular fertilization (roses, for example) should go with other plants with the same need (annual flowers, say), so that Tom wouldn't have to travel all about the yard sprinkling bits of plant food here and there. He could do all his fertilization at once.

The Advantages of Unnatural Gardening

Marty's hands-off approach to maintenance bears a superficial resemblance to the current horticultural fad known as "Natural Gardening," a style of gardening on which Tom had pinned great hopes at one time. He had believed it would free him from all garden drudgery. Tom still believes that Natural Gardening represents a great American tradition—the same tradition that produced Elmer Gantry and Dr. Whiplash's Amazing Indian Snake Oil Remedy.

The basic premise of Natural Gardening is that the gardener must remove from his or her yard all those nasty foreign plants and replace them with good American plants, plants native to the site. If the gardener will only do this, why then, his garden will take care of itself. It will require no irrigation, no pruning, and it will be bug- and disease-free. One Natural Gardener insisted to Tom that she spent no more than six hours a year in maintaining her property.

Unfortunately, when Tom tried this in his own yard, things didn't work out as promised. What the Natural Gardeners hadn't told Tom was that his yard would soon come to look like a run-down version of what the Native Americans burned off before they built their houses.

Maybe the problem with Tom's Natural Garden was his lack of ideological purity. He could never bring himself to get rid of all his foreign-born roses and flowers. Was that why some of his natives proved unruly, and why others seemed to sulk and wouldn't grow at all? Anyway, Tom never could figure out exactly what is native to the little city in which he lives now.

The Natural Gardeners told him he should start all his plants from seeds collected within a mile of his house. That pretty much ruled out everything except Kentucky bluegrass, Norway maples, and plum tomatoes. (Tom's neighborhood consists mostly of Sicilian-American families.) But none of those plants were growing in Middletown, Connecticut, in 1491—and only "precontact" plants (plants that were present before the arrival of the first Italian, Columbus, on these shores) are acceptable to Natural Gardeners. Though for the record, what the Native American gardeners in Connecticut planted were mainly Mexican plants. Their favorite crops—corn, squash, beans, and sunflowers—all originated in Central America.

When he was a student, twenty years ago, Tom actually spent six months working in the native plants garden of the New York Botanical Garden, and he admired many of the native American plants he learned about there. Some he has since found to be relatively common garden plants. Mountain laurel (*Kalmia latifolia*) is something of a garden cliché, but that's because it is so undemanding and rewarding. Tom loves the glossy evergreen leaves and the delicate, pentagonal pink-and-white flowers of the mountain laurel that grows by the northwest corner of his house.

However, Tom also encountered plants in the native plants garden that are only now becoming popular with American gardeners. Joe-pye weed (*Eupatorium maculatum*), for example, had to wait until European nurserymen sent back outstanding cultivated strains such as 'Gateway' to earn the respect of American gardeners. Tom is enthusiastic about the work of institutions such as the Mount Cuba Center in Greenville, Delaware, which is dedicated to re-exploring the native North American flora, so that it may identify other such overlooked treasures.

During his stint in the native plants garden, though, Tom learned that many native plants flourish only in very specific circumstances. The same plants that are so robust in a pristine bog or old-growth forest often cannot tolerate the disturbed environment they find in a suburban yard. In such a setting, they demand far more coddling than garden-bred "foreigners" who do feel at home in a subdivision.

So, having admitted to himself that he lacks ideological purity, Tom is shameless now about planting "exotics"—plants of foreign origin. He has two rules about these. Before he will buy anything, it must have been tested in North American conditions, so that Tom knows he isn't promoting a plant that will become a horrible weed, like the purple loosestrife that has come from Europe to overrun our wetlands. In addition, any plant Tom buys (actually, this applies to natives as well as exotics) must come from an area with a similar climate and soil to those of his central Connecticut garden, so that he can be confident the plant will be happy there.

An interesting footnote to this issue is that in many cases, the exotic plants have actually proved more pest- and disease-free in Tom's garden than the natives. A biologist who Tom consulted explained that this is customarily the case. When an Asian or Australian plant is moved to North America, it commonly leaves its pests behind, and it often takes decades for North American pests to zero in on the import.

Natural Gardeners reproach Tom for not turning his yard into a preserve for our endangered native flora. But the biologist told Tom that a quarter-acre island of native flora in the middle of the city (or a suburb, for that matter) wouldn't be self-sustaining, and that if he really cared about the native flora, he should send a check to The Nature Conservancy.

Anyway, Tom heard recently from a friend who had visited the garden of the greatest Natural Garden guru of all. She said that she saw (gasp!) Japanese plants there. Apparently, Tom's not the only back-slider.

Tom also arranged his landscape plantings so that plants with a need for more nurturing—especially watering—would be closer to the house and garage. That made it easier to reach them with the hose or any other tools. Tom was clued in to this trick by Marty's reproaches. At Tom's suggestion, Marty had landscaped part of his front yard with mushrooms—'King Stropharia' mushrooms, which are supposed to produce delectable caps as large as eighteen inches across. Tom had told Marty the sight of these would stop passersby dead in their tracks, even in Westport.

They would have, too, except that the streetside along which Marty planted the mushroom spawn (in a heap of wood chips) was 150 feet away from the nearest faucet. Typically, Marty read the cultural instructions that came with the spawn only after he had planted it. When he did, he learned that the mushrooms had to be watered daily. So every evening he had to couple together four lengths of hose and drag all of them out, water, and then gather up the hoses and put them away. Sometimes Marty just couldn't face this task, and because of his lack of diligence the mushrooms never sprouted. Tom heard about this many times (in detail), and he was determined that he wouldn't make the same mistake.

So Where's the Garden?

By this point, Tom was feeling very much on top of his landscape—but he was a little troubled as to how and where he should stake out space for his garden.

"Don't," was Marty's reply.

"The 20-minute gardener measures his garden not in feet and inches, or even meters," Marty intoned. "The 20-minute gardener measures his garden in increments of time."

Tom figured that he owed Marty one for the mushroom fiasco, so he let this pass. But he did demand an explanation in plain English, PDQ.

"We don't begin by setting aside a garden space and then figure out how to fill it," Marty said. "We begin by figuring out what we like to do, and we let the garden create itself around that."

Tom still didn't understand, so Marty laid it out in detail. What they were going to do was to plan a number of 20-minute projects, projects like Tom's nocturne. Like that planting, these would be modest projects shaped around the likes and dislikes of the gardener. Marty, for example, wanted simple, all-American plants and activities. Tom said okay, but he wanted something a bit unusual, something to pique his more jaded horticultural appetites. Marty aspires to quiet elegance; Tom prefers the flamboyant.

The two gardeners agreed that in any case the projects had to be planned for impact; the results had to be high profile and distinctive and whenever possible yield a double payoff—like the gourd vines, which were starting to provide Tom with tasty fruits as well as handsome flowers. Why not shade and nice foliage, too, Marty wanted to know. Let's go for a vine that grows like kudzu, Tom added. Both gardeners wanted to get the most out of their 20 minutes.

That, of course, was the most important common theme: a gardener should be able to carry out any one of the projects with just 20 minutes of work each day. A project might continue over several days, or even several weeks, from beginning to end, but it couldn't require more than 20 minutes of attention each day.

Marty said that there had to be some leeway. Like you could skip a day once in a while if you felt lazy or it was disgusting out or if your boss had been more vile than usual. On the other hand, if you got inspired on a sunny Sunday in May, maybe you would actually put in a full hour or even two. But the *average* had to remain 20 minutes a day.

How would they organize these plantings within the landscape? That would be dictated by the projects; the nature of those would determine where each garden would go (growing zinnias requires a sunny spot, growing ferns means shade) and what space it would occupy—Tom's kudzu garden would be expansive, Marty's bonsai garden would be small.

Having overcome yet another set of hurdles, Tom and Marty settled down to a furious session of project planning. As they tossed ideas back and forth, strange and marvelous gardens appeared and disappeared like mirages in the desert. Then Marty's watch alarm sounded—20 minutes were over.

So the gardeners shook hands and put their feet up. Francis Bacon wouldn't have approved, but he never sounded like much fun, anyway.

2◷-MINUTE PROJECT

Window Boxing

Simple pleasures are the best, and Marty likes to keep them within easy reach. He and Judy maintain an assortment of aromatic herbs along the path that runs from house to driveway, and that's fine, but he likes to keep a few essentials right at arm's reach while he is cooking. That's why for his first essay at a 20-minute project, Marty set a window box outside a south-facing kitchen window. When he's putting together a soup or a salad now, all he has to do is slide up the window sash, reach out, and pinch off a sprig.

Marty loves to do this when there are dinner guests—it looks so chic. Besides, the fresh herb leaves have a much livelier savor than those dried flakes from a can. And the window box really is handsome. Sun-drenched and well-drained, it provides perfect conditions for herb plants, and they flourish there, filling the bottom half of the kitchen window with a tangle of fragrant shrubbery.

Marty had planned to buy a tasteful plastic window box from Home Depot, but Tom refused to include that in this book. Eventually Tom agreed to make one for Marty. At a lumberyard Tom bought a 12-foot-long, 1″ × 12″ cedar plank for $18.45, and within two hours he had turned that into the item pictured on the next page.

A skilled carpenter with a real workshop could have finished the job in half an hour; Tom took longer (he used up almost a week's worth of 20-minute increments), but he thoroughly en-

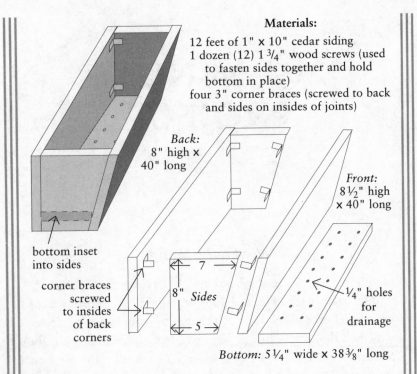

Materials:

12 feet of 1" x 10" cedar siding
1 dozen (12) 1 ¾" wood screws (used
    to fasten sides together and hold
    bottom in place)
four 3" corner braces (screwed to back
    and sides on insides of joints)

Back:
8" high x
40" long

Front:
8½" high
x 40" long

bottom inset
into sides

corner braces
screwed
to insides
of back
corners

7

8" *Sides*

5

¼" holes
for
drainage

Bottom: 5¼" wide x 38⅜" long

joyed hacking away at the fragrant (and rot-resistant) cedar wood, and now his Christmas present to Marty is taken care of.

Before bringing the window box to Marty's house, Tom had drilled a pattern of holes across its bottom to ensure that water would drain out freely (though, actually, it would have escaped just as easily through the gaps in Tom's less-than-perfect joinery). Marty, after the obligatory comments about Tom's workmanship, lined the box with a scrap of fiberglass screening, to make sure that no soil would wash out with the water. Then he filled the box with ordinary potting soil that he had mixed with an equal amount of clean sand (the sort that is used to fill sandboxes). Tom had warned Marty that herbs prefer a sandy soil.

Marty planted the window-box garden with herb seedlings he had purchased at the garden center down the road. The first year, he planted with roasts and stews in mind: he set a rosemary plant in the middle, flanked it with sage plants, and tucked in creeping thymes and oregano around their feet. Five plants were enough to fill the whole box. Marty set the garden up on sturdy angle irons he had screwed to the clapboards outside the kitchen window. He watered it, and voilà!

Regular watering was just about the only maintenance this garden needed. Marty fed the plants only once a month, and then with a half-strength solution of ordinary houseplant fertilizer. He skimped on the fertilizer because Tom had warned him that lush growth would have little flavor, that herbs grow best in nutrient-poor soils.

The first year's harvest would have been a great success, except that Marty's daughter, Madeleine, converted him to vegetarianism by the middle of the summer. The heavy-flavored herbs Marty had planted to spice his meat dishes overpowered his delicate vegetable broths and parsnip ragouts; rosemary tastes great with lamb, but lousy with tofu. Still, the window box was beautiful, and Tom used to cut bunches of seasonings every time he stopped by. He's a hopeless carnivore.

This past summer Marty replanted the box with an assortment of purple and red chili peppers that Tom had gotten in a seedling swap (see page 115) and one plant of Neapolitan basil—lighter spices for his healthful diet. Tom keeps pushing for a return to rosemary—his lamb chops are really suffering—but Marty is considering a Thai theme (lemongrass and coriander) for next year. Maybe he'll sneak in an early spring crop of arugula first. Can you imagine the guests' faces when Marty picks a salad without ever leaving the kitchen?

Chapter 3

Who Does the Hard Work?

"A man should never plant a garden
larger than his wife can take care of."

—T. H. EVERETT, author of *The New York Botanical Garden
Illustrated Encyclopedia of Horticulture*

"Just you wait, 'enry 'iggins, just you wait."

—ELIZA DOOLITTLE, floral sales consultant,
London, England

"Ah, but," we hear you saying. "Sure, turn your back on the
lawn mowing, hedge clipping, and tree trimming. Call it landscape maintenance and dismiss it. See what happens. No,
somebody has got to do the grunt work. This 20-minute business is all a scam."

To which we say: right, and wrong. You are right that someone has to do all the tiresome work of tidying up the yard. But you are dead wrong in calling 20-minute gardening a scam. We are well aware of the need for regular landscape maintenance (that is what has been putting bread on Tom's table for more than twenty years, after all). The genius of the 20-minute gardener, though, is that he or she knows how to delegate this work so that it is done by someone else. Read on and we will share with you the skills and wisdom needed to accomplish this.

This section will be brief. Indeed, if Marty had his way, we would skip it altogether. Marty has no interest in manual labor. He assumes that as such work becomes necessary, others will appear to do it. And when Tom asked, "What if they don't?" Marty suggested leaving a message on his assistant's voice mail.

Tom insisted, however, that as the pioneers of 20-minute gardening, he and Marty must develop a solution that will serve a broad population. So Marty agreed to let Tom include a guide to the types of labor available to the average suburban gardener—as long as Tom promised to write a true 20-minute guide: you should be able to read and digest this chapter in just that interval of time.

Professional Gardeners

Forget it. True gardeners—men and women who have devoted years to mastering this complex craft—are not to be found in the average community. If, by some chance, you do locate a real gardener, keep in mind that 1) you can't afford what they charge, and 2) real gardeners don't want to spend their time on the kind of routine maintenance which is what you need done.

Landscape Maintenance Contractors

This is a more realistic alternative. Landscape contractors are found in the Yellow Pages of every telephone directory, and such a service can relieve you of most of your routine yard work. This help does not come cheap either (the amount you pay will be based directly on the amount the contractor knows you can pay—ask Marty), but on the other hand, a good contractor is self-supervising, so that you really will be able to put those chores out of mind.

How do you find a good maintenance company?

Word of mouth is best. Ask the manager at the neatest, best-organized garden center in town. He does business with all the contractors and will know the type of jobs at which each contractor excels.

Is a big landscape service better than a one-man or one-woman operation?

Depends on what you want. Big services with lots of employees offer diversity of experience. Different employees have different skills, so that whatever you need done, whether it is trimming the hedge or renovating a lawn, chances are there is someone who knows just how to do it. One man/one woman operations typically have more marked strengths and weaknesses.

The advantages of a small service:

In a bigger service there is a chain of command, and messages may be misunderstood as they are passed up and down. Tom has a friend who hired a large tree service to remove a dead oak tree from his property. When the crew arrived, the foreman who had negotiated the job was not with them, and as a result, the crew cut down the wrong tree. They cut down a magnificent, healthy oak that was the centerpiece of the landscape. Insurance adjusters estimated the loss in value to the property at $30,000.

What a landscape contractor can do:

Anything that can be done with power equipment.

What you shouldn't ask a landscape contractor to do:

Handwork, such as weeding a flower bed. Quite likely contractors won't know how to do this properly, and even if they do, they will be reluctant to undertake the job since it will tie up their personnel and they probably can't charge what the work is really worth.

For the same reason, it's a mistake to ask a maintenance contractor to attempt complicated operations where mistakes can cause lasting damage. Don't ask the maintenance contractor to prune your lovely old Japanese maple, for example. He's not going to spend a morning figuring out how to enhance its intrinsic beauty. Instead, he'll give the tree the same treatment he gives all other small trees, and you will end up with a generic shade source.

How you can save money:

Take a walk around the yard with the contractor before he or she prepares an estimate. Discuss the changes you can make that will simplify upkeep. Are you really committed to those perfectly trimmed evergreen cones and spheres that line the front of the house? Maybe you'll prefer a shaggier look after you learn the cost of barbering.

What you should demand:

Make sure the contractor is fully insured. That means the company must carry not only liability insurance but also workman's compensation on its employees. If it doesn't and one of the employees injures himself in your yard, you will be liable.

If the contractor will be applying dangerous chemicals—even just spreading "weed and feed" on the grass—make sure the applicator has proper state certification (in most states, a license is required to apply pesticides). Certification means that the applicator has completed a safety course and passed a test of basic knowledge. Your insurance company will care, even if you don't.

Teenagers

Tom maintains that teenagers offer a virtually untapped labor pool of fabulous proportions. Marty maintains that most teenagers are unemployed because they are unemployable. He is the father of two such chronologically challenged persons (Dan and Madeleine), and he says he would rather buy a new car than go through what it takes to get them to wash the old one. And, as he proudly points out, Dan and Madeleine are great kids.

Tom agrees with that last statement. But he also knows that teenagers can be persuaded to work. During the ten years that Tom maintained the gardens of an old estate for Columbia University, he relied heavily on teenagers to fill out his crew in the summertime. Actually, this seasonal help was Tom's favorite labor source. They provided a delightful contrast to the regular staff.

This regular staff consisted of three university groundsmen, and they all had but one ambition: they wanted to spend 7.5 hours of every weekday hiding in some boiler room smoking cigarettes. The other half hour they spent on coffee break, discussing what they would do if they won the lottery (smoke cigarettes outside the boiler room), and why it was unreasonable of Tom to expect them to do the work they had contracted to do.

By contrast, the teenaged summer help was amazingly energetic—Tom used to shed ten pounds every summer trying to keep up. The teenagers always made a point of telling Tom that they had no interest in flowers or shrubs, but they would do what he asked in return for the wages they received. They had fun—gardening might seem ridiculous to them (who cares about all this flower sh*t?)—but that didn't mean they couldn't have a good time while they indulged Tom. Overall, Tom found their attitude to be a healthy corrective: whenever he thought some professional challenge was overwhelming, he would mention it to his teenage assistants, who would explain that he should be chasing babes instead.

Working with teenagers was something for which Tom's professional education at a leading botanical garden had not prepared him. In fact, this was never mentioned in all of his horticultural studies. But Tom has made his own study and developed the following guidelines.

Rule 1: Never hire your own children. Even if you fire them, you'll still have to deal with them at the dinner table.

Rule 2: Never hire a relative's child. Sooner or later you'll have to deal with their mother or father over dinner.

Rule 3: Never hire the child of a boss or an important client. Your employee may fire you.

Rule 4: Never hire a pair of friends. It will be a great experience for them, but little work is likely to result.

Rule 5: Do hire the children of friends—or, better yet, the children of friends of friends. Most teenagers hesitate to embarrass their parents by messing up in front of family friends. And if they do, the humiliated parents will take care of retribution.

Rule 6: Insist on punctuality. While working for Columbia, Tom used to allow teenage employees one late arrival. After that, if they arrived even five minutes late, they were told that there was no work for them that day and they had to go home. Otherwise, as Tom discovered, you get no gardening done at all; you spend all your time negotiating.

Rule 7: For the first few days, work with your teenage employees and set as grueling a pace as you can sustain. If you can do it, run them right into the ground. Make it clear that you aren't asking them to do anything you wouldn't do yourself. That matters a great deal to most teenagers, who haven't yet acquired a mature taste for hypocrisy.

Rule 8: Foster paranoia. Make a point of slipping back quietly to check on the teenagers at odd intervals throughout the day, and approach from a different direction each time, so that they never see you coming. Stand there, expressionless, until they notice your presence. Then tell them they are doing fine, really, but suggest how they can do the job even better. This is a technique Tom learned from an old head gardener. Tom hated him, but Tom used to work like hell.

Rule 9: Remember that the teenagers who work for you don't intend to stick with the job past the immediate period of economic need. That means they are essentially untrainable. So give them obvious, self-explanatory tasks. Tell them to remove all the weeds from a bed of pachysandra, for instance—and make sure they understand what pachysandra is—and they will probably do an adequate job. Ask them to weed the perennial bed and you are liable to lose as many flowers as weeds.

It's okay to entrust teenagers with more demanding jobs, but only if failure won't create problems. Let them trim the privet hedge—if they scalp it, it will soon grow back. And expect problems. Teenagers will *never* take a lawn mower to the gas can and refill the tank in the garage, where a spill will create only fumes. Instead, they always carry the gas can out to the mower to refill its tank where a spill will burn a brown spot into the lawn. To rage at the offender is as foolish as blaming a crow for stealing seeds from the garden. That's just what they do.

Rule 10: Pay a bit more than the minimum. Professional maintenance contractors expect you to go for the low bid, and they respect a customer for being businesslike. The same behavior makes teenagers feel exploited. They still expect adults to be generous and to watch out for their interests. Don't disillusion them just yet.

Marry in Haste
and Garden at Leisure

Theoretically, a marriage, or even an agreement to move in together, could solve virtually all of a gardener's labor problems. If one gardener does 20 minute a day, then two can do 40 minutes, and life is sweet. Right?

Alas, it is not that simple. Where once partnerships were based on naked exploitation—mutual exploitation when things were working right—now we have relationships. Nobody understands how they work, least of all us. So we can't give you any general rules for how to delegate to a partner. That sort of gardening has become as unpredictable and complicated as sex—which is what makes it so interesting.

Tom volunteered to research this subject, before he found out that what Marty wanted him to write about was the gardening. What follows is his report.

Tom's discovery that Suzanne actually enjoyed raking leaves and mowing lawns wasn't what made him propose to her. Tom had known he should marry her on their first date, when he took her to a garden and she corrected his identifications of the plants. As a professional horticulturist, he was impressed by that. But Tom did feel that her enthusiasm for garden chores he wanted to escape made her an ideal partner.

Tom marched to the altar with romantic visions of gardening together. One pair of hands would dig the hole while the other pair planted the flower, and all in perfect harmony. Reality proved different.

Indeed, Tom and Suzanne's garden developed into an arena for their most heated disagreements. Surely there is no argument like the one you have on a hot and humid afternoon when one party (the one that studied gardening) takes time out from swatting bugs to point out to the other that they aren't supposed to ever step in the flower bed—remember? At times, Tom has wondered if his marriage could survive a mutual love of gardening.

A few months ago he sought counseling. He began tracking down gardening couples—couples whose personal partnerships were strong and whose gardens were flourishing, too. He asked them how they managed to work together.

Tom learned to his relief that the problems he and Suzanne had experienced are the rule rather than the exception. In fact, he discovered that their horticultural relations could have been far worse. A prominent nurseryman confessed that his wife had so disapproved of the way he pruned an apple tree that she had banned him—indefinitely—from their backyard orchard. He supplies plants to gardens all over the East Coast but is not welcome in his own.

Tom learned that, in fact, partnerships which successfully mix personal and horticultural closeness are quite rare. But they do exist. And the rewards of successful collaboration are great. Besides the obvious benefit of doubling the labor supply, there is another. In an effective partnership, each participant brings different strengths to the garden. When these are harnessed together, the result is a landscape more exciting than either partner could create individually.

Tom also learned that there is more than one way to share a garden.

The most common mode is for each partner to lay claim to an area of the landscape and to make that his or her own. Thereafter, the other partner is typically allowed in only by invitation and is expected to keep their hands in their pockets. Opinions should not be volunteered but commonly are sought. Once the threat that the other may interfere with your space has been eliminated, then you can relax and share.

The most outstanding example of this separate but equal policy Tom encountered is in the gardens of Gwen and Panayoti Kelaidis, a Denver couple whose names are familiar to rock gardeners worldwide. Panayoti is the man responsible for turning the Denver Botanic Gardens' alpine garden into the finest in the country, while Gwen serves as the editor of the North American Rock Garden Society's journal, the *Quarterly*, and operates a mail-order business that supplies rock gardeners in several countries with seeds of uncommon and especially fine alpine plants.

Panayoti is an insatiable collector. His current field of interest is the flora of South Africa, but he continues to gather plants from high-mountain and steppe areas worldwide. Gwen has a collection of some two thousand species herself—but her plantings in their small urban yard were threatened by the tidal wave of Panayoti's acquisitions. They decided that because Panayoti had ample space at the Botanic Gardens, the range of miniature peaks Gwen had constructed around their bungalow would be hers alone.

According to Gwen, Panayoti will still arrive home in the evening with dozens or even hundreds of seedlings and a casual request that she "work them in." Often she does. For whereas once she preferred to add plants in deliberate numbers, Panayoti, she says, has expanded her appetite. He, for his part, has learned to trust Gwen as a gardener and to take orders (at least at home): her methods sometimes seem odd to him, but he nearly always likes the results.

❀

Fred and Mary Ann McGourty have worked out a very different sort of horticultural relationship. Gardening is what brought these two together. They met in 1972 at the annual meeting of the American Horticultural Society, and as a partnership they have turned Hillside Gardens, their five-acre garden in Norfolk, Connecticut, into one of the most outstanding displays of "uncommon perennials" in the country. The garden has become a cottage industry that supports them both: they sell divisions of their plants in a driveway sales area, they design gardens, they lecture all over the country, and in the wintertime they write books and articles about perennial flowers.

But the greatest triumph of these two passionate plantsmen may well be coexistence. As Mary Ann brags: "We have managed to garden together for many years without killing each other."

"Barely," Fred replies. Then laughs.

A sense of humor and an elaborate "unwritten contract" has been the McGourtys' salvation. Hillside Gardens had been Fred's family home before he married Mary Ann; she took care not to propose any dramatic changes when she first moved in. Instead, she helped with the maintenance and only gradually suggested new projects.

The first step to gardening harmony, the McGourtys agree, was coming together on a basic goal for the garden: they agreed that their mutual aim would be to enhance the informal charm and flowing land form of this former dairy farm. Then as each new project arose, they appointed a chief and a laborer; the chief was the partner who had stronger feelings about the direction the project should follow.

Clearly these feelings could be very strong. But both recognize the importance of compromise. Mary Ann gestures toward some midsized (and, to Tom's eye, innocuous) bushes. "I hate these damn snowberries."

"I think they are one of the most beautiful shrubs in the garden," Fred replies. They laugh again—they have worked this one out. Mary Ann campaigned vigorously against the snowberries (*Symphoricarpos albus*) until the most prominent one, the one that blocked the view from the house of the upper lawn, was removed. The unstated understanding was that once this happened, Mary Ann's suit against the others would be dropped. So it went.

Tom stayed silent when the McGourtys scoffed at the romantic idea visitors have of Fred and Mary Ann working together: one digging the hole while the other plants the perennial. They almost never work in the same area at the same time. Yet they share and each is quick to learn from the other. Fred tells of a lecture they delivered jointly some years ago in Cincinnati. His responsibility was to assemble the slides, and he slipped in a photograph of a plant he admired but knew Mary Ann despised—the silver-leaved but spiny Scotch thistle (*Onopordum acanthium*). When this appeared on the screen, there was a very public difference of opinion. In the course of the argument, however, Mary Ann realized that what she really hated about the thistle was that it was planted right by the barn door, so that it stabbed her every time she went in or out. Planted in the middle of the "sun border" as it is now, she likes it.

"Shouldn't we have a few more?" Fred asks.

"Never mind."

❖

Sometime a shared gardening experience changes not only the garden but also the gardeners. That was Marco Stufano's experience. Since 1967 he has been director of horticulture at Wave Hill, New York's most remarkable public garden. Yet Marco questions whether he would have stayed if nineteen of those years hadn't been shared with John Nally, "if it weren't for the fact that we were having so much fun."

John Nally (who died in 1988) signed on at Wave Hill in 1969, two years after Marco's arrival. John was a printmaker who had no training in horticulture. But John had a perspective that Marco badly needed.

Wave Hill is nationally famous now for its rich selection of carefully chosen plants and for the flair and imagination with which those plants are combined. But when Marco looks at photographs of the flower arrangements he created in his first years, he finds then "so uptight and scary—and ordinary." John Nally's contribution was to change that—though in the process Marco changed John.

Marco recalls the fights, "incredible fights about all kinds of things." John worked on getting Marco to loosen up; Marco worked at teaching John how to be ruthless enough to garden well.

Marco knows that you can't afford to be sentimental about plants that have passed their peak, and that even a plant that is flourishing may be in the wrong spot. If so, it must be removed. He does this without compunction: "There is nothing I like better on a particularly bad morning than to come in and throw things out."

John, by contrast, saw beauty in every plant—and often he was right. There is an aster at Wave Hill called 'Chicago Bus Stop'; that is where John found it, rescuing it from a crack in the sidewalk to bring it back to Wave Hill's "wild garden" (his special charge). This past spring Marco included as part of Wave Hill's display at a Rockefeller Center flower show in Manhattan a *Pachypodium* that John found for sale at a price of $1.25 in a New Jersey diner. Marco agreed to buy the palmlike succulent from Madagascar because it was rare and cheap; John bought it because it had been knocked out of its pot and unless taken home was going to die.

Marco says that though he was always greedy for plants—Wave Hill is a collector's paradise—John Nally made him greedier. And though Marco's natural inclination is to do everything himself, John taught him the strength that comes from collaboration. For the first couple of years after John's death, in fact, Marco recalls that when he was designing new plantings he would find himself standing in front of the beds saying, "Where are you? Help me—I don't know what I am doing here."

It bothers Marco to hear the garden described, as it often is, as his garden. It is still John's garden, too. And it is the garden of every staff member who works with and for Marco. Though Marco couldn't point to any special aspect of the garden that was just John's—because his work became their work—perhaps that is his legacy. A gift for sharing.

❀

Whether you choose to delegate to a landscape maintenance service, a teenager, or your life partner, the thing to keep in mind is that it is your garden (well, maybe part his or hers, too). Ultimately, what you like is what's right (at least in your half). While the contractor he hired may not approve of Marty's philosophical garden, it suits Marty just fine. Meanwhile, Tom and Suzanne continue to hammer out their gardening relationship. Marty sympathizes with Suzanne. Can you imagine being married to someone who is right all the time? Or at least thinks he is? And who is always quoting some old Botanical Garden tyrant named T. H. Everett?*

* as on page 36.

2⏰-MINUTE PROJECTS

Flowers That Plant Themselves;
Houseplants That Never Get
Planted at All

The Perpetual Garden

Tom *loves* annual flowers. He believes they are the horticultural equivalent of ketchup. Just as a judicious splat of the red stuff improves the flavor of every dish from eggs to fish sticks, so too a sprinkling of annual flowers enhances the beauty of virtually any garden. In the old days, his enthusiasm for these blossoms was tempered by the fact that he found the plants to be a lot of work. But that was before he learned about reseeding annuals.

Tom used to cultivate annuals in the traditional way. He'd sow seed in shallow trays in a greenhouse, and after the seeds germinated, he would "prick out" the seedlings—transplant three or four thousand of them into individual pots. He'd nurture this army of little plants for a couple of months, and then after the last spring frost he'd move them into the garden, setting them out in meticulously calculated patterns. To accomplish all this required a massive input of labor, and the results were, well, a little obvious. The pinwheel of scarlet salvias and silver dusty millers Tom planted one year was colorful but predictable, and so was the sunburst of yellow and orange marigolds he planted the next.

No one could call Tom's annuals predictable these days, and that's because he has stolen a trick from the old farmers he met during the four years he lived in central Texas.

These people descended from many different ethnic groups and cultures, but they were united in their love of flowers and their pragmatic approach to gardening. They didn't have much energy or money to give to their gardens, so everything they did was calculated to get results. That's why the Texans had space only for annuals that grew themselves.

Over the generations, the Texans had identified a number of annual flowers that, once planted in a garden, seed themselves. These are hardy species that grow and flower with no more help than a sprinkling of fertilizer in the spring and an occasional watering during the dry parts of summer. They don't bear flowers as big or as colorful as those of the wonder hybrids Tom used to plant in pinwheels. But the hardy annuals do produce lots of fertile seed. This they scatter around all summer long. The seed lies dormant over the winter and then germinates in the spring to produce the next year's crop of annual flowers.

This is easy—as close to effortless as gardening gets—and it offers endless surprises. Because the seeds fall where they may, you never know where the flowers will emerge. Your design tool is a hoe. A few weeks after the flower seedlings have emerged, you hoe out the ones in inconvenient places. If you make a point of leaving only sturdy, vigorous seedlings (and who wants any other kind?) you will gradually improve the character of your annuals as a whole, so that in a few years you, like the Texan farmers, will have only plants that like your soil and your climate and that can take care of themselves.

Tom's favorite self-seeding annuals include marigolds, petunias, cleomes (which are also called spider flowers because of the extended, leggy look of their pink or white blossoms), portulacas (which love dry, sandy, and sunny spots), four o'clocks, and Johnny-jump-ups (a sort of miniature pansy). Generally, you know that an annual has potential if the gardening experts describe it as "weedy." They think reseeding is a bad habit, since they want flowers to grow only where they put them. Tom thinks that a plant that grows like a weed but bears beautiful flowers is something to be treasured.

Some reseeding annuals are modest in comparison to their hybrid relatives. Petunias, for example, bear smaller flowers the second year, and the blossoms are uniformly colored a wine red. Other reseeding annuals, however, maintain their original brilliance generation after generation.

The most exquisite flowers in Tom's Connecticut garden are the marigolds his five-year-old son, Matthew, planted three years ago. It took considerably less than twenty minutes to break up the earth and plant out the original seedling. (Matthew had grown it in a Dixie cup at preschool.) There was plenty of time left over to hunt for worms that first afternoon, and the flowers have required almost no care since. Every year they bear the same cloisonné blossoms of red petals edged with gold, and they have spread from that single seedling to a patch that entirely covers the hot, dry, infertile space alongside the driveway. The summer-long drought of 1995 that cooked so many others of Tom's flowers didn't even faze the marigolds—they seem unstoppable. Tom has visions of them increasing year after year, jumping the curb and overrunning the neighbors' yards, eventually covering the whole city in a carpet of blossoms.

That's almost better than ketchup. Almost.

Tom's Extraterrestrial Houseplants

Tom hates houseplants. He has found them to be whiny, nagging little organisms. Come home from a hard day of weeding somebody else's garden and there's the ficus—or the philodendron or the begonia—looking sad because it's dry. Or it's too wet. Or maybe its soil is okay, but the *air* is too dry or too wet. Besides, too little sunlight comes through your window, so the plant is stretched and anorexic; and it's growing toward the sun but you keep forgetting to turn it, so it's got a profile now like Quasimodo.

What fun.

As a rule, Tom believes that plants are for outdoors. But there is one kind of plant with which Tom does enjoy sharing his living quarters. That's tillandsias.

What are tillandsias? They are relatives of the pineapple, except that most are epiphytes, which means they don't grow on the ground. Instead, they cling to tree branches and rocks, or even telephone wires. Their roots serve only as anchors, for the plants absorb the moisture and nutrients they need from the water that washes over them in rainstorms or that condenses on them as dew or fog.

Tom got to know tillandsias during the years he lived in Texas. The Spanish moss that hangs from the live oaks there is a tillandsia (*Tillandsia usneoides*). Tom never brought that into the house, though he suspects it would have been quite striking had he draped it over the furnishings. Suzanne, however, did domesticate another tillandsia: *Tillandsia recurvata*, "ball moss," which made little Dr. Seuss–style puffs of spiky grayish foliage along the tree branches. Despite Tom's protestations, she broke off one well-decorated branch and hung it over the kitchen sink. To Tom's amazement, this impromptu houseplant flourished, thriving on a diet of steam from the dishwasher and an occasional misting. Some of the puffs eventually sprouted odd little greenish flowers, though this effort seemed to exhaust them; the plants died soon thereafter. All in all, however, ball moss was the least demanding roommate Tom had ever had.

Alas, there is no ball moss in Connecticut; the tillandsias' natural range is from Virginia southward to Argentina. But Tom found a nurserywoman in California, Barbara Holladay, who specializes in raising these gems and has a collection of more than 250 varieties. Barbara listened to Tom's description of his Yankee kitchen—airy, with bright but indirect light from skylights—and told him it was the perfect opportunity. Then she selected four plants for him: a *Tillandsia caput-medusae*, a wild head of snaky Gorgon locks; a *Tillandsia capitata* 'Peach', which offered a tousled but more mannerly head; a bold, almost cabbage-sized *Tillandsia brachycaulos*; and a meandering stemmed *Tillandsia queroensis*.

All the plants were grayish green, and a close look revealed that the stems and foliage were entirely covered with tiny scales. These protect the plants against dehydration, and their presence is a sign that Tom's tillandsias originated in a region with a dry climate. Barbara recommends the gray tillandsias for the average household situation because the atmosphere in a centrally heated house often is desert dry.

Tom knew, from his days at the botanical garden, the horticulturally correct way to grow an epiphyte: you affix it to an old tree limb and create a sort of museum-of-natural-history diorama effect. To fasten the epiphyte to the "trunk," you first wrap the roots and base of the rosette (tillandsias typically produce their leaves in compact whorls, or rosettes) in damp sphagnum moss, and then you sandwich the moss-wrapped roots between a sheet of cork or bark and the "trunk," lashing the whole thing in place with fishing line.

But Barbara had more interesting suggestions. She says that lots of her customers lash a tillandsia's moss-wrapped base onto a piece of driftwood, or insert it into a large shell or an ornamental rock. She knows one person who redid her kitchen cabinets with tillandsias—the woman sanded the cabinets to give them a porous surface, then used staples and wire to attach the plants. The tillandsias rooted right into the cabinets and gradually spread into a sort of jungle veneer.

Interesting; but Tom decided to suspend his plants. He hung them with nearly invisible lengths of fishing line beneath the skylights, and now the tillandsias float about the room like furry little aliens. Once or twice a week he takes them down and soaks them in a sinkful of water. Rainwater is recommended for this bath, but Tom uses ordinary tap water, and his tillandsias don't mind. Once a month he soaks the plants in a half-strength solution of an ordinary, balanced, water-soluble houseplant fertilizer.

Tom's tillandsias are growing, slowly but noticeably. They haven't bloomed yet, but Barbara told Tom he has to be patient. Young plants may take from one to eight years before producing their blue, pink, white, or red flower spikes. You'll know the flowers are imminent if the plant flushes, changing from grayish green to maroon or purple or red. The flowers emerge on a spike and may last anywhere from a few weeks to a couple of months. When they have done their job and the seed is ripened, then, as Barbara put it, "the moms die." But before they do, they produce a whole brood of "pups"—little rosettes that sprout around the older rosette. The pups actually feed on the nutrients released by the mom as her foliage decays.

Barbara warned Tom to watch the tillandsia leaves. If they start to roll up into quills, that is a sign of dehydration. The cure for that is to soak the plant more often. If the leaves brown at the tip, that's probably a symptom of overfertilization. So far, though, Tom's tillandsias have not shown a single hint of dissatisfaction.

Tom always heard that his ancestors left the old country because they were tired of sharing their living quarters with livestock. But they never knew about tillandsias.

Chapter 4

Shopping Without Prozac

One of the most appealing aspects of gardening is the sheer simplicity of it. Just you and the soil there, the birds singing, a gentle breeze wafting through the blossom-fragrant air. And certainly as long as you're physically in the garden (or watching a Disney cartoon), it can be like that. But what if you need to buy a plant? Or a bag of fertilizer? Or a pair of pruning shears?

Why, that's simple too. You just go to the local garden center, or the "home center," or the supermarket, or the local gourmet shop that also sells flowering plants, or you order it by mail, by modem, or . . . or you can blow it off, go back inside, and watch reruns of *Gilligan's Island*, which probably seems like the most attractive option about now.

For in shopping lies one of the great contradictions of modern gardening. Most of us garden to escape stress. Doctors even prescribe gardening as a treatment for stress. Yet once we start gardening, we find that we need all sorts of stuff. And acquiring that stuff can be a bewildering, frustrating experience—in other words, stress.

That's not your fault. Somewhere over the course of the last decade, the MBAs started conducting surveys, and this instantly transformed gardening from a hobby into a huge consumer market. Now the marketing geniuses are working overtime to complicate the field. Their plan is to shame you into accessorizing while at the same time so confusing you that in desperation you will buy whatever overpriced, inadequate "solution" they put on the shelf.

Tom and Marty recognize this as one of the most serious challenges confronting the 20-minute gardener. He or she (i.e., me or you) has a total of just 121 hours and 40 minutes of gardening time a year (122 hours in a leap year). Yet in the past Tom has often spent that much time agonizing over the selection of a single rose bush.

That's because when confronted with the need to fill a hole he worries about choosing the best cultivar of the class best adapted to his garden. He worries about whether he should get a plant that has been grafted onto a rootstock (grafted plants grow faster and tend to be more vigorous) or a plant that is growing on its own roots (these live longer). He has to decide whether he should buy the rose locally and get one in a pot or whether he should order by mail and get a bare-root plant (one that was dug while still dormant and shipped without any soil around the roots). He also has to check the grade of each plant, to make sure he isn't getting a runt. By the time Tom has this all figured out, the planting season is over.

Marty isn't about to embroil himself in all of this. In the past, his solution was to go generic: he bought whatever was cheapest, figuring that one rose was as good as another. (He claimed that Gertrude Stein personally told him so.) Tom says that's why the rose Marty planted outside his kitchen door almost never bloomed and when it did, you wished it hadn't. Marty agrees that the hours of time he devoted to planting, watering, fertilizing, and spraying this bush should have earned him more than the three scrawny flowers he harvested last year. Indeed, he's shopping again now because this past spring he consigned that Lost Generation special to the compost heap.

How can Marty avoid getting stuck with another loser? How's Tom going to loosen up? These two pioneers have spent a good deal of time exploring this. They consulted with their own experts and pursued their own in-depth market research. They toured the different types of garden marketplaces and identified which to go to for each type of garden supply. They also developed easy-to-follow guidelines for shopping in each of those markets—let the salesman beware.

Discount Stores: Marty Saves Big Bucks While Tom Has a Nervous Breakdown

Tom and Marty's market research began with a trip to the type of market most Americans patronize these days: the local discount superstore. This store can belong to any one of a number of chains, and honestly, we can't tell one from the other: they are all as interchangeable as their merchandise.

There was lots of parking—and lots of stuff. Marty was in his element. The two shoppers hadn't even passed through the front door before he'd fastened on a cedarwood tub. This was priced at only $8, and Marty decided it would be perfect for the 20-minute water garden he was planning (see page 158). Tom remarked that the tub looked as if it had been crafted by a beaver with an orthodontic problem. Marty tossed it into a cart and pushed on.

Entering the store, Tom and Marty were greeted by the perfume of hazardous waste—a bag of lawn-grub killer had fallen off a shelf and split. Shoppers were scuffing through the heap of pesticide, kicking it down the aisles. When he asked a clerk for directions to the hoses, Marty was answered with a vague wave toward the third aisle over. There, eight feet up on a shelf, were the hoses Marty needed to water his mushrooms (see page 30). Even Tom had to admit the price was right. Afterward, he joined Marty in snapping up plastic trowels from Finland. How could you go wrong at $1.98 apiece?

Outdoors, in the plant sales area, Marty found a 12-foot-tall crab apple tree that was selling for $39.95. Tom pulled aside the burlap wrapped around its roots and found that the ball inside was composed of an artificial peat and soil mix. The tree was being sold as balled-and-burlapped stock—that is, it was supposed to have been dug from a nursery field with a ball of soil around the roots, and the ball wrapped in burlap so that the roots would not be disturbed during shipping and transplanting.

From his inspection of the root ball, though, Tom could tell that this tree was really bare-root—just like those roses he never ordered. This is fine—almost every nursery sells bare-root trees in early spring, and though the success rate in transplanting these is less than with balled-and-burlapped trees, the bare-root ones are far cheaper. Here, though, someone had practiced a deception: they had packed the tree's bare roots back into soil, forming an artificial ball that they then wrapped in burlap. Presto! An overpriced bare-root crab apple becomes a super-bargain balled-and-burlapped one, while the price actually increases! Sadly, the packing of the artificial ball had quite likely so traumatized the roots that they would never recover. But that's show biz.

To be fair, we should mention that not far off Tom found a fair selection of no. 1 grade roses all properly packaged and, at $7.98 apiece, very competitively priced. The flower and vegetable seedlings looked shopworn—most were wilted, mangled, and often just plain deceased. Marty ferreted out a pot each of parsley, dill, and oregano that looked, well, okay, and at a dollar apiece, he took a chance. The dill died within a week, but the others took root in his garden and provided cuttings for the salad bowl all summer long. Not bad for three bucks.

By the time the two shoppers had reached the end of the plant gulag, Tom was in the midst of an anxiety attack. Maybe it was the woman with a shopping cart full of toilet fixtures and azaleas who back-ended him and then demanded that *he* apologize, or maybe it was the two kids sniping at each other with bargain-size bottles of no-brand window cleaner. Maybe it was the fumes from the grub killer. Whatever— Tom bolted for the car, leaving Marty to pay the check. ("Charge it to the publisher," Tom shouted over his shoulder.)

The Verdict:

• For generic items such as fertilizers and pesticides, the discount stores offer an adequate selection at good to excellent prices.

• The tools are of fair to poor quality but are priced accordingly. Tom finds such bargain tools awkward to use, and for him that robs gardening of much of its pleasure. Marty finds *all* tools awkward, so why not save the money?

- Sales help is nonexistent, and if you do happen to find a clerk they will know nothing about the stock except how to computer scan its bar code. If you are to shop successfully in this environment, you must know what you need or want, and you should be aware that the plants are commonly mislabeled or not labeled at all.

- Regard money spent on plants at a discount store as money spent on a lottery ticket. The plant you buy there may survive the move to your garden and flourish. Quite often, though, because of the abuse it has suffered in the store, the plant will die soon after you get it home or else sulk for years, not dying but also not growing. Figure that at least a third of the time the plants you buy at a discount store will die, so add 50 percent to the price of any plant when you are trying to decide if it is a bargain. If it passes this test (and it may), go ahead.

A Family Nursery: Tom Brushes Up on His Latin, Marty Checks Out REM's New Album

Not ten miles away from the megastore, Tom and Marty found Oliver's, a nursery Tom had been hearing about for years through the horticultural grapevine. Founded by John Oliver Sr. in 1964, this business soon became famous for its choice selection of uncommon trees and shrubs, alpine plants, and dwarf conifers, as well as for the "display gardens," which John Sr. had planted to help his customers visualize how the plants might be used.

When John Sr. retired in the 1980s, the nursery passed to his son, John W. Oliver. When he in turn retired, the sale of the nursery would have caused consternation among a by now very loyal clientele, except that the buyer was Scott Jamison, who had been working at Oliver's since 1974. John W. returned to help out during the busy spring season for several years, and Scott gradually expanded the nursery's scope to reflect new interests: first perennials, and lately annual flowers. These new interests prompted the planting of yet more display gardens.

Pulling into the parking lot at Oliver's was like arriving at a particularly beautiful private garden. Marty stood at the entrance muttering things like, "Wow, this is really cool." Tom wondered if the staff had placed the bird's nest in the fashionably skinny hornbeam (*Carpinus betulus* 'Fastigiata') that was selling for a tidy $850. Marty looked at that price tag and blanched. Tom reflected that the tree was nearly full grown, of a choice type, and obviously had received years of meticulous care—it had not a single brown leaf or broken twig.

Marty wandered from tag to tag: each plant was carefully labeled with its name, the size to which it would grow and how fast it would reach that size, as well as such details as what sort of location it preferred, the color of its flowers (if any), and the plant's winter hardiness. Some of the plants—a 'Blue Princess' holly, for example—Marty recalled having seen at half the price at his discounters. But he suspected that those bargains had had abusive childhoods, while the ones at Oliver's were fat and glossy, clearly poised for distinguished careers. Anyway, at $32.50, the Oliver's hollies were not unreasonably expensive.

Tom, meanwhile, was running from tree to tree, spouting Latin faster than a Roman senator. Most of the nursery staff fled in terror. Only the true horticulturalists remained. To Marty, the conversation sounded like this:

"Is that a flowering *Arbiticus ridiculous*?"

"It is indeed, the *verbulous* variety."

"I thought the last one of those had expired in Madagascar in 1784."

"No, they managed to get one on a boat to Cuba, where they grafted it on to a *Rhizonomous perpendiculous*."

❖

Two hours later, Marty was sitting in the car listening to REM and admiring the hen and chicks (a plant—*Sempervivum tectorum*—that he had bought for $5 after a ten-minute discussion with the sales help) when Tom emerged with about six cartons of "specimens" and no cash. Marty agreed to loan him the money to buy an ornamental sweet potato ('Blackie') that Tom had to have, as well as a couple of bucks for gas so that he could complete the trip home.

The Verdict:

- Prices somewhat higher than at the discount store, but the plants at the family nursery were immeasurably healthier.

- Friendly, informed sales help made sure that Marty got a plant that would be happy in his garden.

- Oliver's guarantees that the plants they sell are "true to name"— if you find that your *Ilex × meserveae* 'Blue Princess' is actually 'Blue Prince' and so doesn't produce berries, they will refund the purchase price.

To Marty, Oliver's was definitely a fun place, although, truth be known, there were many more varieties of things than he could really deal with. Things did cost more, but since they were in such great shape and often so much bigger than their relatives at the discount outlets, the price differential wasn't as great as it might seem. Sometimes, surprisingly, the prices were no higher at Oliver's, or the size of the plants was so much larger that Oliver's was actually cheaper than or at least equal to the discount store. But the biggest difference lay in the quality of the help; Oliver's staff was so knowledgeable and so generous with their instructions you would think you were adopting a child. Marty half expected them to call the next day to see how the hen and chicks were doing.

For Tom, the great attraction of family nurseries like Oliver's is the more interesting selection of plants you find in such places and the way that the selection varies from nursery to nursery. That reflects the different interests of the owners. Tom also likes the sense of personal responsibility in family businesses. Scott Jamison has his name and a phone number in Oliver's catalog, and you can call Scott if you are looking for something special or you are unhappy with your purchase.

This kind of personal involvement can be useful in unexpected ways. Years ago, when he lived in New York, Tom used to shop at D'Ercole Farms and Garden Center in Norwood, New Jersey. He stopped in one Saturday to pick up some chrysanthemums, and Joey D'Ercole wanted to know why Tom was so depressed. When he found out that Tom had a big date lined up that night with this woman Suzanne, and that the cash machine had just eaten Tom's cash card, Joey pulled a roll of bills out of his pocket and peeled off

$90. "Pay me back whenever." When was the last time you heard that at the discount store?

Tom Consults an Expert

Tom has bought a lot of plants and peat moss over the years, but he knows he isn't a particularly savvy shopper. He knows someone who is, though: Dean Rossman, who with his partner, Kenneth De-Falco, operates a garden design and maintenance business on the North Shore of Long Island, New York. Dean shops constantly: in the spring he stops in at some nursery every second day, on average. Dean does this because he has to—buying plants for his customers is his business—but he also clearly enjoys the quest. For him, shopping is an art form. So in the hope of picking up a hint or two, Tom asked Dean if he could accompany him on an afternoon of nursery hopping.

Tom had a great time and would tell you about it, except that Marty insists he cut right to the chase. So listed below (in skeletal form) are the gems of shopping wisdom he gathered from Dean:

Shopping for Trees and Shrubs

Dean began by teaching Tom how to really look at a plant (check its teeth, as it were). You can tell a lot about a tree or shrub just by a close visual inspection.

1. When shopping for deciduous trees and shrubs (the ones that lose their leaves in fall) during the spring and summer planting seasons, check for leaves that are torn or brown along the margin; Dean found such damage in a *Hydrangea paniculata* 'Tardiva' that caught his eye and confided to Tom that this was probably a symptom of trauma experienced during shipment. What shipment? Dean explained that almost no retail nurseries grow their own plants anymore—virtually all of them buy their stock from wholesale nurseries. In fact, it's common for the same wholesaler to supply all the retail nurseries in town: over the course of the afternoon, Dean showed Tom how the same type of plant sported identical labels at every place they shopped—that's because the plants all got labeled at the same place, some wholesale nursery in Virginia.

When that is the case, when all the plants come from the same supplier, then any differences in quality at the retail level must originate in the kind of care each retailer has given to the plants. And a big difference may lie in the way the plant is handled after the retailer picks it up. If the plant is kept cool, well watered, and out of the wind during shipment, it won't even notice it has been moved. But a less conscientious nursery owner may stack plants in the back of an open truck and subject them to hours (or even days) of scalding sun and dehydrating hurricane-force winds while in transit. The plant may recover from such a trail of tears, but why take a chance?

2. Also check for yellowed leaves. These are usually a sign of damaged roots. Maybe the nursery help isn't conscientious about watering the plants, or maybe this tree or shrub has been left sitting out in a too hot sunny area. Dean chose a plant with this symptom and slid it out of its pot. Then he showed Tom how the roots were blackened at the ends rather than crisp and white. Dean's verdict: forget that plant, because in the long term, the health of the plant's visible parts depend on the health of the roots.

3. When shopping for trees, check the trunk. There should be neither bruises in the bark nor the scars of old bruises. Such an injury—a legacy of rough handling—may look superficial, but if the bark has been damaged, the growing tissue underneath has also been injured, and as it dies back it will create a point of entry for disease and decay.

4. Check to make sure there are no splits in the crotches where major branches emerge from the trunk. That's another symptom of rough handling. Such damage may not be apparent unless you squat down and look closely, since the injured branches remain partially attached and may even continue to grow for a period of months or years. Then wind or snow applies pressure and the damaged branch snaps off, leaving you with a crippled plant.

5. Check trees for "double leaders"—a trunk that has been allowed to fork. Generally, the fork creates a weak point and leaves the tree much more prone to splitting—even decades later, when the tree has grown into a monster that overhangs your roof.

6. Check for stubs of cut-back branches. At best, this is a sign of unskilled pruning and suggests that the tree or shrub hasn't gotten good care. At worst, it's a clue to a cover-up: because of disease or some sort of mistreatment, the plant's branches died back, and rather than discard the injured specimen, a less-than-scrupulous nurseryman simply removed the evidence as best he could.

7. When shopping for conifers, run a hand over the foliage; if it feels dry, that's an indication that the plant's root ball has been allowed to dry out at some point, even if it is moist at the time of inspection. Conifers rarely recover from that kind of stress.

8. Step back and check out the profile of the root ball; this is a clue to how long the plant has been sitting in the nurseryman's yard. A sagging, flattened ball is a sign that the plant has been there for a long time. That's not good. Ideally, the interval between the moment when the plant is lifted out of its nursery bed and when it is set into the customer's garden should be no more than a few days to a few weeks—the longer the interval, the more trauma the plant suffers. Weathered or, worse yet, rotting burlap is another sign of long-term residency in the nurseryman's yard. So is a rank growth of weeds sprouting out of the burlapped root ball or out of the pot— they weren't there when the plant arrived from the wholesaler.

9. When shopping for trees and shrubs, buy young. Impatient gardeners may insist on buying trees and shrubs that are already large, but they should be aware that to dig such plants requires a butchering of their root systems. Smaller trees can be moved with a root ball that is much larger relative to the plant, and so they suffer much less trauma. That means they recover from transplanting and resume growth much more quickly. Often a small tree will shoot up to overtake the larger specimen within a few years. That makes the smaller tree a terrific bargain, for they commonly sell for a fraction of the price of the larger, more imposing specimens.

If you are determined to buy a large tree or shrub, Dean suggests that you have a landscaper you trust buy it for you. You will pay more for the plant, but the landscaper will make sure you get the best plant possible, and he or she has the experience and equipment to move and transplant your purchase without unnecessary harm.

Shopping for Flower and Vegetable Transplants

When shopping for annual or perennial flowers, Dean says, the most important thing is to make sure they are pest free. Check the tops and undersides of the leaves and along the stems—and if you find any sort of bugs, or even empty egg cases, leave the plant alone. Otherwise, you may be bringing home some parasite that will keep you spraying all summer. Dean and Kenneth use truckloads of lantanas each year in making up flowering tubs and baskets for clients, and Dean drives to Rhode Island (well over a hundred miles) to get the plants. That's because he knows the plants at the nursery there are reliably pest free.

And when buying any flower or vegetable seedlings, avoid the tall ones that are already in bloom. Such plants have been sitting in the pack too long and they most likely will remain stunted no matter what kind of care they receive after you set them out in the garden. A far better buy is the seedling that is stocky but compact, with rich green foliage but no flower buds. Such a seedling is still in its most active phase of growth and will root quickly into your garden and fill out properly before it begins flowering.

In General

If one plant is markedly more expensive than its fellows, find out why. Dean pointed out a handsome, cinnamon-trunked tree marked *Betula nigra* 'Heritage'. This special clone of a river birch was priced almost twice as high as some similar-sized European white-barked birches (*Betula pendula*) nearby. But the 'Heritage' birch is worth the money, for it is resistant to the borers and leaf spots that soon disfigure or kill those bargain European birches.

And Before You Leave the Nursery . . .

After you've bought, there is one more thing you must do: get the nurseryman to water your plants before you cart them home. Remember that a windy drive down the highway will dehydrate the plants otherwise.

Marty's Two Cents' Worth

According to Sal Gilbertie, who in a fifty-year career has turned Gilbertie's Herb Gardens in Westport, Connecticut, into a horticultural landmark, the bulk of his annual sales occur during two weeks in April. Sal cautioned Marty that if he insisted on shopping during this period, he would find the sales help extremely harried, the shelves depleted, and the crowds unpleasant. If Marty would make a point of shopping earlier or later in the growing season, Sal added, he would find sales staff members far more friendly and helpful, and he would be more likely to find the merchandise on sale.

Tom noticed when he went shopping in October this past fall that the trees and shrubs in the nursery yards were marked down 50 percent; and though not many gardeners know this, late fall is actually the best time to plant deciduous trees and shrubs. Late fall or even early winter is also the best time to plant evergreens and perennials in the South; September is a good month for planting evergreens in the North.

Shopping by Mail

Mail order has become the virtual mall in which millions of Americans shop for virtually everything. The advantages are clear: you shop at your convenience; the selection is tremendous; the prices, because of the volume of business, are always competitive, if not rock-bottom low; and the quality is for the most part good, with many mail-order companies offering a money-back guarantee on their merchandise.

Ordering plants and gardening supplies by mail can be a real time-saver or a real pain in the neck. As usual, a little knowledge goes a long way.

For a knowledgeable, organized person like Tom, ordering by mail is a natural. Before Tom plants anything, he usually knows exactly what he wants, exactly where it will go, and exactly when he wants to plant it. He can look at catalogs and make an informed decision. Mail-order shopping saves Tom the time he would otherwise spend driving from nursery to nursery, and often it spares him trouble in the garden. That's because he can get precisely what he needs through the mail—he can get a plant or a tool specifically designed for the situation at hand.

With roses, for example, shopping by mail opens up a huge selection of diverse plants, whereas at the local nursery Tom has to choose from the tiny assortment of roses that the retailer has chosen to stock. None of those garden-center roses are likely to survive in his mother-in-law's arctic landscape in the Berkshire hills of western Massachusetts. Via mail order, though, Tom can get ultra-hardy hybrids bred from *Rosa rugosa*, a rose native to central Siberia. These rugosa roses relish Berkshire winters, and if Tom is looking for a rose for a tight spot—like the narrow strip between the house and lawn—he can order special compact rugosa roses that never grow more than 2½ feet tall or wide. No wonder Tom loves mail order.

For Marty, on the other hand, catalogs are a nightmare. Maybe if he just received one or two, he would have a fighting chance. But a season after he ordered six bulbs by mail, he received no less than seventeen catalogs, all arriving within a period of two weeks. Give Marty a choice between two varieties of tulips and he can make an intelligent decision. Give him a choice between fifty and it's Prozac City. Marty, being an editor, finds directional atrocities like "Height: 18 inches to 3 feet" maddening. Which is it? If it's 18 inches it goes one place; if it's 3 feet it goes somewhere else.

And when the plants arrive, there's another problem. Maybe eventually they will grow to be the perfect specimens pictured in the catalog, but right now they look like clumps of, well, green stuff. Sometimes they come packed with great directions; sometimes they come wrapped in the local newspaper. And what if the weather's lousy for a few weeks after you order the stuff? Like it snows in April? What do you do with the plants to keep them alive? Open the box? Start them indoors?

Sometimes Marty doesn't even remember what he's ordered, although this can have surprisingly good results. (See the 20-minute projects at the end of this chapter.) Nevertheless, mail-order gardening fills Marty with anxiety. To relieve this (and maybe to relieve your anxiety as well) and to ensure that you always get your money's worth, we have developed ten rules for ordering by mail:

1. Order only from catalogs that include a telephone number to call for customer service and, ideally, the name of the proprietor. Sending money to a post office box is never a good idea (unless it's Marty's).

2. Never order from a catalog that doesn't list the winter hardiness of each plant and include a copy of the United States Department of Agriculture Zones of Hardiness map. The hardiness of plants is basic information you will need to get plants that will survive in your area. If the mail-order company doesn't bother to provide it, chances are it doesn't bother with other important things, such as the health of the plants.

3. Order early and you are much more likely to get the plants you want. Tom, for example, has found that to get the antique apple trees he needs for his hard-cider orchard, he has to order in November or December for spring delivery. Even when ordering vegetable and flower seeds, he tries to get his orders in by mid-January.

4. Specify when you want the plants delivered. Generally, four to six weeks before the average date of the last frost in your area (your Cooperative Extension agent can tell you when that falls) is a good planting time for plants such as apple trees or perennial flowers that will shipped to you bare-root and dormant. Plants hate to be kept waiting, so make sure you can put them in the ground as soon as they arrive.

5. But identify a storage spot just in case the plants do arrive early, or spring arrives late. A cool, frost-free place is what you want. A spot at the back of an unheated garage, against the wall of the house is good. Tom stores his mail-order cartons under the bulkhead over the basement's outside door. He opens the cartons as soon as they arrive, moistens the plants if they are dry, and then puts them into his do-it-yourself cold storage until he can plant them out. They'll keep two or three weeks in there.

6. Does the catalog list plants by botanical names and specify the cultivar? The cultivar is the registered strain to which the plant belongs; its name will be listed between single quotes, as in *Betula nigra* 'Heritage', where Heritage is the cultivar name. Or does the catalog use Madison Avenue–type names cooked up to snare the unwary: "Nebraska Beauty Vine" or "Tree Tomato"? How can you figure out what you should buy if you can't tell what it is that they are selling?

7. Look askance at any catalog that advertises a "compost activator." That's a common product, but it's also a useless and totally unnecessary one, since the bugs and microorganisms of decay already live in every backyard. Any catalog that sells it is run either by organic gardening ideologues or by rascals. You are a fool to do business with either. Likewise, immediately dispose of catalogs that advertise cute bunnies made out of compressed manure. You shouldn't encourage that kind of behavior.

8. If you garden in the North, where winter hardiness is the main concern, try to order your plants from a region with a somewhat colder climate so that you know your purchases will be hardy. Tom orders all his roses from Canadian nurseries—he can practice his conversational French while he orders by phone, and the roses he gets think they have moved to Miami and flourish accordingly.

9. Ordering regionally is also important in the Deep South; when Tom lived in Texas he watched many a Yankee and Californian plant melt in the heat and humidity of summertime. Transplanted gardeners insisted on ordering Dutch bulbs, which had to be refrigerated through the winter before they were planted out to bloom in spring; the catalog of Ty Ty Plantation in Ty Ty, Georgia, was Tom's introduction to all the bulbs that lo-o-o-ve Texas summers. It takes all kinds.

10. Above all, be sure any catalog from which you order includes a guarantee on the plants the nursery ships; shipping plants by mail is a risky business, but good mail-order nurseries will replace anything that arrives looking like lettuce that has been in the crisper drawer too long.

How can you find mail-order sources for the plants, tools, and supplies you need? The best aid is Barbara Barton's book *Gardening by Mail,** a 375-page directory to everything you might conceivably want to order (and even some things, such as compost activators, that you don't want).

How can you tell the quality of a mail-order nursery before you invest in an order? Ask other gardeners about it and you are likely to get an earful. The most efficient way Tom has found to get in touch with satisfied and unsatisfied customers is via the Internet. He searched the World Wide Web for "plants by mail" and tapped into a couple of home pages that had served as clearinghouses for critiques on the quality of service provided by hundreds of mail-order nurseries.

* Houghton Mifflin Company, Boston, 1994, $18.95.

Other Stuff

We aren't going to advise you on shopping for specific chemicals, since 1) you shouldn't be using them in any significant quantities (we rarely resort to anything more lethal than liquid soap), and 2) the regulations change so fast that any advice we did share would be dangerously outdated by the time you read it.

Our only suggestion is that you check the expiration date on any bottle or canister before you buy. Modern insecticides, fungicides, etc., are designed to break down over time (so that they won't persist in the environment), and they lose their effectiveness fairly rapidly. For the same reason, you should buy these things in small quantities so that you use up each purchase promptly.

We do have some advice on shopping for fertilizers. Ignore the brand names; instead, look at the labels. On any fertilizer label you will find a series of three numbers, such as 5-10-5 or 10-10-10. These numbers tell you the actual nutrient content of the fertilizer (most of what a sack of fertilizer contains is actually some sort of filler, such as ground-up corn cobs). Add the three numbers up, then compare the totals of the different products and their prices. If ten pounds of 5-10-5 fertilizer (total nutrient content: 20 percent) costs $10 and ten pounds of 10-10-10 fertilizer (total nutrient content: 30 percent) costs $12.50, then the 10-10-10 is the better deal.

Gardening books recommend the use of different fertilizer formulas for different sorts of plants. However, we have found that, in practice, a fertilizer in which all the numbers are fairly similar (as in those cited in the preceding paragraph) works fine for just about everything. All other things being equal, we prefer products that promise slow release, since that's how plants like to be fed, slow and steady.

That's why Tom mostly makes his own plant food by collecting raw materials a barrelful at a time from the local barnyard and then processing it in his compost bin. He has tried lots of different manures over the years, from elephant (when he lived near the Bronx Zoo) to mouse (he got that from a pharmaceutical laboratory). The results have been, well, mixed.

Cow manure we found to be too dangerous. With manure, the fresher it is, the more nutritious it is. But cow manure is very soupy when fresh. Put a barrelful of that in the back of your Toyota Tercel and you are liable to end up knee deep the first time you brake for a light on the way home from the farm (ask Tom). Elephant manure is excellent, but it only comes in bulk lots and, anyway, the zoo told Tom that it no longer gave a poop the last time he called. Chicken manure is strong but smelly, and it's hard to find—most of the big chicken farms are themselves composting all they produce and selling the results. Dog and cat manure are generally available (just watch where you step), but both are a haven for parasites and diseases and should be kept out of the compost heap and garden.

Tom's rule (and on the subject of manure Marty concedes that Tom is the expert) is that manure must be of a sort that comes in neat, easy-to-handle pellets; it can't have too unpleasant an odor; and it must be locally available. Horse is the manure that best fits this profile. It is easy to find even in Manhattan, and stables are almost always glad to give it away. Tom takes Matthew along on these shopping expeditions, and they always bring a bag of wilted carrots to share with the horses. Tom and Matthew regard this as an investment.

2🕐-MINUTE PROJECTS

Cultivating Chaos; Tom and Marty Slug It Out on Composting

Marty's Chaos Garden

Maybe it was because Marty opened the Dutch bulb catalog on a rainy summer afternoon that was otherwise completely lacking in color. Or maybe he just couldn't resist the exotic charm of the Netherlandish English. ("In the ground, yes?" "So attractive for friends to visit.") Whatever the reason, a few month later he found himself the recipient of dozens of bulbs, which he shoved in the back of a closet and promptly forgot about until an unseasonable November snowstorm brought him back to reality. He realized that if he didn't plant the bulbs immediately, he was going to have to sauté them for dinner.

It was a singularly disgusting day to be out in the garden. The soil was covered with five inches of slush, and a fine, freezing rain was glazing that with ice. Marty had neither the time nor the inclination to indulge in garden design. Then he remembered how the artist Jackson Pollock used to paint by randomly tossing buckets of pigments. His contemporaries had sneered, but Pollock's paintings had come to be worth hundreds of thousands of dollars.

In a fit of inspiration, Marty dumped all his bulbs (tulips, lilies, anemones, hyacinths, daffodils, and crocuses) in a large sack and shook them up. Then with his trusty trowel he scooped holes at random in the not-quite-frozen ground. He dosed each hole with a shot of bulb fertilizer, mixing the granules into the soil at the hole's bottom. Finally he reached into his well-mixed sack, grabbed the first bulb that came to hand, and dropped it into the nearest hole.

This was not the treatment recommended in the bulb catalog. This glossy, colorful booklet specified exact, and different, planting depths for each kind of bulb and recommended marshaling the different species with military precision. But the bulbs did not seem to mind Marty's iconoclasm. The next spring they shot up in a delightful chaos, large flowers intermingled with small, short with tall, purples with yellows, reds, and pinks.

Like the Pollock canvases that had inspired it, this bulb garden had no apparent order and yet was strangely beautiful. Its pattern changed unpredictably throughout the spring as each type of flower bloomed, faded, and gave way to others. Marty likes the result so much that he's made it a permanent feature of his backyard. As his kids say, now the garden matches the rest of his house.

A Pair of 20-Minute Compost Bins

Deep spiritual feelings stir in Tom whenever he goes out to visit the compost heap. (He does this several times a day—it's more fun than writing.) I mean, here it is, the miracle of life in Tom's own backyard. From the dross of last week's potato salad is being born a new vitality for his garden. Compost adds nutrients to his garden soil, giving the plants the sort of slow, steady feed that they like best. It loosens the soil, letting air and water work down to the plants' roots. Compost also acts like a sponge to absorb and hold water that would otherwise run away. By lacing his soil with compost, Tom has eliminated almost entirely the need for irrigation; he only waters new plantings and the vegetable garden. Tom's homemade compost even helps cleanse his soil of diseases and plant parasites. But what moves Tom most is the knowledge that all of this is going on with virtually no work from him.

Still, because this is such a miraculous process, Tom cannot bear to approach it as casually as does Marty. Dress it up with any kind of rationale you like, Marty's do-it-yourself dump is an eyesore. To compost in this fashion, Tom believes, is like holding services at the landfill.

Tom creates his compost neatly, in a pair of bins. One bin he bought, the other he built himself. Neither took more than 20 minutes to assemble. Each has its advantages.

The main advantage of the homemade bin is price. It's cheap. To build it, Tom collected five wooden loading pallets from the local building-supply center. The manager gave these to Tom. And why not? Most wooden pallets are used only for one delivery and then are sent to the landfill, at considerable cost to the disposer (i.e., the building-supply center). Chances are, the businesses in your area will let you haul away pallets for free, too.

Because he wanted a really handsome bin, Tom was choosy. He took only pallets made of oak. (Many loading pallets are made of softwoods, such as fir, but this product is nevertheless

Materials:
5 wooden loading pallets
(4 small, 1 large)
8 wire hangers
Total construction time: 40 minutes
Cost: nothing

Note: wire should wrap around and through the ends of both pallets to fasten them together.

Construction: stand four small pallets on their sides, arrange in a square, and fasten together at corners with wire from hangers. Use two hangers per corner, one at top, other at bottom. Tighten wire wraps by twisting ends with pliers. Set finished box on top of larger pallet.

the number one consumer of hardwoods in the United States; we make 540 million pallets from hardwoods such as oak every year.) Tom took five in all: four small ones and one large pallet.

When he got home he laid the large pallet flat on the ground; on top of this, he set up the other four on end, arranging them in a square. Tom wired the four small pallets together at the corners with old clothes hangers that he twisted tight with a pair of pliers. Then he was done. All that his handsome, oaken bin lacked was rubbish, and he soon remedied that. Over the next few weeks he filled it with grass clippings, apple waste from his cider press, the Halloween pumpkin, poop from Matthew's rabbit, and so on.

To make sure that the composting rubbish didn't start to stink, Tom took care to add twice as much dry, brown stuff (dry leaves, sawdust, straw) as green and juicy stuff (animal manures and any fresh and wet vegetable material). In dry weather he waters the bin occasionally, so that the materials inside it are moist but not sopping wet. A year later, he removes the finished compost. This may not look like highgrade coffee grounds as the compost gurus promise it will, but it's much more uniform and granular than the wads and chunks that emerge from under Marty's heap.

Tom loves the sense of self-sufficiency that he derives from his homemade bin, but he wouldn't be without his storebought one, either. It's called a Green Cone—Tom bought it for $70 (shipping and handling included) from SolarCone, Inc., of Seward, Illinois. This bin is actually a double-walled, conical plastic silo that sits atop a perforated plastic basket. To install it, Tom attached the hinged lid to the silo's top and sank the basket into the soil in a sunny spot in the middle of the garden.

This is a wonderful device. Because the silo is fastened to the basket with screws and because the basket is buried, whatever you put inside remains inaccessible to hungry critters. Actually, Tom did find evidence one morning that an animal had been digging around the base of the cone, but a sprinkling of mothballs took care of that (see page 165). Tom uses the Green Cone to compost all sorts of kitchen wastes:

vegetable peelings, meat scraps, old yogurt, and last week's forgotten spaghetti. If he put this stuff in his wooden bin, it would turn it into a feeding station for cats, dogs, and worse. The Green Cone handles it without a hitch.

Another advantage of the Green Cone is that it allows Tom to compost year-round. Regular compost bins—such as Tom's pallet bin—are strictly seasonal. In wintertime, the contents freeze, at which point composting is put on hold until spring. The Green Cone's double-walled design, however, means that it acts as a collector of solar energy. On sunny winter days when the temperature outside was well below freezing, Tom has measured the temperature inside the cone at 50° or 60°F. Even in January, the miracle continues in the Green Cone.

But the best feature of the Green Cone, from a 20-minute gardener's point of view, is that it produces very little compost. Instead, it seems to digest most of whatever material you put into it and leak it into the surrounding soil. This makes the Green Cone a sort of solar-powered fertility generator. You don't have to unload its contents into a garden cart and haul them to the garden. Instead, set the Cone in the garden and plant around it. The tomato seedlings Tom set out around his Cone sent vines up eight feet high and yielded buckets of fruit. The grapevine growing there now bore a bushel of fruit last summer. Only once in 2½ years has Tom actually had to remove the cone from its base and unload the basket. For the rest, it's been strictly buffet style, with the plants helping themselves.

Marty's Composting for Mere Mortals

While Tom fills you in on all the scientific reasons to compost, I thought I could give you the two real-life reasons why my family does it.

First, it gives you something to do with banana peels and coffee grounds so you don't feel quite as guilty about all the useless packaging you're constantly bringing home from the supermarket. Also, since nothing edible goes into the garbage, the neighbor's mutt doesn't knock over the can anymore. Raccoons hate composters.

Second, it's a lot cheaper than fertilizer.

Now even though Tom and I have written a whole book about composting and much as we and our publisher would like you to buy it, all you really need to know are these two words: COMPOST HAPPENS. Whether it happens in six weeks, six months, or six years is purely up to you. But happen it will. You can use one of Tom's scientific methods or you can use Marty's Random Theory of the Universe Method, which works as follows:

1. Find a place behind a tree not visible from your house or those of your neighbors (except for the one with the dog; put it directly in his line of vision).
2. Dump stuff there (nothing that ever walked, swam, or flew).
3. Wait.
4. (Optional.) Poke it with a stick every once in a while. If it screams, run.
5. Twice a year go out and see if it's compost yet.
6. Using this method, unless you're prepared to bequeath this pile to your offspring, you will probably get something that Marty has cleverly labeled "not quite compost," which means you will see clumps of soil shaped like banana peels and maybe an occasional persistent eggshell.
7. If you don't need compost, give it more time.
8. If you do need compost, take some of your not quite compost and mix it into your soil a month or two before you do any planting.
9. Start over.

Answers to Stupid Compost Questions

1. Yes, it smells, but it doesn't smell *bad*.
2. No, it doesn't attract animals unless you put animal foods in it—meat, bones, or old sour cream, the type of stuff the neighbor's dog likes to drag out of your garbage cans. Those can be composted, but only in a sealed, high-tech bin like Tom's Green Cone.
3. Yes, compost does attract bugs, but these are good bugs, natural recyclers, and they are not the types of bugs who will attack your house or invade your kitchen.

4. No, it can't explode.
5. When in doubt, don't put it in the heap. There's nothing magic about composting, and it won't turn toxic waste into fertilizer. Save your old batteries, scraps of pressure-treated wood, and other evils for the toxic waste drop-off box. (Your town clerk can tell you about that.)
6. No, the finished product probably won't look like Colombian coffee grounds, no matter what the organic gardening magazines may claim. Your compost is probably going to be lumpy and ugly, but your garden doesn't care and you aren't going to put it in your coffeemaker.

Chapter 5

The 20-Minute Toolshed

One of Tom and Marty's most energetic discussions focused on what exactly is the selection of tools that any gardener needs. Marty suggested that for Tom, buying tools was a way to avoid actually gardening. Who, Marty wanted to know, aside from a fetishist, really needs twenty-six pocket knives? Or five different kinds of compost bins?

The compost bins, as Tom pointed out, had been essential for this book's research, and besides, he needed them if he was going to process all the leaves that his neighbors kept giving him for nothing. As for the knives, Tom has lots of those because he likes to have the right tool for the job.

For instance, he finds that his German pruning knife's hooked blade is less liable to slip when he is cutting water shoots off his apple trees. Of course, the American-made pruning knife has the same advantage, but Tom has found that once his hand gets sweaty, the American knife's plastic handle is harder to grip than the walnut handle of the German knife. If the water shoot is a large one, well then his Japanese pruning knife—the one that looks sort of like a machete—is clearly the tool for the job. But for a really precise cut, there is nothing as good as his Swiss grafting knife. Unless it is his American grafting knife, which . . .

Tom hadn't suspected that Marty even knew that kind of language. To make sure that there would be no repetition of this unpleasantness, however, Tom agreed to come up with a list of the twenty essential tools—tools that would fill every basic need of the 20-minute gardener. Think normal, Marty urged. He promised to come up with his own list and boasted that his would be even more concise, a list for the real purist.

Tom's 20-Minute Toolshed

1. Short-Handled Garden Spade: This has a squared blade that is good for cutting an edge or digging a straight-sided planting hole for a tree or shrub; the short handle (which ends in a D-shaped grip) makes this a far more efficient digging tool than a long-handled shovel. Look for one whose blade is about eight inches wide and twelve inches long; the blade should attach to the handle with a forged socket that completely encloses the handle's end.

2. Round-Pointed, Long-Handled Shovel: You'll need this for digging compacted soil or cutting through tree roots. Fiberglass-handled models are the strongest, but they are also heavy and tiring to use.

3. Spading Fork: This is the best tool for turning soil in a bed or digging out perennial flowers when you want to divide a big clump into smaller ones ("lifting and dividing" is what the horticulturists call that). Such a fork should have four tines, and in the better forks, the tines will look square in cross-section. The broad, flattened tines found in cheap spading forks bend as soon as you hit the first rock.

4. Scuffle Hoe: Marty thinks that the scuffle hoe is a square dance he did one time when he was down in Texas for a sales conference. But Tom knows that a scuffle hoe is the ultimate weeding tool. It looks like a stirrup mounted at the bottom of a regular hoe handle. Lean on it, push it forward, and pull it back, and it slices through the soil just under the surface. Along the way, the scuffle hoe slices through weed roots, too, leaving the tops to wither and die.

With a scuffle hoe you can clean up a good-sized flower bed or a mulched display of shrubs in a matter of minutes. That makes it a very valuable tool. Yet it needn't cost you much. Quality of workmanship isn't important in scuffle hoes; even the cheap ones work well.

5. Hand Pruners: You'll need these to shape up trees and shrubs. Get yourself a good pair of by-pass shears. This kind of shears has two curved blades that cut neatly like scissors. Blade-and-anvil shears—the cheaper alternative—sever branches by crushing them between a blade and a stationary anvil, and this leaves a wound that is much slower to heal. Felco #2 shears are the standard choice of professional horticulturists, and though they cost about $30 a pair, they have replaceable blades, so that they will provide years of clean cuts.

6. Lopping Shears: This tool is designed to cut branches of diameters from one-half inch to an inch or more; you should keep a pair on hand so that you aren't tempted to do this type of heavy pruning with your hand pruners (which you will thereby ruin). Once again, by-pass models are the best. Tom prefers loppers with aluminum handles, since they are lighter than the wooden-handled ones and so easier and less tiring to wield.

7. Pruning Saw: Put the old woodworking saw back in the garage. It cuts as you push the blade through the wood—that's fine when you are leaning over a board, but it will wear you out when you are cutting an overhead branch. So get a pruning saw that cuts on the pull. One with a curved blade thirteen to fourteen inches long and a pointed tip is the best all-round solution; the blade's pointed tip will let you work the saw into tight places, like the center of a rosebush. Make sure the saw is made of tempered steel (really cheap saws often aren't) so that the blade will flex without bending. A blade with four to six teeth per inch is good for fast cutting in soft woods; harder woods require a finer-toothed blade, with six to eight teeth per inch.

8. Garden Cart: Wheelbarrows are great for mixing concrete, but you'll find a wooden-sided, big-wheeled cart much better suited to moving stuff around the garden, or from the garden back to the compost heap. Get one with a front end that swings open—it's easier (and neater) to dump forward rather than tipping the cart back so that stuff spills into your rubber boots.

9. Hose: Spend some money and get a good hose: a four-ply, ⅝-inch-diameter rubber number with heavy-duty brass couplings. Cheap vinyl hoses kink and leak and are almost as annoying as cheap spading forks.

10. Hose-End Sprayer: This ingenious device uses water pressure to turn a jar and nozzle into a power sprayer. It's much cheaper than all those pump-up tank-type sprayers, and it works far better. Marty uses it to douse soapy water over the aphids on his dahlias.

11. Leaf Rake: You pays your money and you takes your choice. Bamboo rakes are cheap and nice to use; they have a natural spring to them. Steel spring rakes are more durable but can do a lot of damage to a lawn or bed if you wield them too brutally. They are also more expensive.

A handy tip: Soak the tines of the bamboo rake in soapy water before using it and they will be less liable to break.

12. Garden Rake: Quality of construction isn't important here. All you'll use this tool for is levelling out beds before planting, so you'll never wear it out. Purists insist that a wooden-toothed rake does a better job. We've never tried one. But they are cheap, so maybe we should.

13. Trowels: You need two: one with a long narrow blade for digging out weeds and planting bulbs, and another broad-bladed trowel for planting flower or vegetable seedlings. Make sure that the trowel is either a very cheap one (like the plastic ones Tom and Marty bought at Home Depot) so that you won't care when it breaks, or else an expensive, forged one that can withstand the pressure you'll put on it when you hit a rock or root and try to make the trowel do a spade's job.

14. Pocket Knife: Gardeners need a good knife—they'll find themselves using it for everything from taking cuttings to opening shipping cartons. If you must limit yourself to just one, Tom advises that you get what is traditionally called a "florist's knife," a folding knife with a single, especially keen, straight-edged blade. A. M. Leonard (Tom's favorite source of tools—more on that later) sells one of these (they call it a "pocket grafting knife") for $15. Cheapskates can make do with a barlow knife, a sturdy one- or two-bladed pocketknife of time-tested design (Tom Sawyer carried a barlow) that sells for as little as $8. Marty loves his (even though he fancies himself as more the Huck Finn type).

15. Old Table Knife: Forget all the gizmos in the catalogs and garden centers; these make the best hand-weeding tools. And unlike the gizmos, table knives are made of stainless steel (at least in Tom's house) and so won't rust if you leave them out in the garden.

16. Boots: High rubber boots that you can slip off at the door will keep your floors mud-free and your feet dry. Get the $15-a-pair kind you see at the local feed or surplus store; the $50 "wellies" you'll find in catalogs are strictly for suckers. We've never tried garden clogs, but generations of European peasants swore by them. Of course, they also subsisted on cabbage and died by the age of thirty.

17. Hat: Tom's wife, Suzanne (*Dr.* Suzanne, as she is known to her students), insists that he wear a broad-brimmed hat when gardening, and she's right. She knows from her research on climate change that the ozone in the upper atmosphere over North America has decreased by some 13 to 14 percent since the end of the 1970s, and that every 1 percent of that drop *seems* (scientists hate to commit themselves) to have resulted in a 2.5 to 5.0 percent increase in the rate of skin cancer.

Even the mathematically illiterate ought to be able to figure out what that means: it's time to cover up. Straw hats are light, cool, and inexpensive; Tom got a really snappy Panama for $19. It not only keeps the sun off his face and neck, it creates the perfect look for effective supervision. Marty claims that his Brooklyn Dodgers cap provides equal protection and looks far cooler. Yeah, right.

18. Gloves: No real gardener wears gloves. They hinder any work that requires a fine touch. Besides, the greatest pleasure of gardening is the feel of a clod of earth crumbling between your fingers,

and you can't savor that with fingers swathed in goatskin. If you *must* wear gloves, take up boxing.

19. Electric Leaf Shredder: Marty makes do without one of these, but then Marty would garden with a pointed stick if left to his own devices. Tom knows that this gadget—a string trimmer mounted at the bottom of a big funnel—is the cornerstone of 20-minute gardening. Tom's shredder can turn a Buick-sized pile of leaves into six trash cans' worth of brown confetti in an hour or less. That's a year's supply of mulch that saves him from weeding, watering, and fertilizing.

Roto-Tillers, Leaf Blowers, Wood Chippers: Rent these as you need them. Homeowner-sized models are rarely powerful enough to do the job properly; the rental companies offer professional-grade equipment, and they have to maintain and store the stuff for the 364 days each year when you aren't using it.

And, of course:

20. Lawn Mower: Cheap is the way to go when you are buying a gas-powered rotary mower, since the kid you hired to mow the lawn will make a point of hitting every rock.

Even cheaper is the rule when shopping for a push-powered reel mower. These will cost you up to $265 new, but if you are smart you will do what Tom does and buy one at the Congregational Church's Fourth of July tag sale.

The push mower you find there should cost $10 (that's the going price, for some reason), and it will be far more solid than anything manufactured in the last fifty years. The mower Tom bought this way is a triumph of Victorian engineering; it weighs about sixty pounds; it is made of cast iron, steel, and oak; and it will outlast him just as surely as it outlasted its previous owner. Tom's going to live a long time, though, because he's getting plenty of healthful exercise pushing that mower around, and he's not breathing toxic exhaust fumes as he does it.

One more tip: Your reel mower needs its blades sharpened annually if it is to work properly, and finding someone who knows how to do that isn't easy. The guy at the hardware store guffawed when Tom asked him. Tom finally found someone with the necessary skill by asking a professional lawn-maintenance company where it took its mowers to be sharpened—professionals use motorized versions of the old reel mowers because they know that such machines deliver a much neater cut.

Marty's Five-Minute Tool Shelf

Because Tom truly believes in First Amendment rights, he has agreed to let Marty include the following.

Lots of Cheap Spades, Cans, or Whatever:

In spite of Tom's preference for tools whose lineage bears two initials (A. M., as in Leonard), Marty has found no difference in the quality of the holes he digs with expensive, hand-forged tools and those he digs with a plastic shovel, stick, or his hands. Therefore, he buys and uses whatever is cheapest. He also buys in bulk, because over the course of a summer he will misplace at least a dozen trowels. Some of these he finds when their blades puncture the sole of his sneaker; many others are pulverized by the lawn mower.

Marty has given up trying to learn the difference between a spade and a trowel. He can, after much practice, distinguish these two tools from a shovel. He doesn't understand, though, why the former are considered superior.

Clippers:

Marty recommends buying clippers with bright orange handles because clippers are more expensive than trowels and you are less likely to lose or leave out in the rain a bright orange tool. This is also a safety measure: clippers hurt more when they puncture a sneaker sole.

Coffee Cans:

To put things like seed and fertilizer in. If you buy fancy gourmet beans in bags (like a certain upwardly aspiring horticulturist I know), lighten up. A few pounds of Maxwell House won't kill you.

Garbage Bag Ties:

To tie up things that need staking. Keep them in a coffee can.

Lawn Mower:

Get a mulching mower. It cuts the grass into tiny pieces that get recycled into the soil. It's also great if you are a less-than-compulsive leaf raker. Marty bought his mulching mower at Sears five years ago.

To keep your mower running well, you are supposed to dump out all the old oil and gas every fall. Marty has never done this, and he knows that eventually his mower will turn on him. But he can never figure out what to do with the old oil and gas, and he's tired of hearing his daughter say that he's polluting the earth.

Old Running Shoes:
Keep 'em in the garage when you work in the mud so you won't crap up the house too much.

Blue Fertilizer:
Marty has never understood why fertilizer is blue.* Nevertheless, stirring it up with a stick in a gallon of water and pouring it over the flowers keeps the economy moving and probably doesn't hurt the plants. Yes, he composts as well, but compost is something you apply in addition to fertilizer, sort of like taking vitamins even though you eat a balanced diet. Tom, of course, thinks vitamins are a socialist conspiracy. That's why his skin is so pasty.

Shopping for Tools

Once you've determined which tools you want (and Tom fervently hopes you have ignored the last couple of pages), you have to buy them. That means re-entering the marketing jungle. Keep the following series of hints close at hand, however, and you will make it back to your garden unscathed. The tools you bring with you will be worth the trip, too.

Before we get into specific tips, however, we want to share a fundamental insight: when shopping for tools, the key to success is not to buy expensive but to buy smart.

For example, Tom has found that if he orders his tools from A. M. Leonard, Inc., a professional horticultural supply house located in untrendy Piqua, Ohio,† he gets better quality at half the price demanded by those purveyors of garden tools and accessories located in the more chic parts of California, New Mexico, and Vermont. Of course, A. M. Leonard doesn't offer the "elbow-high gar-

---

* For his part, Tom doesn't understand why a note on fertilizer has been included in a discussion of tools, but he has promised not to rewrite Marty's prose here.
† See Sources, page 217.

den gloves," the "Japanese farmer's pants," and the "poacher's spade" you need to make the scene. But it does offer thirty-one kinds of pruning shears (including models designed for small hands, for left-handed gardeners, and even for gardeners with arthritis), as well as forty-three different gardening knives. A. M. Leonard's imported English garden spade costs $17 less than the one in the fashionable catalog, and it is the very same tool.

As you may have gathered, Tom shops for most of his gardening tools by mail; the quality and selection are far better than what he finds in the local hardware store. But as part of his effort to wean Marty away from those unsafe-at-any-speed, discount-store horrors, Tom has been accompanying Marty on local shopping expeditions lately. Together, they have developed the following five rules for identifying high-quality tools on sight:

1. Every hardware store or garden center stocks three grades of tools: "good," "better," and "best." Those labels should actually read "junk," "poor," and "fair." Unless self-punishment is your goal, buy only the "best."

2. Never buy a tool with a painted wooden handle. The coat of paint may look cheerful, but its purpose is to hide the poor quality of the wood underneath. Look for tools with knot-free, fine-grained white ash or hickory handles; cheap tools are often fitted with handles of soft, brittle Douglas fir, which will break as soon as you put any pressure on it. Fiberglass or steel handles are even stronger but are expensive.

3. Check the quality of the metalwork. Welds and seams should be even and smooth, and cutting edges should be not only sharp but burr-free. If there are moving parts, they should turn easily (but not loosely) and without a catch.

4. Check how the blades or other metal parts of rakes, spades, and trowels are attached to their wooden handles. In the best tools, the blade will be welded to a forged socket that fits up around the end of the wooden handle. In bad tools, the blade or metal head usually ends in a spike or "ferrule" that is jammed up inside the handle's end. This soon works loose, whereupon the head slips off—constantly. You get to spend 20 minutes each day hammering heads back onto handles and practicing your profanity.

5. A tool should feel comfortable in your hand. Before you buy, grab the spade and set a foot on top of the blade; grip the trowel and poke with it the way you would if you were on your knees in the garden. The sales clerk will stare, but a tool has to fit you, it has to be the right size for you. However well made a spade may be, it's the wrong tool for you if it is designed for someone taller or shorter.

That's it. Twenty tools and five rules, all coordinating to make the tasks of gardening easier and the prospect of shopping less intimidating. Or a scruffy heap of old coffee cans leaking blue fertilizer. It's your choice.

2⏰-MINUTE PROJECT

Round Two: Tom and Marty Slug It Out on Seed Mats

Marty's Designer Seed Mat Disaster

It looked great in the catalog. You just prepare the soil, unroll the mat, and water, and a few weeks later your yard looks like a shot from Martha Stewart's estate. Right?

Okay, so they're a bit expensive. In my case, $20 each for mats about three feet long and one foot wide. I bought one that was designed for a sunny spot and one designed for partial shade. But I knew that they were going to look so beautiful, who cared about a few extra bucks?

What to Do

1. Follow the instructions carefully. Prepare the soil as instructed, even throwing in a bit of compost for good measure.
2. Plunk the mat down.
3. Keep moist.
4. Wait.

The result: Utterly miserable. I can't think of another project that was so disappointing. The "partial shade" mat was a complete bust, sending up a few meager sprouts and then just giving up. The "full sun" mat fared a little better, producing a blue flower whose origin neither Tom nor I could determine with any degree of certitude. This flower basically took over the entire mat. Unfortunately, it grew about a foot high, six inches higher than it was supposed to, and thereby hid all the flowers I had planted behind the mat. Martha Stewart doesn't have to worry.

In an attempt at salvage, I tried moving the blue flowers toward the back of the bed, but after a while it hardly seemed worth the effort. Sometimes you have to know when to just abandon ship. But I still get a lot of pleasure looking at the hundreds of perfectly formed flowers that adorn the handsome cardboard tubes in which the mats were shipped. Those tubes make great storage containers for pasta or crackers.

Tom's Homemade Seed Mat Triumph

Tom still remembers that spring day when Marty proudly showed him the newly arrived designer seed mats. The graphics on the mailing tubes really were handsome; "made with real organic straw," the label said.

"Is there any other kind?" Tom asked. Marty was annoyed, and he was even more annoyed at Tom's reaction to the mats themselves, objects that looked like something you would wipe your feet on if you were really poor. "You spent twenty dollars for each of those?" Tom asked. "For that money, I could make you something better." So do, snapped Marty.

Determined to help his friend, Tom set out to find some talented individual who could design an instant garden for him. He called his friend Jane, a potter who is also a weekend painter and a keen gardener. She has good taste, and Tom figured she could sketch out a garden plan for him in no time.

Jane, it seemed, was preoccupied with motherhood. She suggested that Tom design his own garden. Maybe he could copy a famous work of art—a van Gogh painting, perhaps.

Tom hung up thinking, "I don't draw that good." Anyway, Tom's tastes run more to paintings of Elvis on black velvet. He suspected that would be tough to translate into flowers. No, Tom needed an original design created for the purpose. For this he went to the one member of his family who does draw good: his five-year-old son, Matthew.

Tom wasn't up to weaving a mat out of organic straw, so instead he dropped in at the offices of the local newspaper and picked up a roll of newsprint. Actually, it was the end of a roll, one that was left over from the morning's print run—this he got for free. Then he went to the garden center and picked up six different packets of annual flower seeds. There were red-, white-, and green-flowered zinnias; orange and yellow marigolds; and some chestnut-and-gold miniature sunflowers. Tom's final stop before returning home was the art supply store, where he bought six markers of colors that matched those of the flowers pictured on the seed packets. While he was there, Tom also purchased a box of blank jigsaw puzzles; they looked intriguing, and Tom knew Matthew liked puzzles.

There was no problem in persuading Matthew to draft a design: Tom told Matthew he couldn't decorate the puzzles until he came across with the garden. Matthew immediately obliged, drawing on a 4-foot-long strip of newsprint a vivid figurative painting that employed all the markers. The subject looked to Tom like a duck hunt; Matthew explained with some disdain that those were *monsters*.

Alas, Matthew's design was too intricate. To realize it would require bushels of seed. When Tom asked for something simpler and bolder, Matthew looked blank. That's when Tom employed one of those cunning parental tricks: he handed Matthew a piece of paper measuring 7″ × 12″ and told him to draw a design on that. Matthew quickly scrawled something that looked (to Tom) like a psychedelic snake in need of a chiropractor. (Tom didn't share this insight with his son.)

Thus, less than 20 minutes after sitting down at the table with Matthew, Tom had his design. The next day, he dropped it off at the copy center. The people there blew up the design on their color photocopying machine. They expanded the original by 100 percent—and they expanded that copy by 100 percent, so that the final version measured 4 feet long and 28 inches wide.

Then came the clever part. Tom punched holes at irregular intervals through Matthew's snake, turning the enlarged design into a stencil. Tom then laid this stencil down over a piece of newsprint of identical size and squirted a dab of white glue through each of the holes in the design sheet. Onto each dab of glue Tom dropped three seeds—in each case, the seeds were of a flower of the same hue as that particular length of Matthew's snake.

In this fashion, Tom manufactured two flower mats in slightly over 20 minutes (26 minutes to be exact)—and at a total cost of under $18. To go with these, he reclaimed two of the jigsaw puzzles from Matthew and wrote out a set of directions on each. Why make life too easy? In the directions, he advised the reader to dig a garden bed measuring 28″ × 48″ by turning the soil to a depth of one foot and mixing it with an inch of compost. He told the reader to rake the soil smooth, roll out the mat over it, and then cover the mat with ¼″ of sand or finely pulverized soil. This must be watered daily until the seedlings emerged, at which time irrigation might be reduced to once or twice a week. When Tom had finished writing all of this on the puzzles, he scrambled them and dropped the pieces into two envelopes. Then he delegated: he sent one mat and envelope to his brother, and the others to his mother.

Only one sunflower emerged from the mat that Tom sent to his brother. Tom was reasonably well satisfied with that, since it proved that his homemade product could exactly match the performance of Marty's expensive commercial one. Meanwhile, the mat Tom had sent to his mother proved far more fruitful.

The seeds were slow to germinate. Tom thinks that he should have used a flour-and-water mix to paste the seeds to the mat rather than white glue. But after a period of several weeks the seeds did germinate, and by midsummer Tom's mother was cutting zinnias from Matthew's garden, and her sunflowers and marigolds were the envy of her neighbors in the community garden. She grumbles less and less about smart-aleck sons who send instructions that require assembly.

In the glow of his success, Tom has forgiven Marty for his doubts. Tom has saved the picture of the monster duck hunt. What a garden Marty is going to have next year. And Tom won't charge a penny more than $20 per mat. Payable in advance.

Chapter 6

Tom's Guide to Connoisseur Plants

Tom's got a real problem with plant snobs. That's unfortunate, since most of his colleagues fall into that category. It's part of why Tom prefers to garden alone. But even this has brought only partial relief. For as a professional, Tom has to keep up with what's going on in other gardens. He's spent countless hours touring famous gardens that were planted entirely with oddities and mutants.

This is what is called "plantsmanship." It's a kind of disease in which the gardener has to pack his yard with as many different plants as possible, and preferably plants that are rarely seen anywhere else, even in the wild. If the neighbors are growing magnificent (but ordinary) red and yellow tulips, the plantsman has to grow some black-flowered tulip that no one has ever seen before. So what if it is scrawny and a magnet for diseases and bugs? And all around the black tulip, the plantsman sets out a miscellaneous horde of wild-type tulips stripped out of some economically underdeveloped part of the Anatolian plateau. That's *real* plantsmanship, and among the gardening elite, it's the accepted mark of the master.

Bah, humbug!

Tom finds these botanical freak shows depressing. Anyway, he believes that having fun is the mark of a great gardener. Who cares if you have one hundred of the most aristocratic English summer phloxes—or the latest astilbe from Germany or Japan— if keeping those plants alive keeps you on the run every waking minute? Is it really worth all that work just to impress the other folks in the garden club? They probably hate you, anyway. What do you expect, devoting all your leisure time to making them feel inadequate?

Still, there is one kind of plant connoisseurship that Tom believes is very important. That kind is knowing precisely which plants will make your life easier. Because plants are like people in this respect: some just put in the hours, but others give 110 percent. The latter are the plants a 20-minute gardener wants—they deliver more pleasure for less pain. These are Tom's "connoisseur plants."

Where do you find these wonders? Well, a lot of them are at the local garden center—you just have to know what to ask for. Some you have to order through the mail from connoisseur nurseries; we'll tell you where. Some of Tom's favorite connoisseur plants you'll find on the nearest street corner. Just because something is common doesn't mean it isn't special.

What exactly makes these plants special? For Tom the most important thing is practicality. A good plant solves a problem or fills a need. It thrives in barren soil where other plants won't, it provides you with flowers when nothing else is in bloom, it weathers the severest drought without trouble—and not even the greediest suburban deer will touch it.

But the true connoisseur plant also offers extras in the aesthetic department. The new leaves are touched with a rosy blush when they emerge in spring, and they expand into a mass of foliage so lush you want to get down and roll in it. The flowers are spectacular, and they smell good, too. The foliage turns a glorious yellow in autumn, and then it drops away to reveal a brilliant-hued bark. Now *that* is a connoisseur plant.

Tom's Sixteen All-Time Favorite Connoisseur Plants

Trees

1. Japanese pagoda tree (*Sophora japonica*) is standard planting around Buddhist temples in Japan and China. Tom isn't sure why, but he assumes that the sages prefer sophoras because they give so much pleasure for so little trouble.

This tree is fast growing when young—a sapling may increase in height by as much as three feet a year—but it settles down at maturity to make a rounded canopy fifty or more feet tall and wide. Although it prefers well-drained, loamy soils, as a member of the pea family, the sophora can cope with poor ones—these plants' roots can absorb nitrogen directly from the atmosphere, effectively manufacturing their own fertilizer. The foliage is a handsome lustrous green, and the individual leaflets are small, so that when they drop in the fall, they don't smother the lawn below. Instead, they wither to little crisps that shatter with the last fall mowing and then sift into the turf to serve as an organic soil builder.

The best feature of the Japanese pagoda tree, though, is the foot-long bouquets of fragrant white flowers in July and August. These appear long after most other flowering trees have finished their performances, which gives an extra impact to the sophora flowers—they are the grand finale. In fact, these blossoms are most handsome as the curtain drops: as they fall from the tree, they furnish a midsummer blizzard that is most refreshingly out of season.

Tolerant of both heat and drought, the pagoda tree is a great tree for the South but flourishes up into Nebraska, Michigan, and central New England.

2. Cedar of Lebanon (*Cedrus libani*). Everyone oohs and ahhs over ancient trees and wails when a hurricane blows one over, but who bothers to plant the next generation? We have got to look out for our great-grandchildren. Tom knows that his cedars of Lebanon will be there for them.

Tom remembers when he planted two of these trees on the Columbia University campus. The head of the grounds department was annoyed at having spent $80 for each of these 4-foot-tall trees—he was clearly disappointed that he hadn't gotten more for his money.

"They'll grow, won't they?" he asked wistfully.

Sure, Tom replied, they will make magnificent, rugged evergreens 120 feet tall and 100 feet across.

"How soon?" the paper-shuffler asked, with a more hopeful note in his voice.

Oh, eighty years, maybe a century.

Tom never did regain his credibility with that administrator, but he likes to know that those trees are on their way. They are his form of immortality.

The cedar of Lebanon is the tree from which Solomon built the temple—and pious North American colonists made a point of planting the tree in their New Jerusalem as early as 1638. Some of those first plantings may still be around; the cedar of Lebanon is not only handsome and sturdy (Solomon didn't build with junk), it's virtually pest- and disease-free, almost as durable as Scripture. Flourishing from the northern tip of Michigan and as far west as Oregon to the mountains of northern Georgia, this tree is handsome even when young—but it's your posterity that will really enjoy it.

3. Sourwood tree (*Oxydendrum arboreum*). Why is this tree so rarely seen in American gardens? Tom bought his present house mainly so he could look out of the living room window at the sourwood tree that grows there. Tom and that tree have been cohabiting joyously for more than five years now.

This tree is a good size for small properties: 25 to 30 feet tall. The branches droop gracefully, and the trunk typically grows with a feminine curve. It's got gorgeous shiny green leaves that turn yellow, red, and purple in fall, and in early summer it drapes itself with white, bell-shaped, perfumed flowers that dangle like charm bracelets. Tom's tree feeds every honeybee for miles around—someday he's going to find out where they are taking the nectar. Sourwoods flourish from New England to Louisiana, in the Pacific Northwest, and through the cooler regions of northern California.

4. American Persimmon (*Diospyros virginiana*). One of the great pleasures of life in central Texas (Tom spent four years there) comes from the 'simmon trees that grow in the hedgerows along back roads. A close relation to the ebony tree, they are really beautiful when fall hangs the angular, rough-barked branches with

countless orange globes an inch and a half across. These taste like concentrated pucker when new, but if left to hang on the tree awhile, they soften to sweet pulp, becoming the basis for the best muffins, puddings, and ice creams Tom has ever tasted.

The American persimmon is a midsized tree that occasionally reaches a height of 60 feet but is more likely to stop at 30 or so. Aside from the fruit, its greatest attraction is its bark, which has the fashionable texture of an alligator shoe. The glossy, dark green leaves are handsome too, especially as they turn color (either yellow or reddish purple) in the fall. This tree thrives in the hot and humid South, but is hardy well up into the North, too. Tom knows of a fine specimen in Connecticut—the farmer has promised Tom that he will dial 911 if he finds Tom in its branches one more time.

5. Tree of heaven (*Ailanthus altissima*). Suppose someone offered you an exotic Chinese tree with tropical, palmlike foliage that was hardy where winters are arctic? A tree that would grow virtually anywhere and that was the closest thing to "instant tree" in the whole world? Suppose they told you that it might expand 5 feet in a single year? And that by late summer that tree would be covered with festoons of salmon-orange seeds? We bet you would say yes, thank you, give me a dozen. But when Tom recommends the tree that grows in Brooklyn, the tree that is famous among city dwellers for sprouting out of every crack in the pavement, clients turn up their noses. Yet these are the same tree.

Ailanthus has become a weed in the poorer neighborhoods of American cities (they call it the tenement palm in the Bronx), but that's because it is the only tree that flourishes in that hostile, polluted environment. In a more hospitable suburban or rural setting (the ailanthus thrives from the upper Midwest down into the upper South and throughout most of the western states) this tree grows just as fast but over the long term cannot compete with stronger, longer-lived trees. Despite its reputation as a weedy pest, ailanthus doesn't invade healthy woodland—it prefers concrete or the compacted unhealthy soil of the average American backyard.

Ailanthus does have two faults: the wood is soft and liable to snap in a storm (so don't plant ailanthus near the house), and the greenish flowers that precede the seeds have a rank odor. Still, ailanthus is the ideal tree where you need a screen right away—like when a stockbroker from the city decides to build a plywood palace on the vacant lot next door. Just wait until he sees ailanthus bursting up all around his "Tara." Tell him that proper English plantsmen esteem this tree most highly—that's the truth.

Bushes

6. Wintersweet (*Chimonanthus praecox*). One of Tom's regrets about moving to central Connecticut is that wintersweet finds that area too cold. It does reasonably well thirty miles to the southeast, along the coast, and even up to Cape Cod, and it loves the South.

Wintersweet is a real Clark Kent of a bush. In summer it is a fountain of acceptable but undistinguished foliage—as much as 12 feet high and wide in the South and milder regions of the Pacific Coast, considerably smaller in the North. Set it in the background, but not too far from the back door, because when it blooms during a midwinter thaw, the small, greenish brown flowers will knock you down with the sweetness of their perfume. You'll inhale one deep breath and remember that the world won't always be gray, that there are flowers, and that spring and love and good times are returning. In that breath, wintersweet has paid a whole year's worth of dues.

7. Rose-gold pussy willow (*Salix gracilistyla*). Pussy willows are one of the great pleasures of childhood—and they can be equally special to adults, especially if you plant a rose-gold pussy willow, whose extralarge silver plush pussies are tipped with scarlet. This species grows only 6 to 10 feet tall, which makes it a much better plant for the average garden than the ordinary pussy willow, which commonly grows 25 feet tall and 15 feet across. An interesting variation of this species is the strain named 'Melanostachys', whose pussies are purple-black tipped with red. This strain's twigs and shoots also turn purple-black in winter.

Try both of these, the rose-gold and the black, as cut flowers: take a vaseful down to the public library and leave them on the circulation desk, where the kids can enjoy them and passing gardeners will sicken with envy.

Rose-gold pussy willows are short-lived—they slip into a messy senility after fifteen years or so—but fast-growing: they should make a good show within a couple of years of planting. They grow well in dry soils but will also thrive in soils so soggy that little else besides snapping turtles can survive there.

Actually, willows can be a remedy for just that kind of problem. Tom has seen shrubby willows planted in hedges to serve as living pumps. By drawing excess water up through their roots and evaporating it out through their foliage, these trees transformed basement-flooding bogland into respectable suburban yards. Which may be an improvement—unless (like Tom) you are fascinated by snapping turtles.

8. Graveyard roses. Roses are a passion with Tom, and he often gives talks about them to garden clubs. Every time someone asks, "What is the best kind of rose for my garden?" Tom's reply is always the same. Next June, he says, go down to the oldest cemetery in your town, one where the groundsmen aren't too compulsively neat, and look for the rosebushes growing up around the graves.

That may sound morbid, but it's sound advice all the same. A couple of generations ago, it was the custom to plant a rose by your mother's grave—and even now, fifty or seventy-five years later, many of those sentimental plantings still survive. When you find such a bush, look at the nearest headstone: the date on it will give you an idea of about when the bush was planted. Then consider that in the years since then, the rose has probably gotten no spraying, no feeding, and no pruning other than an occasional butchering with a weed whacker. Any rose that can withstand that treatment and continue to bloom is tough. Any rose that can flourish year after year without any help obviously likes the local climate and soil—and is self-sufficient enough to be perfect for the 20-minute gardener.

You can't buy graveyard roses, so the only way to get one of your own is to take a cutting and root it yourself. Tom has included instructions for that at the end of this chapter; not only is the process easy, but it costs nothing (Tom likes that), and it will give you a rosebush with a provenance guaranteed to impress (or maybe alarm) any visitor.

9. Japanese stewartia (*Stewartia pseudocamellia*). This is often described as a small tree, and it will grow 20 to 40 feet tall, but the one Tom planted threw up a cluster of trunks, so he calls it a shrub.

However you classify this plant, you have to admit it is out-standing. Hardy from coastal New England to southern Alabama and throughout the Pacific Northwest and down into northern California, the Japanese stewartia has trunks that ripple with muscle and sinew; the reddish bark scales off in flakes, giving the tree-shrub a camouflaged look that is very dramatic when set against a background of winter snow. (Eat your heart out, Alabama.) The leaves turn purple before falling away in autumn, and the white camellia-like flowers that open in mid-July are quite elegant.

The very best feature, though, comes right before the flowering: the stewartia's expanding flower buds turn opalescent like giant pearls just before they open. Grab a cup of coffee and venture out to admire this in the soft light of early morning. It may be the very best moment of your gardening year.

Hedges

10. Hardy orange (*Poncirus trifoliata*). Citrus groves in the Bronx? Sure, if your yard offers a moderately sheltered spot. Hardy orange survives temperatures down to −10°F. It grows wild in Tennessee, and Tom has harvested fruit in New York City. (This is one tough plant.) The fruit looked just like little oranges, too, though it was seedy and sour enough to provide a good substitute for lemon juice; it makes a tasty marmalade.

Hardy orange also produces white and fragrant orange blossom–like flowers. Still, this plant's greatest benefit is the sense of security it can provide. It bears needle-sharp, 1–2-inch-long thorns all along its stems—nobody pushes his way through a hardy orange. Set several plants out in a row, shear them back once a year to keep them compact and dense, and hardy oranges make an impenetrable hedge. In fact, this plant attracted a brief flurry of publicity a few years back when a security firm began planting it around military ammunition dumps and nuclear facilities.

Even in the Bronx, Tom recalls, no one messed with this plant. He has since seen it growing in the South, where it was far more vigorous and bore much more fruit. It doesn't mind salt spray, and it makes a good seaside planting, though it doesn't appreciate the huge seasonal temperature swings of the upper Midwest and the Rocky Mountain states. Gardeners there will have to content themselves with razor wire.

Climbers

11. Scarlet runner beans (*Phaseolus coccineus*). Tom has found that his style of gardening involves a good deal of patching and masking. Sometimes, that's due to his mistakes—for example, the clematis he planted in too sunny a spot, so that it never grew. Sometimes the problem is a natural disaster—the blight that polished off his crab apple. And sometimes the problem is just a question of priorities—sure, the old half-rotten arbor is ugly, but the cost of having a carpenter rebuild it would be two months of his son's tuition at day care. Not to worry, though. Scarlet runner beans are equal to all of these problems.

Plant the big seeds in rich, moist soil as soon as the weather has warmed in spring, and these beans are off and running. The vines shimmy up strings, poles, tree trunks, or rotten arbors with equal ease, wrapping their hosts in garlands of lush green leaves. They'll climb to 8 feet, and by midsummer the vines are bearing their scarlet blossoms. These in turn give rise to 8-inch bean pods that are delicious when steamed. When not burning up the tuition money at day care, Tom's son, Matthew, used to eat the beans raw, right off the vine.

Scarlet runner beans are annuals, so they solve a garden problem only for one year. That's okay though—you can always replant the following spring and postpone that repair yet again.

Flowers

12. Okra (*Abelmoschus esculentus*). Marty detests okra, but then, what can you expect from a guy that thinks a hunk of grilled tofu is acceptable barbecue? Tom knows that okra is one of God's great gifts to man—indeed, it has caused him to suspect that the Ten Commandments (the *real* Ten Commandments) were dictated in a drawl.

Yankees know of okra only from the frozen blocks they buy in their soulless supermarkets. Pop one of those into the microwave and what you get is a slimy horror. If only they could know okra as Southerners do: step out into the dews of the evening and gently pluck the perfectly ripe pods from the head-high stalks. Roll the pods in corn meal and fry them in hot oil. Eat them while they are still hot and crunchy. Or don't cook them at all: pickle the pods and then alternate them with gulps of cold beer. If you are feeling exotic, curry them. Heaven.

But Tom has discovered a use for okra that apparently the Southerners never suspected: it makes a wonderful flower and foliage plant. Which is not surprising, for okra is a close relation of the hibiscus, and the big yellow okra flowers are very similar to those of that subtropical beauty. A well-grown okra plant stands 4 feet tall even in the less-than-tropical North, and in the South Tom has seen okra reach 6 feet and more. Planted in a mass, okra makes a good backdrop for a flower garden, especially if you use the red-leaved cultivar 'Burgundy' that's got creamy flowers our Mississippian friend Felder Rushing describes as "thigh-colored."

One summer not too long ago, Connecticut suffered a drought, and though many of Tom's other plants suffered, the okra he had planted around a sunny garden seat obviously relished the extra heat. Tom used to sit amid his okra in the evenings, picking and eating the crisp pods as he contemplated the beauty of the blossoms. Knowing that Marty was at the same moment hunkered down over a slab of charred bean curd made the okra (and beer) taste all the finer.

13. Sunflowers (*Helianthus* spp.). Listing sunflowers as a single entry is cheating, since this plant comes in so many different sizes and colors it can supply a whole garden of flowers all on its own. We haven't tried all of them (there are about 150 species of sunflowers and as many more domesticated types), but we'd like to.

Tom loves the annual sunflower 'Russian Mammoth'. This grows gratifyingly fast to a height of twelve feet and bears yellow-petaled flower heads the size of dinner plates. He planted 'Russian Mammoth' in thickets one year to screen his house from the road and harvested the seeds to feed the birds and himself. He's heard of planting it in circles and then tying the stalks together at the tops to make a living tepee. His son, Matthew, has promised to help him with this.

There are red-flowered annual sunflowers too, and a white-flowered Italian kind ('Italian White') that is very chic. Tom grew that one year. He hasn't yet tried 'Teddy Bear', a cultivar that makes thick stalks and monstrous flowers but grows only two feet high. This is advertised as ideal for a child's garden, but it looks like a pituitary problem to Tom.

The perennial sunflowers are less often seen in gardens, but that's what makes them a badge of horticultural sophistication. (Plantsmanship rears its ugly head!) Tom grows a prairie species, the willow-leaved sunflower (*Helianthus salicifolius*), whose stalks do sort of look like willow shoots. So far it hasn't flowered, but Tom is much too sophisticated to care. He's getting clouds of flowers already from the Jerusalem artichokes he planted last fall—they're perennial sunflowers too: *Helianthus tuberosus*. "Jerusalem" comes from a bastardization of the old Italian name, *girasole*, which means "turn to the sun." That's exactly what sunflower blossoms do: over the course of the day they turn to track the sun as it moves across the sky.

In addition to this aesthetic pleasure, though, Jerusalem artichoke offers a more practical reward. Its fast-growing tuberous roots may be dug up and boiled—they taste like artichoke hearts. Indeed, experienced growers have warned Tom that he better eat a lot of them if he doesn't want to have his whole front yard transformed into a solid patch of sunflowers. Think of that: a solid block of yellow flowers turning in unison like a yardful of gilded satellite dishes.

Ground Covers

14. Lavender (*Lavandula* spp.). Soon after Tom met Suzanne, he sent her a bunch of lavender cut from his garden—and in the accompanying note, he suggested that she use it to perfume her drawers. Tom meant her *linen* drawers; he was trying to be subtle.

Subtlety is a mistake, especially with lavender. Plant it in great swaths wherever the soil is well-drained and the sun is intense. It's bug-proof and drought-proof, and the elegant, polished silver foliage is delightfully aromatic. English lavender (*Lavandula angustifolia*), which is hardy to −10°F, bears lavender-colored flower spikes in early summer; there are pink- and blue-flowered cultivars, too. Though classified as an herb, this is actually a shrub that will grow to a height of 2½ feet—though Tom finds it makes a better ground cover if sheared back low in the spring. French lavender (*Lavandula dentata*) and Spanish lavender (*Lavandula stoechas*) make bigger, bolder plants (to 3 feet tall), and French lavender has handsome cut leaves. But alas, these are not frost hardy.

A bunch or two of lavender in your drawer(s) really will keep your linens and woolens moth-free and smelling sweet. Will it bring you true love? It's worth a try. Lavender is a very seductive plant. Take it from Tom.

15. Woodruff (*Galium odoratum*). Tom got a start of this plant when he visited the garden of a friend who mans the plant-information hotline for the New York Botanical Garden. Her transplanting technique was to drive a spade into the woodruff bed and pry loose a couple of clumps. Tom took these home in a plastic trash bag. The next morning he spaded up a shady patch of earth. He mixed in a bucketful of compost, popped in the woodruff, watered, and it was off and running.

Given a moist and humus-rich soil, woodruff spreads rapidly to form a plush blanket of whorled green leaves 8 to 12 inches deep. The foliage is glossy green and elegant; the plant is a vigorous spreader and is hardy to −20°F. Woodruff would be worth growing even if the vigorous foliage were its only attraction. But it isn't. In May it breaks out in parasols of tiny, four-petaled white flowers, signaling that the time has come to drink May wine.

This is a German concoction that is as simple to make as it is to drink. Begin by picking, cleaning, and crushing ¼ cup of woodruff leaves. Drop them into a large ceramic or stainless steel bowl and mix with ¼ cup granulated sugar, ½ cup cognac, and ½ bottle of white wine. Cover tightly and let sit for twelve hours. Then strain the liquid into a punch bowl and add the other half of the bottle of wine. Chill, add a bottle of champagne, and garnish with a cup of sliced strawberries.

The woodruff leaves add a vanilla flavor and fragrance to the drink—and also, supposedly, help "make the heart merry." Tom has found that if taken in moderation, May wine very definitely has an uplifting effect—gardening in this fashion has provided him with some of the best 20-minute intervals of his entire life.

16. Garden cress (*Lepidium sativum* var. *crispum*). This plant's peppery leaves make a tongue-awakening addition to salads and sandwiches. Its highest use, however, is as vegetable graffiti. This is one of the most gratifyingly fast-growing plants in the gardener's arsenal. Sow cress seeds, and shoots of green begin emerging from the soil within a week. Two weeks later you've got a nice tuft of curly, lacy leaves; these are ready for harvest within another week or two. That makes garden cress a most convenient plant for gardeners (like Tom) who have trouble planning ahead—if you are late with the second sowing of lettuce, you can paper over the gap in harvests with a quick planting of cress.

But cress has other virtues far more poetic. It grows best in the cool weather of early to midspring and mid- to late fall, when Tom's front-yard vegetable beds are otherwise bare. They aren't bare for long, though. Dribbling powdered lime between his fingers, Tom sketches patterns of white lines over the carefully raked soil. Last year the pattern was a series of wild arabesques; this year it was five-year-old Matthew's initials (M.G.C.). Once he has worked out the pattern to his satisfaction (mistakes are raked into the soil and re-drawn) Tom inks it in by scattering cress seeds wherever he sees lime.

He waters the seeds and sprinkles them daily thereafter. A week or two later, the first green ghost of the pattern emerges. The first year, neighbors and dog walkers made daily visits to watch the arabesques darken and thicken. They made a point of returning the next spring but were mystified by the initials which were that year's pattern. So was Matthew. He didn't really believe his father's story: that the garden itself was writing to Matthew. But he wasn't sure.

Tom also used cress seed to decorate a new garden (a sort of pyramid of raised beds) he built behind his Texas home. Suzanne was planning a celebratory barbecue; Tom chose his planting time by counting back three weeks from the date of the party. He doo-dled knots, curlicues, and mystic symbols. Right after the guests ar-rived, he turned on the spotlights. They were amazed.

These are some of Tom's favorite connoisseur plants (only some). He doesn't expect you to slavishly adopt them all as your own (though you could do worse). Tom hopes, though, that in reading through his plant descriptions, you have figured out how he selects those plants that have been granted space in his garden. But because he believes that subtlety is generally a mistake (and not just in affairs of the heart), he has listed below the six criteria for true connoisseur plants. Apply these to the plants that surround you, and you can create your own connoisseur's list.

1. A connoisseur plant must be realistic. Nursery catalogs are going to try to sell you on whatever is new and odd because they can charge more for such novelties. Pay no attention. Instead, think about the realities of your yard and your life, and choose a plant suited to them. A plant connoisseur with a shady yard and allergies

doesn't care where the plants come from—she wants plants that flourish in low light and bear sterile, pollen-free flowers.

2. A connoisseur plant must be vigorous—not necessarily fast-growing; that's not always what you want. A dwarf chamaecyparis that increases in height only an inch a year is a much better planting for the spot under your picture window than a Japanese black pine, which will add a foot of height each year and soon give you a view of only needles. But fast-growing or slow-growing, you want a robust plant.

3. A connoisseur plant must be bullet-proof. It must be disease- and pest-resistant—in your garden, not just in its native habitat. That qualification is important to keep in mind, for native plant enthusiasts will try to sell you all sorts of plants, with the rationale that since they come from the wild, the plants know how to take care of themselves.

That's true—as long as the plants are left to grow where they like. But you want the plants to grow where you tell them to, and that's a different matter. Take, for example, the high-mountain natives that rock gardeners call "alpines." In the wild, those delicate-looking plants grow amid conditions of wind, cold, and drought that would kill a Sherpa. And they flourish. Yet those same plants are as temperamental as can be in a coastal lowland like New York City. Tom knows. As part of his botanical garden apprenticeship, he had to help care for a whole gardenful of alpines. Those suckers hated New York summers, and the only useful purpose they served was to provide take-out dinners for a streamful of tough, urban muskrats. Tom couldn't wait to get out of that garden.

4. A connoisseur plant must be adapted to your soil and climate. Often, the best choices are plants, like graveyard roses, that you find flourishing in abandoned gardens or by overgrown cellar holes in state parks or forests. Such a plant obviously needs no special care.

If you don't have the time or inclination to track down these lost plants, you can get lots of information about plants that like your region from gardeners at the nearest botanical garden, or from your local parks department. Even if you decide not to plant the species they suggest, the recommendation can give direction to your shopping. If the parks department tells you that 'Burford' holly is the shrub they plant everywhere, you may not want to follow suit—too boring. But you should definitely look into the holly family, because the relatives of boring 'Burford' are likely to do equally well in your area.

5. A connoisseur plant must have something special to offer. Maybe it offers a different beauty through every season: the stewartia is a good example of that. Or maybe it offers a combination of shade, an ability to deal with poor soils, and a reduced need for maintenance (like the sophora). It may be a plant that knows how to delight with a surprise—like the wintersweet that fills the yard with perfume during a winter thaw, when life otherwise seems bleak. Occasionally a connoisseur plant offers an intriguing twist on a familiar favorite, as in the case of the rose-gold pussy willow.

6. Above all, a connoisseur plant must be one that you like. Just because public opinion may say that perennials are the thing to have and annuals are gauche, there's no reason you can't go on growing the marigolds that you like. Anyway, marigolds are a very special flower: domesticated by the Aztecs, they were brought back to Europe by the conquistadors as one of the treasures of the New World. Tom has found that he can develop a rationale for practically any plant—and he is confident that as a fellow connoisseur, you can, too.

2🕐-MINUTE PROJECTS

Rooting for Roses; Starting from Seed

Grave Robbing: Tom Roots a Rose

If you want to plant a new rosebush in your garden, you have two options. You can stop by the garden center and buy one; that costs money (which is anathema to Tom), and the chances are excellent that the plant you get will never again look as good as it does on the day you take it home. You can spray it, feed it, mulch it, and wrap it up with a burlap comforter over the winter, but unless you live in southern California, you can't provide the unvarying mild climate in which your off-the-shelf rosebush was bred and raised. Transplant this Californian to Memphis or Dubuque, and most of the time, it is going to sulk.

The second way to get a rosebush is to find a bush that likes your soil and climate, an established bush that is already thriving in your area, and take a cutting. The ideal hunting ground for such a rose, as Tom has already suggested, is a graveyard or some similar setting, such as an abandoned garden, where the bush has had to get along without coddling. In that way, you may be sure that the rosebush you are introducing into your garden is a self-sufficient one—a 20-minute gardener's dream that flourishes without spraying or winter protection.

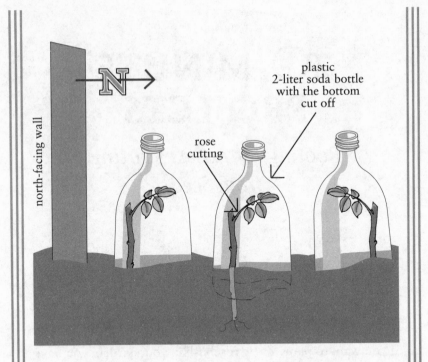

north-facing wall

N

rose cutting

plastic 2-liter soda bottle with the bottom cut off

Of course, you'll probably never know the real identity of such a plant, and if you did, it would be of little use, because in all probability, your locally adapted rose is of some type that long ago dropped out of fashion and vanished from the catalogs. Even if you make a pest of yourself at some botanical library and establish that the rose you collected is 'Lady Inchiquin' or 'Flame of Fire', so what? No one is going to recognize the name anyway. But do you care? You'll have a bush that likes your climate, likes the soil in your garden, and will bloom for you without spraying or special care. A rose like that, who cares if it's anonymous?

The best part of this is that starting roses from cuttings is not only cheap, it's easy. And it requires practically no equipment: just a pair of pruning shears, a couple of one-gallon zipper-lock plastic bags with a moist paper towel in each, plastic labels, an indelible pen, and a cooler. You gather these things and then you wait for the height of rose season. That's the time of year when the rosebushes in your area are producing their biggest and best flowers and in the greatest numbers.

In the North, this usually happens sometime in June; in the South, the rose bloom peaks twice, once in mid- to late spring and again in early fall.

You'll know when peak rose season has arrived because your neighbors' bushes will seem bent on blooming themselves into oblivion. When that is happening you load your equipment into the car and head down to the cemetery. Take a walk around (with your pruners in your pocket and plastic bags in hand) and look for rosebushes—as Tom has already explained, you are more than likely to find several, if you have chosen a properly neglected cemetery. When you do find the ideal rose, and the date on the headstone indicates it is an old one, you make the cut.

With your pruners, you amputate at its base a cane (gardener talk for a rose stem) with a flower. Snip off the flower and stick it in your buttonhole. Then cut the severed cane into pieces about the length and thickness of a pencil, making sure that each piece has three to five leaves (each one of which will be divided into 3 to 9 tooth-edged leaflets) sprouting from it. Seal the cuttings in one of the zipper-lock bags, together with a label on which you've scribbled a description of the flower—its color, fragrance, and so on.

Checking the date on the headstone is important not only because it reveals whether or not the rose is a real survivor but also because it will spare you embarrassing encounters. Common sense dictates that you should take cuttings only from roses growing on gravesites old enough that the survivors aren't still paying visits. Cemetery groundsmen won't care about what you are doing (see Tom's description of groundsmen on pages 39–40), but it is embarrassing to be discovered in the act of grave robbing by the bereaved.

If you have chosen your cemetery well, you should locate several promising bushes in a single walk. Tom once visited a Victorian cemetery in Pennsylvania in which he found twenty-three distinct kinds of roses; he had exhausted a full box of plastic bags by the time he got back to his car.

When guilt or shame or simply running out of roses puts an end to your collecting and you have returned to your car, place the cutting-filled bags in the cooler to keep them fresh during the ride home. If it's a warm day, you should keep a bag of ice in the cooler, too. Once you've done this, there's no hurry—cuttings stored in this fashion will remain viable for a day or even two. So by all means, return by the scenic route and keep your eyes open. Many's the time Tom has spotted a collectable rose on his way back from a collecting expedition, and often this was the best find of the day. Indeed, he makes a practice of keeping collecting gear in his car right through rose season—you never know when opportunity will present itself. And if the opportunity happens to be growing in someone's front yard, well, there's no reason you can't ask for a cutting. Make sure the owners don't claim to be gardeners, though. You don't want the kind of fussy roses that real gardeners grow.

When you get home, dig up a bed in a partially shaded, protected spot—against the foundation on the north side of your house is ideal. Mix lots of sand and peat moss or compost with the soil, so that when irrigated it will remain moist but not wet. You won't need a large bed unless you have been exceptionally greedy: a bed two feet deep and three feet wide will accommodate dozens of cuttings.

Process the cuttings one bag at a time—if you mix cuttings from different roses together, you won't be able to sort them out until the cuttings have grown into bushes and borne flowers of their own, and that may take a couple of years.

Prepare each cutting for planting in the bed by snipping off all of its leaves except the topmost one. Then dip its base in rooting hormone (this is a powder that may be purchased at any good garden center; it contains chemicals that promote the formation of roots). Tap the cutting to shake off any excess powder. With a pencil, make a hole a couple of inches deep in the bed, drop the cutting in, and firm the soil in around its base with your fingertips. Water the cutting and cover it with an upended one-quart canning jar, or with a two-liter plastic soda bottle from which you have cut the bottom. That's it.

Set the cuttings about four inches apart, and be sure to keep them well-watered—in hot, dry weather, you may have to irrigate every second or third day. During hot weather, you'll also have to ventilate. This you do by tipping the jar slightly and standing one side of its lip on a pebble or stick, or by unscrewing the cap from the cut-down soda bottle.

The cuttings may root within a month, but the process may take considerably longer. Give them time; if, like Tom, you are impatient, you can test for root formation by tugging gently on the cutting's leaf; if the cutting starts to slide out of the ground, it is still rootless. If that's the case, slip the cutting back into the bed, refirm the soil around it, and replace the jar or bottle. If the cutting resists your tug, it probably is rooted. Don't disturb it, though. Leave the cutting in place, but remove the cover.

The following spring is the time to transplant the rooted cuttings. You can plant them right into the spots you have set aside for rosebushes, though if the plants are really small, it may be safer to set them in a sunny corner of the vegetable garden and let them grow up before moving them out to where they must compete with other garden plants and weeds. Within a year or at most two, your collected rose should be ready to bloom.

How much time does all of this take? Depending on the size of the cemetery, collecting may take minutes or an hour or more—but a stroll among the headstones is quite relaxing. It's a healthy reminder that no matter how badly things are going for you, they could be worse. Digging the bed and processing the cuttings should take no more than 40 minutes—a weekend's worth of 20-minute gardening. Subsequent care of the cuttings is negligible. And once they are out in the garden, you'll be saving time, because your magnificent graveyard roses will need no spraying, no winter wraps, none of the special care that off-the-shelf roses would need. In Tom's experience, there's no other kind of gardening so shrewd and satisfying as grave robbing.

Tom Starts from Seed
(in 20 Minutes a Day)

To Marty, starting your own plants from seed seems an unnecessary complication. Why keep chickens when eggs are a dollar a dozen at the supermarket?

Tom, however, is always lusting for life's less common experiences. If you buy your eggs, your only choices are grade A or jumbo; but if you raise your own (and Tom would do that if Suzanne and his neighbors weren't so unreasonably opposed), you can have giant turkey eggs (one makes an omelette), tiny quail eggs (hard-boiled, they are the perfect accompaniment for champagne), even blue and green eggs from Araucana chickens—and think how handy those would be at Easter. Likewise, how can Tom be satisfied with off-the-shelf flowers when he knows that the catalogs are full of really special things: lime-green zinnias, tobaccos that flower at night, tomatoes that will actually ripen in New England. He can have all these things and more—if he will start them from seed.

This can be easy, too, if you forget about doing it the natural way. Sow the seeds outdoors, and the bugs and birds will eat most of them. Try to start them on a windowsill, and they will catch a chill the first cold night and then cook the next day when the sun comes out. No, to raise seedlings efficiently, you have to build a nursery box.

Tom managed to assemble the unit pictured on the opposite page in a single Saturday morning—and he did this in January when, frankly, his other gardening duties were slight. He can't predict how long assembly will take you; Marty says that to him it looks like a six-week project. Figure on two hours for the normally adept. The costs are minimal—scrap lumber will do for the frame, so your only out-of-pocket expenses should be for a sheet of foil-backed foam insulation (available at any building supply store) and two 4-foot fluorescent shop lights (these require a total of four ordinary fluorescent tubes). Tom's bill came to $42.50, and that included the duct tape he used to fasten on the doors.

This wholly artificial environment offers a number of advantages. Keep the doors closed, and the lights will warm the soil to the perfect temperature for germinating most seeds. Enclosing the seed pots will also help keep the soil moist until the seedlings emerge, and this is important since even a brief drought will kill sprouts. After the seedlings emerge, you can prop the doors open to improve the air flow. (Plants need fresh air, too.) Thanks to the fluorescent fixtures, you

Materials:

⅝" plywood for ends, top, and bottom
two 4' fluorescent fixtures ("shop lights")
eight 2½" corner braces
thirty-two ½" wood screws
4' x 8' sheet of ½" foil-backed
  foam insulation
roll of duct tape

duct tape
hinges

sides of box made of 15" x 50" pieces
of ½" foil-backed foam insulation attached
to box with strips of duct tape

two economy fluorescent fixtures, each with two
4' fluorescent tubes (one warm white, one cool white)
attached with ½" wood screws to inside of box top

duct tape
hinges

End pieces:
13" high
18" across top
24" wide across
bottom

Top: 18" x 50"

Sides: 15" x 50"

Bottom: 24" x 48¾"

sides and ends fixed to top and
bottom with 2½" corner braces
(eight braces, four to each side)
and ½" wood screws

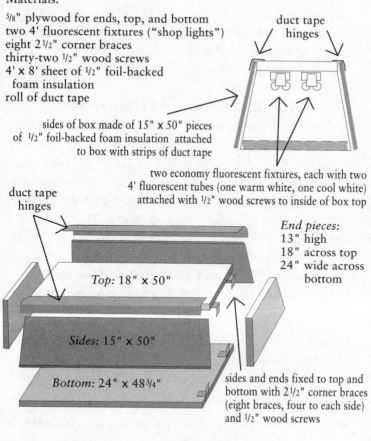

can give the plants as much light as they need; Tom leaves the lights on twenty-four hours a day until the seedlings emerge, and then cuts back to fourteen hours of light daily. This feature also means that you can do your seed starting wherever it is convenient—you don't have to fill the living-room windows with pots.

The very best feature about this nursery box, however, is that it is so small. A greenhouse will nurture seedlings equally well, but it offers too much temptation for many 20-minute gardeners. If you are like Tom, you will feel obliged to use every inch of available space—which means that you'll be raising hundreds or even thousand of pots of seedlings. (Tom grew 3,400 seedlings one spring when he was given the run of a small greenhouse.) That turns your hobby into a job, one that may well be more exhausting than the one you are already holding down. The homemade nursery box, by contrast, will accommodate only a couple dozen pots. It forces type A gardeners to behave like type Bs, which is one of the fundamental secrets of 20-minute gardening.

A Few Tips on Using the Nursery Box

- Don't sow your seeds too early. Wait *at least* until the time recommended on the seed packet, and maybe a couple of weeks later than that, since the seed company figures you'll be making do with a windowsill. Tom got spooked one year by a friend's inquiries ("You haven't started your seeds yet? I've had mine in for almost a month!") and sowed a month and a half before the recommendation. His plants outgrew their pots long before it was warm enough to set them outside, and he had to transplant them into bigger pots. That was a lot of work and a big mess, and the plants never really recovered.

- Wash all pots or other containers with Lysol (and be sure to rinse them well) before planting. This is especially important with pots recycled from the previous year—they may carry the germs of plant diseases.

- Fill the pots with commercial seed-starting mix. It is disease- and pest-free, and since seedlings are very vulnerable, this is essential.

- After planting, water the pots from the bottom. Set them in an inch of water in the sink or dishpan, and the moisture will wick up through the seed-starting mix, gradually moistening it throughout. Subsequent waterings may be done with a spray bottle; keep the seed-starting mix moist but not sodden.

- Once the seedlings have emerged and produced their first pair of real leaves, use a pencil tip to lift the little plants out of the seed-starting mix and transplant them to individual pots. Tom likes to transplant into those molded plastic cell packs that sit in trays, and he always plants into a peat-based soilless potting mix, since this too comes out of the bag disease- and pest-free. The soilless potting mix is also nutrient-free, so a couple of weeks after repotting Tom has to start feeding the seedlings with a half-strength solution of houseplant fertilizer (he applies it weekly).

The most important thing to keep in mind is that the bulk of what you grow in your nursery box you are not growing for your own use. The seedlings are bargaining chips. Many of the plants you would like to start from seed—rare chili peppers, coleus like Marty's got, and most wildflowers—are difficult to germinate and slow-growing; growing them will be far too laborious for a 20-minute gardener. What the 20-minute gardener does is to find some really expert, serious gardeners like Tom's neighbors, the P——s. Then you figure out what sorts of plants the P——s find irresistible, and you grow the most accommodating of these.

The P——s, for example, have a weakness for heirloom tomatoes. They are easy to grow, so Tom always orders seeds of several kinds with intriguing names, such as 'Brandywine', 'Cherokee Purple', or 'Mortgage Lifter'. These seedlings you barter for the seedlings the expert gardeners grew, like the P——s' 'Firecracker' pepper, which bears royal purple chilis, or their white Italian sunflowers. Or you can trade a dozen of your cold-loving 'Stupice' tomato seedlings for a load of llama manure, like Tom did.

Of course, whining and pleading will often get you what you want, too. Tom has been known to try that. But he has found that starting seedlings requires less effort.

Chapter 7

Marty's Top Ten Garden Plants

Now that Tom has regaled you with all sorts of expensive plants with Latin names that will impress your neighbors but drive you crazy (unless you know Latin), the voice of common sense here would like to ask for three cheers for some good old *American* plants (and by American I don't necessarily mean native—I mean plants that were associated with our American heritage, before gardening became Gardening).

1. Grass. May as well start with the obvious. Is grass a plant? I say if it's green and it grows, it's a plant.* Grass has been getting a bad rap because the kinds we grow in our lawns are

---

* When Marty showed the manuscript of this chapter to Tom, Tom considered sharing a little basic botany with Marty. But messing with anything so pure as Marty's scientific ignorance seemed like sacrilege.

mostly not native; you need to mow grass, fertilize it, water it, it's bad for the ozone and blah blah blah.

To me grass is like pizza. There's great pizza and there's good pizza—but there's no such thing as bad pizza. Grow your grass perfectly if you're anal compulsive; crawl on your hands and knees and pull out every weed and your grass will be a bizarre thing of beauty, like a map of the United States made entirely of dryer lint. If that's what makes you happy, who has the right to criticize?

The great thing about grass is that you can also use it as a generic name for anything smaller than a tree that grows on the ground in large quantities and won't break your lawn mower. Grass can be dandelions or moss or onions. Let nature mix your grass with whatever other green stuff it wants to add in. If it covers the ground, it's grass.

Some of us wouldn't think of fertilizing it or insecticiding it. Yet, chem-lawn commercials to the contrary, our grass comes back year after year and looks just fine. Some of us even like to mow the stuff—especially if we have a loud power mower that makes us feel like Arnold Schwarzenegger.

The slower growing, drought-, bug-, and disease-proof varieties on the horizon will make grass ecologically more acceptable. As for the native grasses Tom keeps talking about, I'll invest as soon as someone explains to me why I have to pay less for domestic cars and domestic beer but more for domestic grass.

There's one foolproof method to cure an antigrass snob. Have them walk across the lawn in their bare feet and not smile. Go ahead. Dare them.

Tips on growing grass: Growing grass is laughably simple, but you can make it even easier. First, when you buy your grass seed, put together a mix of different species recommended for your region. The chances are that different areas of your yard offer slightly different conditions—more sun, more shade, drier soil, wetter soil, and so on. The conditions in each area will favor a different type of grass; by sowing several different species at once, you cover all the bases.

Second, when you buy the grass, avoid the fancy named types: 'Tifdwarf' Bermuda grass, 'Touchdown' Kentucky bluegrass, 'Loretta' perennial ryegrass. Get generic seed, seed that is sold by the species name, such as perennial bluegrass, and that lacks a personal name, such as 'Touchdown'. Why? It's like dogs. A pedigreed dog may be more elegant and predictable in appearance, but it's also inbred and probably susceptible to all sorts of weird (and expensive) health problems. The mutt from the pound won't be as pretty, but it will thrive in almost any kind of conditions.

One last bit of advice: put a lot of work into the lawn before you plant it. Pile on the organic matter—compost or peat moss, for example—to a depth of one inch and then rototill the soil to a depth of at least six inches (eight or more is better). Sow the seed, rake it into the soil, and water it well every couple of days, until it makes a nice thick cover.

Then ease off. Cut back on the watering to once a week, and by midsummer stop altogether. Don't rake up and remove clippings, and don't bother to fertilize. Grass can take care of itself, as long as you don't train it to depend on handouts.

2. Pachysandra. Snobs can leave the room right now. Pachysandra is to plants as Cheerios is to food—predictable but good. It's the first plant I learned to identify when I moved to the suburbs: I liked it then, and I like it now. It requires no care and will grow anywhere. It's great for a place where you don't want grass (because it's too hard to mow there) or where grass won't grow (because it's too shady).

Pachysandra does have a tendency to overrun everything in its path, but to my mind that makes it the perfect plant for the '90s. It's like grass on caffeine.

The real reason that horticulturists (Tom) dislike this very practical import from Japan is because any idiot (even me) can grow it. There's no glory in it for *them*. It's too easy to establish, too. Ask your neighbor if you can clip back the pachysandra that's overrunning her walk, and throw the clippings in a plastic trash bag. When you get home, bury the end of each clipping in soil—set them six inches apart, and mulch around the tops with shredded leaves. Keep the planted clippings well-watered for a couple of weeks, and they will take root and start to spread. No wonder nurserymen don't promote this plant.

If you're truly ashamed to be seen with pachysandra, try referring to it by its Latin name.* Or you could grow the native Ameri-

* Tom's note: pachysandra *is* this plant's Latin name.

can pachysandra, Allegheny spurge (the regular pachysandra comes from Japan). Allegheny spurge isn't evergreen in the North, and it's much pickier about where it will grow—it demands a humus-rich soil. But if you have to be different, you must expect hardship.

Tips on growing pachysandra: Avoid dropping a match on it after dousing it with kerosene. Otherwise it will do just fine.

3. Blueberries. I didn't think of blueberries as ornamentals until I planted them one year and got really pissed off when the birds ate the berries. I tried netting. I tried scarecrows. Forget it. I was about to tear up the bushes in frustration. Then I realized two things: 1) the berries didn't taste nearly as good as the ones I could buy in the supermarket for a dollar a pint; 2) the bushes were real pretty, especially toward the end of summer, when the leaves turned all kinds of red and gold; and 3) they required virtually no care.

Conclusion: If someone told you you could have a bush with attractive inedible berries that required no care, had striking leaves, and attracted beautiful birds to whom the berries were not inedible, would you hesitate?

Tips for growing blueberries: They like acid soil. Mulch them with pine needles if you have them or use a fertilizer designed for acid-loving plants. Cut the bushes back in the early spring. You can order them by mail from the nurseries listed on page 220. There are many varieties, with leaves of different sizes and colors and berries that ripen at different times.

4. Strawberries. Same deal as blueberries, except I think the birds that like these either are stupider or can't swoop in on the fruit as quickly as do the blueberry-loving birds because the strawberries are down on the ground. Whatever the reason, my strawberry plants bore so many berries that I actually picked some before the birds got them all.* Unlike the blueberries, my strawberries tasted a heck of a lot better than the rot-proof ones in plastic containers. The plants also make a great ground cover, only slightly less dense than pachysandra.

Tips for growing strawberries: A lot of sun, a little fertilizer, and you're in business. Some people say clipping the leaves after the

---

* For a really ingenious (if slightly Kafkaesque) cure for strawberry eating birds, see chapter 10, page 196.

plants have produced their berries makes them bear more fruit the next year. Some people say clipping off some of the blossoms improves the quality of the remaining fruits. I take no position on either point except to say that they're pretty, easy, and tasty (the berries, that is). And they come back year after year.

5. Daisies. They have all kinds of technical names. Some are annuals. Some are perennials. Let Tom worry about that. As far as I'm concerned, any flower with a yellow center and a ring of white petals qualifies.

Show me a person who's too snobbish to enjoy the innocent beauty of a bunch of daisies and I'll show you someone who's been drinking too much café mochaccino; we're talking basic flowers here. Daisies harken back to a simple, innocent aesthetic. They're also completely painless to grow, provided you've got a sunny spot.

Tips for growing daisies: Tom says there is no such thing as "daisies"—that this name has been applied to hundreds of different species, and they all require different levels of care. He's deigned to describe a few of these species here.

Crown daisy (*Chrysanthemum coronarium*). An annual that may grow 4 feet tall, bearing yellowish-petaled flowers 4 inches across. Prefers cool (but frost-free) weather, full sun.

English daisy (*Bellis perennis*). A perennial. In the South, sow seeds in late summer for flowers the next spring; in the North, start seeds indoors in midwinter. This plant prefers cool (but frost-free) weather, moist soil, and full sun. It is compact, the plant reaching a height of only 6 inches, and in addition to white flowers, garden types of this plant may bear blossoms with pink or red petals.

Feverfew (*Tanacetum parthenium*). This fits Marty's definition of a daisy, so even though it isn't called a daisy, we're including it here. Feverfew is a perennial in the South, an annual in the North. Two to three feet tall with bunches of white-petaled flowers ¾ inch across. Prefers warm weather and full sun or partial shade.

Marguerite daisy (*Argyranthemum frutescens*). A 2–3-foot-tall plant that is perennial in the Deep South, annual elsewhere. Blooms repeatedly throughout the summer if cut back after each flowering. Bears flowers 1½–2½ inches wide with white, pale yellow, or pink petals. Prefers full sun.

Oxeye daisy (*Leucanthemum vulgare*). A perennial to 2 feet tall that bears long-stalked white-petaled flowers 1½ inches across in summertime. Hardy as far north as any sensible gardener cares to live, this plant seeds itself around the garden to fill those spots you forgot to plant. It prefers full sun.

Painted daisy (*Tanacetum coccineum*). Hardy to northern New England, a summer-blooming plant that grows 1–3 feet tall, bearing 2½-inch-wide flowers that may have white, pink, red, or lilac petals. The ferny leaves are pretty.

And finally: African daisy (*Arctotis venusta*). This resembles any other kind of daisy, except that it is bigger (up to 4 feet tall) and bolder—the African daisy bears 3-inch-wide flowers of cream, yellow, pink, bronze, or red. This plant flourishes in full sun and warm weather.

6. Birch trees. Okay, they're not technically a plant, they're a tree.* Sue me, I like them. They look Japanese in the spring. They give moving, graceful shade in the summer. Golden leaves in the fall. Bare in a poetic way in the winter. Downside is that they're prone to all kinds of bugs and diseases and they don't live very long. Upside is that a diseased birch looks better than an undiseased most anything else, and if you let a few of the suckers that emerge around the base grow up, your birches will replace themselves indefinitely.

Tips on growing birches: Shop for a pest- and disease-resistant sort, such as paper birch (*Betula papyrifera*) or river birch (*Betula nigra*). The 'Heritage' river birch is a particularly vigorous and healthy type.

7. Parsley, Sage, Rosemary, and Thyme. Herbs are easy, beautiful, edible, smellable, and about as easy to care for as can be. The four from the song are great, but so are oregano, basil, mint, and whatever else you fancy (unfortunately they don't rhyme as well). Some of them can be a little fussy about the sweetness of the soil; they

---

* This statement is so inexplicable that it leads Tom to suspect Marty isn't ignorant after all. Maybe Marty gardens according to some pre-Linnaean system of botanical classification in which trees are not grouped with plants. Didn't the Druids worship trees as spirits? And how did the Neanderthals classify them? A connection of this sort would also explain Marty's choice of garden tools.

need an occasional dose of lime in areas where the soil is naturally acidic, as it is in most of the eastern half of the country. Other herbs—mint, for example—will take over a football field in a week if you don't trim them. Some of the most aggressive ones are best left in pots, or they may climb up the stairs to your room and strangle you in your sleep.

Think of herbs as garnish, not just for your cooking, but also for the garden. Fill gaps between flowers or shrubs with carpets of parsley or basil, or a sprawling bush of rosemary. Their foliage is handsome, and the herbs will give your garden a very sophisticated bouquet.

Tips on growing herbs: Most herbs originated on the shores of the Mediterranean. (That's why French, Italian, and Middle Eastern foods taste better.) As a result, they prefer warmth, full sun, and dry weather. Herbs develop the best flavor when grown in infertile soil, and they are practically drought-proof once they have rooted into the garden. Buy them as young plants in the spring— they take forever to start from seed. Remember that fertilization and irrigation do not benefit most herbs; that sort of mistaken kindness encourages rank, soft growth, which has little flavor but is attractive to pests of all sorts.

8. Daffodils. "And then my heart with pleasure fills, And dances with the daffodils."—William Wordsworth. The ordinary can be the most sublime when we allow ourselves to see and experience it.

Plunk in the bulbs in fall and forget about them. Get depressed during the winter. Then, wow, what a happy surprise in the spring. Daffodils bloom before you have to do anything for them—when just being able to look at them after all the ice and snow is such a kick.

Tips for growing daffodils: Put them where you're not likely to step on them, bozo. And plant them deep enough so the neighborhood rodents can't get to them. Or sprinkle moth crystals over the bulbs after you plant them to turn off the squirrels and mice. If by chance it doesn't, well, at least you'll have moth-free rodents.

9. Ferns. These go in my category of "plants so beautiful that they must be hard to grow only these aren't." Who'd've thought that something as delicate as a fern was a perennial that requires virtually no care and comes out just when summer is getting a tad hot

and you're so grateful for their delicate coolness? Maybe mankind did something right in a previous life.

Ferns love shade. The new shoots are edible (I can't pick 'em; they're too pretty). I've taken ones that grow naturally under pine trees and transplanted them where I wanted them—then watched them happily grow. I've never given them anything, done anything for them, or seen them have any problem with any kind of weather or soil.

Tips on growing ferns: They don't like too much sun.

10. Hosta. Almost as easy as pachysandra to grow. They take sun; they take shade. They crowd out weeds; they will handle as much or as little water as you give them. As an extra bonus, you get some flowers in July or August. I've never done a thing for mine and they don't seem to care. They just happily come back year after year to provide graceful and seemingly weed-proof ground cover.

Tips on growing hostas: This is the ultimate designer plant; it comes in thousands of different sizes, shapes, and colors. Take your pick.

Hostas will survive almost anywhere but really thrive in a semi-shaded spot with moist soil. Watch out for deer, though. They graze hostas right back to the roots, unless you protect them with some of the truly clever tricks outlined in chapter 9.

So there you have it. You can choose from Marty's simple, down-to-earth, easy-to-grow, all-American plants or Tom's pretentiously Latin-monikered rarities guaranteed to break your bankroll, impress your friends, and give you a nervous breakdown. Or maybe you can mix and match. Ferns and pagoda trees, daisies and stewartias, ailanthus and . . . uh . . . uh . . . crabgrass.

Politically Incorrect Gardening

Marty likes to be right. He may seem detached and philosophical ("spaced out" his kids call it), but beneath the cool veneer there is a world-class competitor who lives to get in the last word. That's why he hates it when Tom talks down to him about plants. Or he used to hate it, until he developed his secret weapon.

Marty's secret weapon has brought him all sorts of magnificent, unusual, and easy-to-grow plants that leave Tom speechless with envy. These are plants that are specifically adapted to succeed in the soil of Marty's yard and in the climate of his region. In short, Marty's weapon is the ultimate source of 20-minute plants, and Marty's going to share it with you, in case you ever run into Tom and his hotshot catalogs. That may sound generous, but really, Marty's secret weapon is a secret only because he can't figure out an acceptable name for it.

"Those old ladies" is what Tom calls Marty's plant source. Marty knows that "old lady" is no longer an acceptable term, at least in his world, that to call anyone by such a disrespectful term is to practice ageism of the worst sort. Tom insists that a hundred miles in from either coast, "old lady" is a term of respect, that it is a position one *aspires* to, that old ladies run everything worth running in the South, for example—and that if Marty doesn't believe him, he should try venturing west of the Hudson River once in a while.

Marty knows that this diatribe is yet another sign of Tom's prehistoric outlook. But at the same time, he can't come up with an alternative term that doesn't irritate his gardening mentors, the women whom he visits periodically to share herbal tea and cookies (Marty's a good baker, but caffeine makes him tense) and to beg for more plants. "Horticultural seniors?" "Elder gardeners?" Marty finds that he's most likely to get the cuttings and seedlings he wants if he sticks with "ma'am."

Here are the facts: while roaming around, walking the dog, Marty discovered that the very best plants in his hometown were all growing in the yards of horticulturally cunning women past the legal age of retirement. These plants are the pick of decades of testing and selection; they provide good garden displays with a negligible investment of work. These women have reached an age where they value true excellence over mere novelty. They know what will work in the local climate and soils, and that's what they grow. Their flowers may not be the most spectacular, but they always flourish, and without a lot of fuss.

Nurserymen have to be businesslike. They know that, generally, novelty sells far better than genuine value, so mostly they aren't interested in the plants grown by Marty's mentors. That doesn't bother the women—they trade starts back and forth among themselves. When they find a rose or azalea they want, they root a cutting. They harvest seeds from favorite flowers and vegetables and save them to sow the next year's crop. They can do this because they favor old-fashioned, nonhybrid plants that offer reliability, instead of the spectacular but temperamental wunderkinds found in catalogs.

The elder gardeners' standbys are precisely the plants that a 20-minute gardener wants, too. If you are Tom, you can beg your starts from Marty, but otherwise, you are going to have to do as Marty does and go to the source.

How do you locate gardeners who maintain collections of these superior plants? Marty recommends starting your hunt in midspring, in lilac season. Snap a leash onto the dog, tell your partner, spouse, roommate that, sorry, you are too busy to clean out the garage, you are doing research, and follow your nose. Literally. Modern breeders have produced lilacs with flowers of all sorts of remarkable hues, but to achieve this they have sacrificed the flowers' fragrance (as well as the bush's natural vigor and resistance to disease). Marty's mentors, however, grow lilacs of the old-fashioned, astonishingly fragrant sort. You'll smell them halfway down the block.

You'll know you've found the right yard because it will contain the most amazing tangle of foliage and flowers. If you wander by early enough in the year there will definitely be daffodils, unnamed daffodils that don't dwindle away over two or three years but that instead spread into fields of yellow trumpets. There will be other bulbs, too—grape hyacinths, crocuses, snowdrops, or other more exotic things, depending on where you live (we know of an eminent specialist in Texas who is putting together the ultimate collection of bulbs for the Lone Star state, and he is collecting these by the bucketful in just this way).

Later on there will be annuals of the commonest species—zinnias, marigolds, impatiens, and so on. But these annuals will be blight- and pest-resistant sorts you can't find elsewhere, and they will all reseed reliably, planting themselves year after year (for more information on this, see page 49). There are certain to be tall bearded irises in late spring and, in summer, rare antique roses (there's a famous California rose nursery that was founded specifically to sell roses collected from such yards). There will be tomatoes that still taste like tomatoes, and in the screen porch there will be a botanical garden's worth of cacti and tropical flowers bursting up out of squalid pots made from recycled paint cans and cut-down soda bottles.

Once you've found your first such expert, your search is in one sense over because these . . . persons . . . constitute a sort of gardening mafia, and once you are accepted by one, she can pass you on to others all over town and, indeed, wherever you go. When Marty travels now, he knows exactly where to go to see the most interesting gardens.

The problem is that acceptance will come only after a long period of scrutiny. These gardeners don't hurry with choosing their plants; why should they hurry with choosing their friends? Marty had the same gates slammed in his face several times before courteous persistence (and cookies) paid off.

Baking the cookies took Marty more than 20 minutes, but the search itself was short—he found his first mentors well within a 20-minute walk of his home, and his dog, Sam, felt that these were the best 20-minute gardening sessions of the year.

Besides, Marty figures that the time he spent on baking is less than what he would be spending on plant shopping if his new-found sponsors weren't providing him with all the greenery he can use. Anyway, it was worth it to hear Tom plead for cuttings and tell him, You want some of these? Hey, start baking.

2🕐-MINUTE PROJECTS

Marty Relives His School Days; A Cautionary Tale

Petite Pinkie and Her Pals

Some gardeners are naturally inept. Marty knows he's among that number. And because he recognizes this, there is very little he has done horticulturally to which he minds admitting. To the rank beginner, any accomplishment, no matter how small, seems like a great one. Still, he'd rather not write about his 20-minute coleus garden.

There's something about coleus that seems so simple and basic that Marty feels silly claiming it as a project. Maybe it's the fact that he remembers it fondly from third grade, and the pot on Mrs. Beck's windowsill.

Therefore, when Tom suggested that Marty undertake the cultivation of this plant, Marty's initial response was, "Tom, I may be stupid but I'm not that stupid." Tom knew enough not to reply to that remark. Anyway, it soon emerged that Tom, sly horticulturist that he is, was not talking about normal coleus. Of course not. No, he was talking about coleuses (colei?) with exotic names like 'Snowflake', 'Camilla', 'Bronze Pagoda', 'Miss Sunshine', 'Black Cloud', and, Marty's favorite, 'Petite Pinkie'. These could all be obtained, Tom informed Marty, from a coleus farm in Florida. Just send in an order.

Tom explained to Marty that he wasn't the only gardener to be embarrassed by a fondness for coleus. Tom knows that coleus is not native to North America—it's a tropical relative of the mints—and that suggests to him that some horticultural predecessor had admired this foolproof flower enough to ship it back to the United States and start growing it here. Who did this? Who knows—apparently no one wanted to take credit. And Tom's search through nineteenth-century gardening books had revealed that all sorts of famous American gardeners had cultivated coleus enthusiastically; there were brief references in their books, but no real descriptions. Who brags about shooting fish in a barrel?

When the box from the coleus farm arrived in late spring, Marty opened it to find a plastic bag full of rooted cuttings. He stood these up in a glass of water overnight and the next day planted them in pots full of premixed potting soil from the garden center. After watering the pots, he set them on a sunny windowsill, where 'Petite Pinkie' and the rest waited for more tropical weather.

This arrived at the end of May. Marty then transplanted all the coleuses out to a semishaded area next to the stone wall. Within a few weeks, this former weed refuge was overflowing with wonderfully varied coleus leaves. These turned out to be Marty's favorite kind of plant. The coleuses didn't seem to care much whether they got lots of sun or none, whether it rained or didn't. They lasted all summer and looked great right up until the first frost of autumn. Marty's wife, Judy, the saver of the family, took cuttings right before that happened, and these are rooting now in a glass of water, so hopefully there will be a repeat next spring.

So simple doesn't necessarily mean stupid. Right, Tom? Uhh, how about philodendrons?

What to Do

1. If you've bought your coleus by mail (and unless you live in Florida, you have little option) open the box as soon as it arrives. Moisten the coleuses' roots (they will arrive as rooted cuttings), but keep them out of direct sunlight for a day while they reawaken.
2. Plant the cuttings on a cloudy day or in the evening, so that they get several hours to recover from the move be-

fore the sun strikes them and they have to go to work at growing.

3. If your garden soil is reasonably good, don't fertilize the coleus plants. Mrs. Beck used to feed hers once in a while, but the instructions that the coleus farm sent with Marty's plants said not to, and his plants didn't seem to suffer.

4. That's all folks.

Night of the Living Nicotine

Beware of horticulturalists bearing gifts. Tom brought over a flat of nicotianas one day and suggested I try them as a 20-minute project. I'm thinking of bringing him a vial of bubonic-plague bacteria for the same purpose. I can't decide whether these peculiar plants should be classified as a project or an emergency.

Here's the good news: they will grow anywhere. Here's the bad news: they will grow anywhere. Tom also claims he has never seen them grow as large as they have on my property. Personally I think this is a case for the *X-Files*.

As you can tell from the name, nicotiana is a member of the tobacco family and a close relative of the stuff that made you gag the first time you smoked it as a kid. If the name didn't clue you in to the relationship, nicotiana's broad, green leaves surely would: they look like something you'd wrap a cigar in. Nicotiana grows to a height of three or four or five feet and eventually shoots out a spike of white, night-blooming flowers that resemble some gizmo you might see emerging from a spy satellite. Judy took to cutting stalks of these (the nicotiana blossoms) and putting them in a vase with a lot of other flowers, where they looked like baby trumpets with antennae. People would always ask, Ooh what's that, as if it were some petite plant they might consider growing. Don't.

What to Do

1. Reconsider. Are you *sure* you want these monsters? (Sorry, Tom.)

2. Give them lots of sun and well-drained soil (although it didn't seem to matter where I put mine. Wherever I dropped one, it flourished, making my garden look like something from *Invasion of the Body Snatchers*.

I decided to trash a bunch of them by throwing them in a compost heap I maintain in the miniswamp behind a grove of evergreens. It didn't stop them for a minute. Before I knew it they were pointing their alien heads above the evergreens as if to check out the roof. All this in the hottest, driest summer on record, when everything around them was wilting, and these guys never got a drop of water.

3. Repent. Tom kept urging me to try smoking them, but I do have teenage children. Anyway, I don't think I'll plant them again next year. But geez, I just looked out in mid-October and saw these big seed pods hanging from the plants. You don't suppose they'll come back on their own?

Tom demands equal time:

Nicotianas *are* vigorous, but most gardeners regard that as a virtue. No doubt because they are a kind of tobacco, they seem immune to every kind of pest—aside from big-league baseball players, nothing chews their leaves. The white flowers, which open at night, seem almost to glow in the dark and are sweetly scented.

If you want to grow flowering tobacco (catalogs prefer to list it as nicotiana, probably to forestall raids by the Bureau of Alcohol, Tobacco, and Firearms), order seeds of the simple white-flowered kind; the fancy pink-, red-, and green-flowered hybrids are less vigorous, and their flowers lack fragrance. Tom grew a variety named 'Only the Lonely' in the hope that the reference to the late, great Roy Orbison would appeal to Marty. (For tips on starting flowering tobacco, see page 17.)

Tobacco is a native American crop, and Connecticut is still famous for the quality of the leaf it produces. The world's finest cigars are wrapped in Connecticut tobacco leaves. Marty should have been proud to become part of that tradition.

Chapter 8

Weeding One Hour a Year

Tom and Marty had witnesses. Still, the guys hanging around the tractor display at the garden center wouldn't believe them. Maybe the problem was Marty's hat: no real tractor-driving man turns his baseball cap around backward. Nevertheless, it was (and is) true. Neither Tom nor Marty spend more than one hour a year *total* on weeding.

Actually, Marty spends a little more time than that, but that's because he enjoys weeding (see page 152). Tom, though he maintains a larger area of garden than Marty (more than a thousand square feet of vegetables, flowers, vines, gourds, and whatnot), couldn't spend more than an hour a year on weeding even if he wanted to (which he doesn't). His gardens are so naturally weed-free that Tom runs out of victims within the first ten minutes of pulling, and he can muster up enough weeds for a slaughter only once every six weeks or so. What's more, Tom *never* uses chemical herbicides in his own garden. He likes to keep the weed termination personal. He deals with weeds by hand.

Think we're boasting? So did those weekend warriors at the garden center. But it's all true, and if you'll read on, you'll learn how you can make your garden equally weed-free. That won't require any special equipment or secret formulas. Mostly what is required is a change in attitude.

Tom takes the credit for discovering this, though he does allow that Marty helped. For it was Marty who introduced Tom to what has proved the 20-minute gardener's most effective weeding tool: the dictionary.

After twenty-odd years as an editor, Marty turns to his dictionary reflexively whenever he has a question to settle. Early on in the development of 20-minute gardening, Tom insulted Marty by calling his beloved daisies a weed—and Marty insisted on bringing in his Random House Concise You-Know-What. He began reading out loud, and what he read, Tom found galvanizing. It didn't change Tom's opinion of those crummy daisies. But it did change, in an instant, his thinking about almost every other plant.

A weed, according to Marty's invaluable volume, is "an undesirable plant growing wild, especially to the disadvantage of crop, lawn or flower bed." Fifteen words; two are key: "undesirable" and "disadvantage." Tom heard these, and it occurred to him that both involve subjective judgments. In other words, a weed is a weed because *you* do not desire it, at least not where it happens to occur, and that is because in that spot the plant is disadvantageous—to *you*. Somebody else, maybe to them the plant isn't a weed.

That means that to eliminate the weed, all you really have to do is change your point of view. Decide that you do desire the plant, that it's advantageous, and presto, the weed is gone. And given that Tom is a notably reasonable person, he knows that changing your opinion is easy (except in the rare case, as with daisies). Certainly, changing your opinion is easier than pulling weeds. Unless you are one of those outstandingly stubborn sorts of people (many of whom, he tells his wife, Suzanne, are still beautiful, wonderful individuals), chances are good you'll find changing your opinion easier than weeding, too.

Ah, but this is merely sophistry, you say. An excuse to avoid work: accepting the weeds because you are too lazy to deal with them. But consider: defining which plants are weeds is truly a tricky matter, for the very same plants have often been viewed as both prizes and pests, depending on the circumstances.

For example, Southwestern gardeners have recognized mesquite trees as being as beautiful as they are tough: bright green, feathery foliage; twisted, picturesque trunk; fragrant yellow flowers in late spring. Not bad. What's more, once a mesquite is rooted in (and the roots may reach 150 feet down into the earth), it will flourish unirrigated even in the desert. Where other trees perish, the mesquite spreads in thickets.

A gardener might like that, but ranchers don't. The mesquite is thorny—the branches really bristle—so even the hungriest cow won't browse on it. As a result, mesquites have overrun thousands of acres of overgrazed rangeland, forcing the cattle out. Ranchers spend millions trying to eradicate this "weed" tree; as a group, gardeners probably spend just as much purchasing "specimen" mesquites to adorn their homes.

The mesquite is hardly an isolated example. Many of what are now considered our most pernicious weeds are plants that were deliberately imported into North America; someone admired them enough to bring seeds or cuttings all the way across the sea. Kudzu (a Japanese plant) was deliberately planted throughout the South— sixty years ago there were even "kudzu clubs" below the Mason-Dixon line that came together for just this purpose. The Puritans brought dandelions and purslane to the New World—to plant in their gardens. The water hyacinths that choke canals and waterways in Florida and Louisiana were also brought to the United States from Southeast Asia—the plant's spikes of blue flowers looked so handsome in the fish pond, and it was so *easy* to grow.

Because these plants have spread out of control, they are almost universally regarded as weeds now; they are "undesirable." But they were admired once, and in the right situation, they still make fine cultivated plants. The Japanese cultivate kudzu as a vegetable. Dandelions are grown for their edible greens, and catalogs have actually begun to advertise seeds of purslane—purslane fanciers say its fleshy stems and leaves taste like bean sprouts (another reason to root it out, says Tom). Water hyacinth is still an outstanding (if short-lived) plant for ornamental pools if you live in the North (where frost kills it off every autumn).

What's our point? With a little ingenuity, you can practice this process in reverse. That is, you can turn your weeds back into garden plants. Before he met Marty, Tom used to regard goldenrod as a weed. Everybody called it a weed; garden books advised on its eradication. But now, with the help of Marty's dictionary, he has come to admire the way that its golden flower heads gild his brawl garden (see page 203) every fall. He wouldn't dream of attacking his goldenrods.

Are there any plants we do recommend rooting out of the garden? Yes. There are some plants so aggressive that if you allow them to grow in your garden, you can grow nothing else. Every Southerner knows the dangers of kudzu; Northerners should be just as wary of Japanese knotweed. Given even the tiniest foothold, these two plants will overrun your garden and swallow your car, the tool shed, and maybe the family dog, too.

Plants of that sort are obvious garden enemies. But we also classify as weeds some plants you might not expect. For a plant may be undesirable and disadvantageous because it happens to be in the wrong place. If the most beautiful rose in the world is invading your tomato patch, sucking nutrients out of the soil and bringing undesirable insects, then as far as you're concerned, that rose is a weed. On the other hand, if, like Tom, you find steamed dandelion leaves the tastiest thing this side of heaven, then you may regard a patch of perfect turf as the weed that is choking your dandelions.

This makes weed identification a very personal matter. Go ahead and borrow that "weed handbook" from the library to help you assign a name to the plant that's annoying you. You need to know something about a plant's habits and weaknesses if you are going to attack it effectively. But when you pick up the weed handbook, be sure to check out a guide to wildflowers and an encyclopedia of cultivated plants, too.* Because you are sure to find out

---

* In truth, the most efficient way to identify a weed is to pluck a sample and take it down to the friendly folks at your local Cooperative Extension office (you'll find its number under county listings in the blue pages of your phone book). Those people really know their stuff, and they can tell at a glance the identity of your plant and advise you on whether it is liable to prove friend or foe.

that the plant you hate, someone else treasures, and the guides may list your enemy as a rare and choice garden flower. That doesn't mean you shouldn't root it out; if you don't like it, it *is* a weed in your yard.

Wildly Successful Plants

Every sensible gardener wants plants that are vigorous and hardy, that flourish without much care. Yet the paradox is the plants that best fill this profile are not welcome in most gardens. They are the plants such as kudzu, Japanese knotweed and honeysuckle, salt cedar (*Tamarix chinensis*), and melaleuca tree that are commonly labeled as weeds.

Weeds are not evil plants; they are just the supreme opportunists. In nature they are the plants that move in right after some environmental disturbance—a flood, say, or a landslide or a fire—to recolonize and stabilize the exposed soil. The weeds are masters of invading what ecologists call "disturbed habitats" because they are amazingly prolific and highly mobile and they grow astoundingly fast.

Check out any of the plants most commonly categorized as weeds and you will find an organism designed for reproduction. These plants are champion seed makers. A single plant of purple loosestrife, the European wildflower that is currently overrunning our North American wetlands, bears as many as 3,000 individual blossoms per plant, and these may produce a total of 300,000 seeds each summer. An acre of this beauty (and purple loosestrife is beautiful) produces almost 24 billion seeds annually.

So maybe in your heart of hearts you don't care about our wetlands (that's okay—in fact, it's likely to get you a government contract these days). But the chickweeds defacing your lawn—maybe you care about them, and even those humble tangles of tiny leaves produce about 15,000 seeds each. A single plant of lamb's-quarters—you'll find that in your flower and vegetable beds—may bear up to 50,000 seeds a year. While your garden plants are putting their energy into handsome foliage, flowers, and tasty fruits, the weeds are concentrating on propagation. That's why when you want to start new flowers, you have to buy and plant seeds, while the weeds—well, at any given time an acre of suburban backyard may host a collection of 100 million weed seeds in the top six inches of soil.

Weed seeds are not only numerous, they are also, typically, designed to travel. As a rule, they are small, so that they are easy to move. Many, such as dandelion seeds, have wings or parachutes so that they can drift in the wind to new territories. Others, such as the seeds of shepherd's purse and plantain, become sticky when moist and can travel long distances by clinging to your shoe. Still others, such as galium or burdock seeds, are covered with hooks, a sort of natural Velcro that grabs onto animal hair or a trouser leg to hitch a ride home with you. A few types of weeds actually supply their own transportation: jewelweed—a wild form of the garden flower impatiens and a common weed of shady places in the Northeast—has explosive pods. Touch one after the seeds inside have ripened and the pod pops open, firing seeds over a radius of several feet.

Weed seeds are numberless, they get around, and they are endlessly patient. Most need moisture and exposure to light and oxygen to germinate. If buried or otherwise packed away, they simply go dormant, in which state they can survive undamaged a long, long time. In 1987, treasure hunters discovered a Spanish treasure ship, the *Nuestra Señora de Atocha*, at the bottom of the Gulf of Mexico, where it had lain since 1622. In the sand that had been packed into the ship's hold as ballast, an archaeologist identified the seeds of a familiar subtropical weed, the common beggar's-tick. When, after 369 years on the ocean floor, these seeds were placed in cups of fresh water, they started to sprout.

Once they've sprouted, weeds typically waste no time. Those chickweeds in the lawn, and the shepherd's purse and bitter cress that spring up as soon as the flower beds thaw in spring, may reach maturity, flower, and set seed in five or six weeks. Being annuals, these particular weeds then die; but they leave behind thousands of seeds each to start the whole cycle again.

This extreme virility makes weeds invaluable from an ecologist's point of view. These fast-growing opportunists act as Band-Aids on any area of disturbed soil, knitting it together with their roots to prevent erosion. Once in place, weeds set about gathering minerals and water and turning them into organic matter, and as this decays, it provides new topsoil. Weeds are wonderful plants until they move into cultivated areas and start latching onto space and resources you intended for other plants.

If weeds are such ferocious competitors, why haven't they conquered the world? Well, remember the tortoise and the hare? Weeds are hares: they start off fast whenever they find an opportunity—a disturbed habitat—but they haven't got the staying power of slower-growing but longer-lived plants. In the summer after a forest fire, fireweed (*Epilobium angustifolium*) may cover ten thousand acres with a blanket of magenta blossoms. But within a couple more years, young trees and shrubs will have grown sufficiently tall to shade the fireweed and force it out.

So why do the weeds return so persistently to your garden? The reason is that most gardens always remain disturbed habitats. Soil is constantly being stripped of its plant cover and then dug up, so that dormant weed seeds are exposed to light and air. Herbicides are used to kill big areas of vegetation, and nothing else is planted in its place. You stuff the soil unnaturally full of fertilizers and flood it with water and then plant species so poorly adapted to the local climate and soil that they offer no serious competition to any vegetable opportunist that happens by.

The remedy for weeds is to disturb the garden habitat as little as possible. Dig, hoe, spray as little as possible. In short, don't bother with all the busywork beloved by traditional gardeners. Plant tough (though beautiful) plants that like your climate and soil and that don't collapse at the first sign of competition. And don't coddle them.

But also expect some weeds. Because if you managed to create a perfectly stable habitat, one that admitted *no* invaders because you never disturbed it, it would be no fun. A garden is a place to experiment and play, to try new plants or rearrange old plants into new combinations. So long as you do this, the weeds—a few of them, not too many—will always be with you.

That brings us to the next point: how do you get rid of the plants you don't like—the undesirable and disadvantageous ones, the plants for which even Tom and Marty can't find an excuse.

To begin with, understand that weed control is an ongoing task—it never ends. No matter how successfully you beat them back, the weeds will reinvade. But weed control should never be a very difficult or time-consuming task either, at least not for the 20-minute gardener.

That's because the 20-minute gardener is an expert in weed avoidance. He or she regards pulling weeds (or worse yet, spraying them with herbicides) as a last line of defense, the agricultural equivalent of bombing when all serious negotiations have failed. And, as with wars, the best way to avoid weeds is to plan ahead not to have them.

That's relatively easy—at least, planning not to have weeds is easy. All it takes to keep the weeds down to acceptable levels (without stooping to pull) are a few intelligent strategies.

The 20-Minute Gardener's Strategies for Avoiding Weeds

1. Solarize your soil. In summertime Marty makes his herbal ice tea by dropping the bags into a jug of water and setting it out in the sun—he knows that the sun will do the job of brewing for him. Recently he has learned to cleanse his flower beds the same way.

Solarizing the soil requires some planning ahead, because it must be done *before* you plant anything in the bed and it only works at midsummer. That means you have to identify where you are going to place your flower beds about eight months before you plant. The best time to solarize, actually, is when you are planning your garden, when you are slavishly following the steps outlined in chapter 2.

Solarization is worth the trouble, though. It removes nearly all the dormant weed seeds from your garden soil, and will also kill the roots of perennial weeds.

Begin by stripping all the vegetation off the area to be occupied by the flower bed; the time to do this is when the really hot, sunny weather has settled in. Cultivate the soil by forking it up or rototilling it. Rake the soil smooth and water it well with a sprinkler. Excavate a narrow trench 4–6 inches deep around the bed. Then cover the moistened bed with a sheet of *clear* plastic (you'll find this for sale at the hardware store). Set a couple of rocks on top of the plastic sheet to make sure that it won't blow around in the wind, and bury its edges in the trench.

The plastic acts as a trap: sunlight passes through it and warms the soil, then the plastic keeps the heat from escaping. On hot, sunny days, the temperature in the soil will be sufficient to steam cook weed seeds. Leave the plastic in place for 4–6 weeks, and virtually all the seeds in the top 6–12 inches of soil will die. The effect of this is to give you an enormous head start: when you plant the bed, there won't be those tens of thousands of dormant weed seeds already in place, ready to germinate.

2. Planned parenthood. The horticultural equivalent of birth control says that you should not allow plants to be brought into the world unless you are planning to raise them, love them, and send them to college. But unlike human birth control, in which abstinence is the most secure method, weed control depends on sowing seed as promiscuously as you can.

Weeds are opportunists: they spread their seeds all over the place, in the hope that some will fall on open ground. When they do find what ecologists would refer to as an unoccupied niche, the seeds germinate, and the weeds start to grow. But when the weed seeds fall on soil that is already thickly covered with plants or mulch, then they sit on the surface and remain dormant—until they die, or some animal eats them, or the gardener removes a plant and creates a space for them.

That's why your goal should be to leave no open, unoccupied soil in your garden. If you dig up an area, plant it—and plant it much more thickly than traditional gardening books recommend. Tom's old handbook on annual flowers, for example, recommends setting zinnia seedlings 8–10 inches apart, or 12–15 inches apart in the case of the taller cultivars. Think about it: a bed planted that way is mostly open soil. It is crying out for weeds. Hybrid tea rosebushes are set 3–4 feet apart—that makes a traditional rose garden a promised land for weeds.

You can fill this empty soil by packing the plants in closer together. That's what Tom does in the ornamental vegetable beds he has created in his front yard. He likes to plant red and green lettuces in elaborate patterns. But instead of sowing the seed in separate rows, he sprinkles it all over the bed and rakes it in. After the seed germinates, he gradually thins the seedlings, pulling out one here, one there, to create room for the remaining seedlings *as they need it.*

Along the way, Tom makes salads of the thinnings—which means he gets a much more prolonged harvest than does the gardener who sows isolated plants and waits for them to mature. And from the moment of germination, Tom has a bed that is completely filled with plants. He never weeds his lettuce. He does have to water more frequently, and he has to enrich the beds with more compost every spring, but that doesn't require anything like the work involved in hand-pulling weeds.

Some plants can't stand being packed together cheek by jowl. Zinnias and roses will soon fall victim to fungal diseases if you plant them too tightly, and they won't flower as well, either, if crowded. So plant something else among them, something ground-hugging that won't try to occupy the same air space but that will occupy the bare soil. Sprinkle seeds of white-flowered sweet alyssum or portulaca underneath the roses—these creeping, shallow-rooted flowers won't compete with the tall-stemmed, deep-rooted roses, but they will exclude weeds. The sheet of white flowers they will create is a great foil for the bright-colored roses, and though portulaca and alyssum are annuals, they reseed themselves, so that they will come up every year.

Plant shallow-rooted, shade-tolerant ground covers such as ferns or sweet woodruff under shrubs and trees. One gardener we know uses pumpkins—which grow almost as fast as kudzu—as a ground cover around larger trees and shrubs on a sunny slope. Of course, a thick blanket of mulch will work just as well at excluding weeds—and has some special benefits of its own.

3. Mulch. This is great stuff for filling an otherwise unoccupied niche in the garden. Cover the soil with mulch and the weed seeds that drift in with the wind never find the moisture they need to germinate. For although the soil may be moist, the top of your insulating mulch blanket remains hot and desiccatingly dry.

Mulch also helps smother the weed seeds that are already in your garden. It does this by depriving them of light. Most weed seeds are keyed to respond to light—they germinate only when exposed to light. Normally this works to the weed seeds' advantage, by ensuring that they don't germinate (and then die) if they have somehow been buried deep underground. A couple of inches of mulch works just as effectively to block the light, preventing most weed seeds from germinating. And while such a mulch blanket is porous enough to let air and water pass down to the roots of established plants (the flowers or shrubs you planted there) it is heavy enough to smother any weed seedlings that do come up.

Acceptable Levels

The number of weeds a particular person can tolerate is as variable as the amount of dust or disorder that you can stand in your house. To some people, one sock out of place is a disaster. To others, being able to see a square inch of floor is a major event. For some gardeners a weed is a sign of moral decadence and cause to send for the chemical equivalent of the National Guard. Others have no problem letting the weeds do their thing, then yanking a bunch of them out when they can no longer find the garden.

Which is right? Either or both—whichever you're more comfortable with. But the 20-minute gardener doesn't dwell too much on controlling weeds. He outsmarts them.

To get the maximum effectiveness from your mulch, apply it early in the spring and replenish it occasionally throughout the season, whenever it seems to be wearing thin. Tom and Marty prefer organic mulches such as wood chips, since as they break down they add humus and plant nutrients to the soil. We are also great believers in using whatever is locally abundant and so is either cheap or free.

Wood chips are available virtually anywhere there is a town maintenance crew, so they are a mainstay nationwide. But just as we like to savor regional cuisines when we travel, so has Tom become a devotee of regional mulches. He loves the brown and springy effect of "pine straw"—a mulch that Southeastern gardeners make by raking up the needles of long-leaf pines. In Florida he can savor the feeling of revenge that comes with a mulch made by shredding a pernicious local weed, the melaleuca tree. Peanut shells and tobacco stems are a mulch for Virginians, redwood bark for Californians.

Since he has settled in New England, Tom has learned to look forward to that region's season of mulch harvesting: autumn. That is when the trees' leaves turn colors to attract the tourists, and then drift down as a natural mulch all over the landscape. In their raw state the autumn leaves pack into impermeable, garden-smothering sheets. But rake them up and feed them through a lawn mower or an inexpensive electric leaf shredder, and you have a superb mulch—as important an element of New England's heritage, to Tom's way of thinking, as Indian pudding, baked beans, or even hard cider.

Tom manufactures this mulch in bulk. He invested $100 in an electric leaf shredder and a bunch of extension cords a couple of years ago, and with these he moves up and down the street every fall, creating a year's worth of mulch from what the neighbors heedlessly put out on the curb. It takes him only a couple of hours to fill a dozen trash bags, which is all the mulch he can use.

4. Target your watering. Nothing can live without water. Not even chickweed or dandelions or quack grass. This means that gardeners in the desert Southwest should really never have to weed, because if nature doesn't supply water in the form of rain and snow, and if you water precisely, if you apply only enough water to satisfy your garden plants and don't spread any extra moisture around, the weeds can't grow. It's that simple.

Unfortunately, in moister regions nature supplies enough water so that weeds can get by—most of the time. But when a dry spell sets in and nature cuts off its irrigation, the weeds will be lolling around with their tongues hanging out. The 20-minute gardener turns on the hose—but gives none of the water to the weeds. They wither, while your plants thrive. Ha!

Watering precisely is simple enough. It means that once your plants are well rooted into the ground, you water only on demand. Wait until the plants show signs of flagging—the leaf tips start to droop, or the color of the foliage dulls. Then water slowly and deeply, delivering the moisture right around the base of the plant and applying it slowly but for a long period so that it soaks deep into the soil, down a foot or more.

This kind of watering can be done in either of two ways. You can install a drip irrigation system in your garden and set water emitters at the base of each plant. Or you can attach a device known as a "bubbler" to the end of your hose and move this from plant to plant. If you keep the water pressure low (open the faucet just a crack), the bubbler will work like a giant drip emitter, releasing water slowly enough that it will soak down into the soil rather than spreading out over the surface.

Whatever you do, don't water your flower beds and shrubbery with a sprinkler. That works well on the lawn and on sheets of ground cover, areas that are completely covered with desirable plants. But because sprinklers broadcast water indiscriminately, they create all sorts of opportunities for weed seeds in any planting where there is the smallest scrap of open ground.

Of course, the best way to keep your garden irrigated is to leave the job as much as possible to nature. Plant only those flowers, trees, and shrubs that like your soil and your climate. There are lots of sources of information about such plants; often the local water company or water board supplies lists of adapted plants as part of the conservation programs that are springing up nationwide.

You'll have to water new plantings. Seeds won't germinate without water, and seedlings are too delicate to stand dehydration; give them a spritz every day or so. Transplanting trees and shrubs damages their root system, leaving the plants vulnerable to drought. Water them weekly through periods of hot, dry weather for the first year. But once the plants are settled in, you should start to wean them off the irrigation habit. Wait until they show those obvious signs of distress before you get out the hose.

Don't coddle the plants—give them enough water, but just enough. Force them to spread their roots wide and search out moisture for themselves. That will make them strong and self-sufficient. By ensuring that your soil is thoroughly laced with roots, it will also help shut out weedy invaders.

5. Fertilize judiciously. Give your plants what they need, no more, no less. Fertilizing too generously will make your plants soft and flabby; it also creates an opportunity for weeds. Remember: weeds are opportunists. If you fill your soil with unused nutrients, weeds will find a way in. If you feed them, they will come.

So how do you know what your plants need? A soil test helps. If you have it done by the Cooperative Extension and specify what plant you plan to grow, the results sent back to you will include exact recommendations for fertilization.

Which, unless you have read this book, may be confusing. The recommendations will specify the amounts of the three major plant nutrients—nitrogen, phosphorus, and potassium—that your plants should get. It might say, for instance, that you should apply .25 pounds of nitrogen per 100 square feet of bed. Often it will say "actual nitrogen"—as opposed to imaginary nitrogen? And how much of that bagged fertilizer makes a pound of nitrogen anyway?

Remember the three numbers on the fertilizer label—like 5-10-5 (see chapter 4, page 69)? These numbers indicate the amount (by weight) of nitrogen, phosphorus, and potassium the fertilizer contains. In 5-10-5, nitrogen contributes 5 percent of the whole, phosphorus contributes 10 percent, and potassium contributes 5 percent. In other words, just 2.5 pounds of a 50-pound bag of 5-10-5 is actually nitrogen; so if your soil test tells you to apply .5 pounds of nitrogen per 100 square feet of flower bed, you spread 10 pounds of 5-10-5.

Whew. With a hand-held calculator, figuring this all out isn't too tough. But we rarely have a calculator with us in the garden. That's why we generally feed by eye. We use a "complete" fertilizer—one that includes all the nutrients a plant needs. And we use a fertilizer in which the three numbers are more or less balanced—such as 5-10-5 or 10-10-10—rather than something like that leftover bag of turf fertilizer (waste not, want not), which is mostly nitrogen. Then we feed at a quarter of the rate recommended on the bag, and we feed often.

The idea is to start feeding with the opening of the buds in spring, and to feed again monthly *if plant growth is weak or seems to be slowing down.* If plant growth is vigorous, we stop feeding. We also stop feeding in midsummer; it gets so hot in Connecticut that the plants shut down and stop growing. Because New England winters are cold, we mostly don't feed in the fall—by feeding then, we would encourage our plants to keep growing when they should be going dormant and getting ready for winter. The main exception to this rule is the lawn, which likes the cool weather of fall and which is going to grow then whether you help it or not. So we feed it in fall. We use compost, but this is also the time to apply bagged fertilizers to the grass.

6. Timing. When you weed is much more important than how often. In general, you should be ultra-aggressive early in the season, when the weed plants are still small. Their roots are shallow then and easy to pull out of the soil.

If you let some of the spring weeds get away from you, don't despair. Wait for a hot, dry day, and hoe them up. In that kind of weather the weeds will quickly wilt and die. If you weed on a cool and cloudy day, or worse yet on a drizzly one, the weeds you hoe or pull up may survive long enough to sneak their roots back into the soil.

Often a succession of weedings is more effective than a single pullfest. If you plan to turn the soil in a flower or vegetable bed, to open up a new area for planting, or to add more compost to an old one, do your digging or rototilling a week or two before you plan to plant. That will give any weed seeds you turn up to the surface time to germinate—and you can hoe the little stinkers out quickly from the otherwise empty bed right before you plant.

Finally, you can help de-weed the beds you use for annual flowers or vegetables by digging the soil up in late fall. This brings buried seeds (and insects, too) to the surface, where the frost can kill them.

7. Sexual frustration. Tom and Marty can procrastinate with the best of them (this is a required skill for writers), but one time they move promptly is when they see a weed getting ready to flower. Flowering is the prelude to setting seed. Attack the weed before it sets seed and you've got only one stem to pull, one bunch of roots to hoe up. Wait until the seeds have ripened and dropped onto the soil, and no matter how thoroughly you remove the mother weed, you can count on a horde of replacements.

Marty insists that this bit of advice is really just another aspect of timing, and should have gone into the previous step. Tom gets so much pleasure out of denying fulfillment to weeds, though, he insisted that it get a step of its own.

8. Night tilling. Rototilling a garden bed may do great things for the texture of the soil. However, it also encourages the weeds to no end. As it brings soil up to the surface from underground, rototilling also brings up old and dormant weed seeds—which germinate, grow, and cause you problems.

But those are not the only seeds that rototilling sets in motion. It turns out that many kinds of weed seeds need only a nanosecond of exposure to light to bring them out of dormancy. So even if the rototiller brings seeds up to the surface only briefly before pushing them back into the depths, it can start the growth process. That means that rototilling may markedly increase your garden's crop of weeds. In fact, stirring the soil for just ninety seconds at midday increased weed germination by 60 percent in one study.

That study was conducted by a pair of German botanists. Fortunately for rototiller owners, the researchers found a solution to this problem. A romantic solution.

In seven years of work and observation, Herr Doktors K. M. Hartmann and W. Nezadal discovered that if the rototilling were done at night—especially toward midnight—the weed seeds that were exhumed and then reburied were not awakened. Indeed, night-tilled soils later showed only 2 percent coverage by weeds, whereas day-tilled soil showed 80 percent coverage.

Hartmann and Nezadal warned that even a tractor headlight or a flashlight could stimulate weed germination. They recommended the use of military infrared scopes and infrared spotlights. Jawohl.

May we recommend ordinary moonlight? That level of illumination is also, apparently, below the threshold of what disturbs the sleeping seeds. Marty thinks it is less likely to provoke a visit from the F.B.I. And, what's more important to Tom, it's cheaper.

9. Have the right tools. The hum of the weed whacker is almost as ubiquitous as the drone of the lawn mower these days. But when you hear the whacker's buzzing rip, what you are hearing too often is the garroting of some innocent tree or shrub.

For when the whirling nylon cord whips the base of a trunk, it commonly bruises the inner bark, the thinner sheath of live cells that is the primary area of growth in a tree or shrub. Often the weed whacker will do this without leaving any very visible mark on the outside of the bark. What follows, though, is the death of the plant, or an invasion of the cambium by some disease that causes stunting and a gradual decline.

You could avoid this problem by keeping the weed whacker away from your trees and shrubs—but trimming the grass around their bases is the only genuine use for this devilish device. What we suggest is that you consult chapter 2 and then redesign your lawn so that the trees and shrubs are surrounded by areas of mulch or ground cover. You should be able to do all the trimming you need to do without having to stop and back up your lawn mower.

Throw that noisy, lethal weed whacker away. Or better yet, trade it in for a scuffle hoe.

We have already described that tool (on page 79) and recommended that you buy one. If you do, you'll find that with it you can clean up most of your garden while hardly working up a sweat. What's more, a scuffle hoe doesn't disturb the soil enough to bring any buried (and dormant) weed seeds to the surface.

Of course, you could instead chop the weeds out with a conventional hoe. It would take longer and involve much more work. Because the conventional hoe cuts deeper into the soil, it's also liable to injure the roots of any valuable plants in the area. But if you choose, nevertheless, to go with the conventional hoe, understand that with it you will churn up the soil and expose to light and air *many* dormant weed seeds. So plan to return, hoe in hand, a week or so later.

10. Eat your weeds. This is Tom's favorite technique for dealing with weeds, and it allows him to transform weeding (which he considers a chore) into harvesting (something that everyone likes to do).

Tom would like to take full credit for this concept, but he has to admit he was inspired by the last genuine Yankee farmer in his hometown, Lew Daniels. One evening Lew told Tom that he had been harvesting his greens from his front yard rather than the fields lately, and he gave Tom instructions for steaming fresh dandelion greens.

Unfortunately, Tom had eliminated dandelions from his front yard years ago by digging them all out with an asparagus knife. His mother-in-law, Gige, though, has better ways to spend her time, and in her yard Tom was able to harvest a potful of the young tender ones in just a few minutes. He washed them and then steamed them for eight minutes or so, and they were delicious. As Gige put it, they taste the way spinach used to taste before it became an agri-product.

Tom can't bring himself to plant dandelions back into his own lawn, but he is able to harvest to his heart's content from Gige's turf—which looks much better for the grazing. Sadly, dandelions eventually pass out of season (once the flowers appear, the leaves become tough and bitter). But as any gardener knows, there is always another weed coming along.

Lamb's-quarters (*Chenopodium album*) emerge in a thicket of seedlings after every summer rain—and from these Tom strips the tender young leaves. This plant is a relative of garden spinach and has a mild, sweet flavor if steamed briefly on the stove. Japanese knotweed supplies a forest of lush new shoots on demand—all you have to do is cut this bamboolike plant back to the ground in a hopeless effort to eradicate it. The tops of the new shoots, if cut before the leaves unfurl, can be boiled and then served chilled with mayonnaise. Tom can't wait for the milkweed pods to appear: picked young and boiled, they taste like okra, according to Euell Gibbons.

Which brings us to an important point: if you intend to eat weeds, you have to be very sure of what you are gathering. You need expert help in identifying the plants, so that you do not accidentally swallow something poisonous. The most sensible help Tom has found is a field guide and recipe book entitled *Stalking the Wild Asparagus* by Euell Gibbons. This book is found in almost every public library, for it inspired a cultlike following during Tom's teenage years. Tom remembers trying all sorts of weeds back then, with never a bellyache. He was a teenager, though, so it never occurred to him that he could do his parents a favor by harvesting in his own backyard.

Buy or borrow a copy of *Stalking the Wild Asparagus*, grab a bucket, and head out on a raid. As any cannibal will testify, there is a special pleasure to dining off the body of a slain enemy.

11. Listen to your weeds. They can tell you a lot about your soil, and so provide tips on how you can garden better. Those dandelions popping up all over your lawn, for example, are an indication that the soil is too compacted and acidic. Spraying them with an herbicide may kill them, but new dandelions will surely sprout unless you correct the underlying problem. Rent a soil aerator and dust the lawn with ground limestone, and grass will replace dandelions.

Other weeds with a story to tell include:

- Field bindweed and quack grass: symptomatic of compacted soil that is deficient in humus. Aerate or till up soil and add compost.

- Cinquefoil, sheep sorrel, swamp horsetail, dock, and knapweed: symptomatic of acid soil. Treat with lime to raise the pH.

- Goldenrod and saltbush: symptomatic of alkaline soil. Treat soil with aluminum sulfate to lower pH.

- Goldenrod, broom sedge, yellow toadflax: symptomatic of sandy soil. Amend soil with manure or compost.

- Chamomile, field mustard, quack grass, and plantain: symptomatic of hardpan (a layer of impermeable soil that lies below the soil surface, interfering with drainage and root growth). Breaking up hardpan may involve deep digging and the addition of organic matter, such as compost.

- Mullein and milkweed: symptomatic of dry soil. Dig organic matter, such as compost or peat moss, into the soil and then cover it with mulch.

- Crabgrass: often an indication of nutrient-poor soil. Feed the grass with a fertilizer rich in organic nutrients or with compost.

- Lamb's-quarters: flourishes in rich soils, especially those that are tilled or dug over regularly; if the leaves have a purplish red tinge to them, however, the soil is deficient in nitrogen.

The remedies listed with the various entries offer chemical-free ways to drive out the weeds in question. But be aware that sometimes the weeds are beneficial, even from the gardener's point of view. Those dandelions in the lawn, for example, are not only tasty but their downward-penetrating taproots help aerate the subsoil and bring nutrients up to the surface soil, where they will eventually benefit other plants.

Follow the clever stratagems outlined above, and your contact with weeds should be minimal. But alas, there are times when an ugly confrontation becomes inevitable. For there are weeds with which a low-key, patient approach just doesn't work. You'll know these weeds when you meet them: they are the hyperaggressive perennial weeds that make a veteran gardener's blood run cold— Japanese knotweed, quack grass, artemisia, nut grass, and the like. You can scuffle-hoe these, pull them out weekly, and eat them until you turn green, but you won't even slow them down. These are not plants you can tame or live with, for unless met with overwhelming force they will annex your whole garden. In short, this is the time to reach for herbicides.

Tom and Marty like birds and earthworms and fish, and worry about things like tumors. (All writers are hypochondriacs.) As a result, they do not resort to herbicides casually. There are very few herbicides they will use. Only two, in fact.

The first one is "organic." It's a derivative of the insecticidal-soap sprays that have appeared on the market in the last few years. What the producers have done is to enhance the soap sprays' tendency to injure plant foliage, so that the "weed-killer" form of the product burns most or all of the weed leaves, even when temperatures aren't especially hot.

The active ingredient in this spray is "naturally occurring potassium salts of fatty acids" (whatever those are); they are relatively nontoxic to mammals, though the label warns that the gardener may experience skin and eye irritation if the product is applied carelessly. This herbicide biodegrades within forty-eight hours of application, and it doesn't pass down the food chain—insects feeding on the plants won't pick up a toxin which kills the bird that eats too many of the insects. It can injure fish, however, if it is sprayed right onto the water, so don't use it at the pond or stream's edge.

Our main problem with this herbicide is that it's expensive (about $6 for 24 fluid ounces, less than a quart of ready-to-use spray) and it is effective in killing tough, perennial weeds only if reapplied several times. It's useful for clearing out the weeds that sprout from cracks in pavement or between flagstones. Such weeds are impossible to scuffle hoe and often extremely time-consuming to extract by hand. In this situation, the fatty acid herbicide can be a genuine convenience. It isn't an effective remedy for big brawny weeds like Japanese knotweed—it's more likely to kill nearby garden plants, for this herbicide is nonselective. That is, the spray injures any plant it touches.

The other spray that we will use is also expensive (about $7 per 24 ounces, diluted and ready to use, or $17 for a pint of the concentrate, which mixes with water to make 8 gallons of spray) but also sure death to any weed it touches. This is glyphosate, commonly sold under the brand names Roundup and Kleenup. It too is organic, although organic gardeners don't accept it as such since it is synthesized in a factory. But because microorganisms agree with the chemists, glyphosate decomposes within a few weeks when it comes in contact with the soil. The products of the decomposition are nontoxic, and because glyphosate attaches itself to the soil particles, it rarely washes through the soil to end up in places you don't want it to go.

The spray itself is, according to the best research, relatively benign. It is practically nontoxic to mammals, birds, and bees, and only slightly toxic to fish and other water creatures. Use glyphosate sparingly and apply it only to the leaves of the target weeds, and you will do the environment little or no harm.

Like the fatty acids, glyphosate is nonselective, but it differs in that it is *systemic* in its action. When you spray it onto the plant's leaves, it is absorbed and travels throughout the plant to kill *all* of the weed, even the roots. This makes it a most effective treatment for perennial weeds, the ones that keep sprouting up from the roots after you hoe them out. For many of these weeds, notably Japanese knotweed, glyphosate is the only effective, environmentally acceptable remedy we know.

Glyphosate works well only when applied to weeds that are actively growing—so spray in spring to early summer or late summer to early fall, when temperatures are moderate and the weather is moist. Don't expect an instant kill: the weeds will take a couple of weeks to yellow and then wither. Be sure to apply glyphosate only to the plants you want to kill, because it will kill virtually any plant. One of the safest ways to apply it is to wipe it onto weed leaves with a sponge; wear rubber gloves if you do this.

❖

In the end, Tom believes, you will do best by coming to an accommodation with the weeds. Get to know them. When a new kind appears in your yard, take a sample down to the Cooperative Extension office and get the horticulturist there to help you identify the plant and tell you about its habits. Does it bear pretty flowers? Does it attract desirable bugs? (See the section on that, page 173.) And just how invasive is it?

Or you can just leave a few of the weeds to mature and observe them. Some, you'll find, are beautiful. Tom particularly likes the rosy, thistlelike flowers of knapweed, which open in midsummer, and the vivid springtime flower clusters of purple cress. You may wish to reclassify some of these weeds as garden flowers and let them fill niches that other weeds would otherwise invade. Take Marty's dictionary and rewrite it yourself.

Martinis—Nature's Secret Cure for Weeds

When Marty comes home from a particularly gruesome day at the office, he pours himself an ice-cold martini and heads out to the garden. Sip and weed. Weed and sip. After a while the activity takes on a rhythm of its own. The cares of the day start to diminish, and the garden starts looking terrific. (Actually the martini may not even be necessary for some people—*The 20-Minute Gardener* does not wish to promote inebriated gardening. A glass of wine or even club soda may work just as well for you.) The point is to allow yourself to enjoy weeding as a kind of agricultural meditation exercise rather than a chore to be completed. You are spending quality time in your garden, getting to know it on its most intimate level. If you listen carefully (especially after the martini), sometimes you can hear a flower go "ahhh" when you pull out a particularly bothersome weed.

The best thing about weeding is that you can't fail at it. No one's keeping score. You do it as long as you feel like doing it and then you stop, knowing that your garden and your head are so much the better for it and that there will be more abuse in the office and more weeds tomorrow.

2⊕-MINUTE PROJECTS

A Pair of Gardens That Weeds Will Never Trouble

Tom's 20-Minute Water Gardening

Though Marty tries to take credit for the invention of 20-minute water gardening, in fact it was Tom's idea. True, Marty did invent the 20-minute wetland, but that was an accident: the "best buy" tub he picked up at Home Depot wouldn't stop leaking. Tom successfully created a water garden because he chose to shop at a good local garden center and buy sturdy, well-crafted containers—tubs made from halves of whiskey barrels. They weren't as inexpensive as Marty's wooden colander, but they only cost $14 apiece (on sale), and they were attractive. Once lined with plastic they were also watertight (almost).

Actually, Tom's thoughts had turned to aquatic flowers the very first time that he and Marty began brainstorming concepts for 20-minute gardens. That's because early on in Tom's horticultural career he had cared for a large ornamental pool. The pool, which was located on the Columbia University campus that Tom maintained, was a concrete basin that measured 16 feet across and 2½ feet deep. It was planted with hardy water lilies and various kinds of water weeds and was populated by six-inch ornamental carp.

This pool was a magnet for everyone who worked at the campus—at lunchtime, its edge was lined with off-duty intellectuals—and it was almost no work to maintain. Once or twice a week Tom would spend five minutes standing at the edge of his pool, fishing out dead water-lily leaves with a long-handled net, and once a month he put on his bathing suit and waded into the pool to slip packets of fertilizer down among the water lilies' roots. The rest of the time, the pool functioned as its own closed community, with each resident getting all that it needed from the neighbors. The water lilies bloomed more or less continuously from late June through October, and the fish kept the water free of mosquito larvae. The only serious pest was a great blue heron who would sail in early in the morning to sample the carp, but Tom came to regard the bird as part of the garden—he loved to watch the heron fish.

Tom hasn't attracted any herons to his driveway in Middletown, but the four tubs he set out there last spring have proved endlessly satisfying. What's more, this impromptu water garden has provided far more flowers with less investment of time than any of Tom's other 20-minute projects.

The secret to creating a water garden that takes care of itself is to create a balanced habitat in the pool, one in which every ecological niche is filled. That's why Tom spent so much time on the orders he placed with water-garden nurseries. He ordered "pygmy" water lilies (compact strains that won't outgrow the tub), whose leaves and flowers would float on the surface of the water, and one compact variety of lotus, *Nelumbo nucifera* 'Chawan Basu', that would also serve as a canopy for a tub. He ordered a variety of free-floating plants, such as duckweed, to fill the spaces between the lily pads. He ordered fish that would eat the insects that might otherwise flourish in the tubs, and aquatic scavengers that would eat algae and plant debris. Finally, he also ordered a number of subsurface aquatic plants that would help cleanse the water and replenish it with the oxygen that the animals need.

Tom sent off his orders to the water garden nurseries (see sources on page 222 for addresses) and was told that the plants would be shipped to him in June. In preparation for that date, he bought the half whiskey barrels and lined them with black plastic sheets, which he stapled to the inside of the tubs' rims. Then, on June 1st, the plants and critters arrived. Tom poured five inches of ordinary loam garden soil into each of the tubs and planted the waterlily and lotus roots into that.

In one tub he put 'Yellow Pygmy', a compact, yellow-flowered water lily that will overwinter outdoors in Tom's area; its olive green leaves are streaked with maroon. In another tub he put 'Aurora', another hardy pygmy; this one's flowers are yellow streaked with apricot when they first open, but darken to red on their second day of bloom. In the third tub he planted a blue-flowered tropical water lily, 'Colorata', and in the tub that he had placed in his night garden under the arbor, Tom planted the lotus, hoping that its contemplation might bring him serenity.

After he finished planting the water lilies and lotus, Tom lifted the leaves that protruded from the soil with one hand while he used the other to cover the soil in the tubs with half an inch of clean sand, to keep the soil from clouding the water. Then he filled the tubs with water and left them out in the sun for a few hours to warm up the water. When it had lost its chill, Tom floated in the tubs the water-filled plastic bags in which the aquatic animals had been shipped. This allowed the animals to adjust gradually to the water temperature in the tubs and ensured that they would suffer no shock when released.

In one tub he released a pair of American salamanders; in another he released four fat bullfrog tadpoles. He released three fancy goldfish—calico shubunkins—into another, and in with the lotus he placed a pair of koi, ornamental Japanese carp. He took bunches of subsurface plants—red hygrophilia (*Hygrophilia polysperma*), a ruddy-leaved tropical water weed, and cabomba (*Cabomba caroliniana*), a two-faced aquatic whose foliage is lacy underwater but round as miniature lilypads at the surface—and tied rocks to their bases and dropped them into the tubs. He dumped a handful of duckweed (*Lemna minor*) into each tub, and in the lotus tub he set a half dozen heads of "water lettuce" (*Pistia stratiotes*), a free-floating plant that sort of looks like a small lettuce fashioned out of green velour.

Then Tom made a mistake: in his WASP zeal for cleanliness he released into all four tubs some "scavengers": live-bearing trapdoor and black ramshorn snails, who were supposed to keep the water gardens free of algae. This they did, but by breeding with Malthusian enthusiasm, they overpopulated the tubs within a matter of days and began eating duckweed, cabomba, hygrophilia, and water lilies, too. Tom picked snails as fast as he could find them, relocating them to an aquarium in Matthew's preschool, but it was several weeks before he had that plague under control.

Dragonflies found the tubs the day after they were filled with water. (Where did they come from?) The plants settled in quickly, so that by the first week of July the water lilies were beginning to bloom. 'Colorata' was the first to flower: the bud rose from the water like Aphrodite on her clamshell before opening into a sapphire star and settling back in to float. Soon there was a blossom or two (or even three) on every tub, except the one under the arbor, which was entirely hidden under parasol-like lotus leaves and a solid field of water lettuces.

About once a week Tom had to top up the water in the tubs; they all leaked slightly, despite the plastic liners. Once a month he pushed fertilizer tablets down through the sand into the soil around the water lily and lotus roots. A couple of the fancy fish died, and Tom replaced them with ten-cent "feeder" goldfish from the local pet store—he probably would have done better to use these generic fish in the first place.

Aphids attacked the water lilies, but Tom washed them off the lily pads with the hose and the fish ate them. Aside from the snails, the water gardens suffered from only one really serious pest: small boys.

Matthew led the attack. He loved to watch the salamanders come out to sun themselves on the rock Tom had put in their tub. He checked on the tadpoles constantly, watching them develop legs and lose their tails, until one day they turned into frogs and hopped off into the woods. All this was good. Matthew also fed the fish sometimes, but they flourished even when he forgot. What he really was conscientious about, however, was his self-imposed chore of stirring the tubs up into pools of muck with a big stick.

This he did, on average, every fifth day, despite his father's pleas, threats, and tears. When Matthew finally lost interest, other little boys appeared to take over the job. Small male children Tom had never seen before began stopping by with their stirring sticks. It took all the serenity the lotuses could furnish to get Tom through this period with his sanity more or less intact. Eventually, however, this plague also ended, as mysteriously as it had begun.

Matthew still exhibits a proprietary interest in the water garden. One recent evening was spent deciding whether the salamanders would welcome a newt that Matthew had found in the woods. Suzanne has said that in her opinion the tubs are far and away the best of the 20-minute gardens. No mess, no work, and far less weird than the scarecrow (see page 176). With fall setting in, Tom is planning to move the fish and salamanders into an aquarium and to dig up the tropical water-lily roots and overwinter them in plastic bags of slightly moist sand in a cool part of the basement; the tubs of hardy lilies and lotus he is going to overwinter by half burying the tubs out by the compost heap, excavating holes for them so that they rest with their lips just above the soil. Meanwhile, he's looking for a heron he can train to chase the little boys.

A 20-Minute Wetland: Marty Goes Egyptian

Marty views Tom's exotic flora with considerable skepticism.

"Heck, Tom," he says, "if I had learned all that Latin I'd be a *doctor*, not a horticulturalist."

But when Tom suggested papyrus as a 20-minute project, Marty couldn't resist. It sounded so weird to have this ancient plant, that you learned in high school was the raw material of paper, growing in a garden in Connecticut, of all places. And Tom said growing papyrus was easy (although Tom's definition of easy and Marty's definition of impossible have much in common).

Anyway, Marty needed a plant that likes swamps. The "bargain" wooden tub he'd bought at the discount store leaked water as fast as he could add it, and over a period of days it had turned a corner of his vegetable garden into a quagmire. If he couldn't find some plant that needed those conditions, he was going to have to clean up the mess. Papyrus seemed a better alternative. What's more, this time Tom was right. Papyrus *is* easy to grow.

If you want to grow this plant, too, but don't have a swamp ready-made, you will have to create one. What follows is Marty's method.

1. Buy the cheapest, shoddiest wooden tub you can find and bury it up to its lip in a sunny spot. Then fill the barrel with any soil you've got handy—Marty used the soil he dug out of the hole in which he put the barrel. Don't cover the soil with sand or anything fancy like that. When the soil turns to goo, you can claim you did this on purpose.
2. Water the soil-filled tub until the contents look like something you'd pack on your face in a really expensive spa.
3. Pop in your papyrus plants (which you have ordered by mail; see page 222).
4. Keep the soil moist and swamplike.

In a couple of weeks you will have a little grove of graceful, reedy plants with lacy palmlike tops. They are utterly beautiful and require virtually no care. Although papyrus is a tropical plant, Marty's even survived a couple of hard frosts in November.

Over the winter, the barrelful of muck will provide a handy retreat for the frogs you raised in your whiskey-barrel lily pond. Above all, though, make sure you point out the success of this project many times to those uncharitable souls who laughed when you were creating the swamp. You knew what you were doing.

Chapter 9

Peter Rabbit
Had It Coming

Tom trained with Sicilian gardeners. So when it comes to garden pests, he doesn't want control, he wants revenge.

Marty, by contrast, never trained at all, and he still keeps in his heart a simple wish to live in harmony with nature—which, of course, is absolutely essential if we as a species are to survive. Even Tom agrees with that. It's just that Tom and Marty have somewhat different understandings of what constitutes harmony.

Marty believes that a gardener should be like Gandhi—so wise, so disciplined and far-seeing, that he or she does not have to resort to violence (hardly ever).

Tom knows he will never be like Gandhi. So he's content to model himself on Fat Tony. Tom remembers how safe, how quiet his old neighborhood in the Bronx was. It was safe and quiet because Fat Tony liked it that way, and nobody liked to upset Fat Tony.

The point is, there's more than one kind of harmony, and we are going to let you choose the kind you like. In the following pages Marty will give you the keys to the peaceable kingdom and Tom will share with you his secrets for how to be king of the jungle. Whichever path you choose, you should be able to make your way without undue work and without more than a very occasional resort to chemicals. As Tom says, So who wants to be king of a Superfund site?

Before we get down to the specifics of strategies, however, we must define exactly what is a garden pest. That category is more inclusive than you might think. At various times in his horticultural career, Tom has had to protect his gardens against everything from a plague of locusts to college students on mountain bikes and a flock of free-range chickens. Basically, he defines as a pest anything that can move and that is, either intentionally or unintentionally, destructive to his plants.

Such a definition includes virtually everything in the animal kingdom—even the carnivores, the more prominent examples of which have large feet (four of them) and not enough sense to stay on the paths. This definition also categorizes as pests many things man-made—tractor mowers (especially as driven by university groundsmen), delivery trucks, strollers, you name it. Living by this definition has helped Tom foresee and forestall all sorts of plant destroyers before they could do any damage—but it has also made him suspicious and grumpy. He doesn't really like to let anyone or anything into the gardens he cares for—not even the owners. They have big feet, too, and they act like they've got a right to step anywhere.

Perhaps surprisingly, Tom worries least about the pests that worry the average gardener most of all—*bugs*. Tom doesn't like the fact that bugs chew holes in his plants, but he also knows that he has to live with them. He has to live with them because they outnumber us, they were here first, and—if Tom's experience in Bronx apartment buildings proves anything—they will outlive us, too.

The fact is that you can't escape bugs: they are everywhere and in the most amazing numbers. Scientist have identified some 750,000 species of insects, and some researchers believe that there may be as many as 30 million more species yet to be identified. Nor

Guys in Steel-Toed Boots

It has been Tom's experience during twenty years as a horticulturist that men in the construction trades do their work in a way calculated to cause the maximum harm to your garden. If the painter can put his ladder on top of your rhododendron or right beside it, he will inevitably crush the shrub. If you have just dug, raked, and reseeded the part of your lawn that abuts the street, that is where the guys repaving the road will go to stomp around and swill down coffee on their break.

Tom remembers working with a big construction firm that was installing sewers on the college campus that Tom maintained. The engineer borrowed one of Tom's landscape plans to use as a base map on which to sketch his excavations. Then he drew up a scheme in which the proposed trench ran directly through every major shade tree on the landscape plan. It looked sort of like a lumberjack's version of connect-the-dots.

Of course, to dismiss this as simply testosterone-driven aggression is unacceptable, since there are now women in steel-toed shoes out there destroying gardens. So Tom called a contractor friend, Mark Brady, to find out why. Mark immediately took Tom to task.

He told Tom that he never should have planted shrubs and flowers next to the house, where they would interfere with maintenance; he said that every home owner should preserve a sort of free-fire zone around their house. But when Tom told Mark that for gardeners this was not an option, Mark grumbled, and then offered useful advice.

The problem, Mark said, is that the builder's bid was based on doing the job in the most efficient way possible, and if that means driving over the lawn and shrubs, well, that's how he came up with the low bid that secured your business. For the customer to accept the bid and then start telling the builder how he has to take extra time to respect the plants is, from the builder's point of view, maddening. Taking more time to finish the job erases much of his profits, so the builder is not going to cooperate any more than he has to.

Make a point of taking the builder around your yard and showing him your plantings during the initial discussion of the job. Impress upon the builder that you want these plantings preserved; discuss with him where he will need access to the house and how plants in the area can be protected. Foundation plantings, for example, can be safeguarded by propping sheets of plywood over them—one end of the plywood rests on the ground outside the plantings, and the other end rests against the house.

If some plants have to be squashed, agree on exactly which plants those are and mark the area with brightly colored plastic tape. Mark suggested getting precast concrete pads, which are available for a few dollars at most building supply centers, and placing them wherever the contractor will have to set ladders—that not only defines where ladders and feet will fall and so protects surrounding plantings, it also gives the builder a steadier base from which to work.

At this time you should also discuss what sort of staging areas the builder will need—that is, places to park machines and stack materials. Outline exactly where these areas will be.

Tell the builder you understand that taking care of plants requires extra time and you expect this to be reflected in his bid. Then when he arrives for work, tell him you understand that a hammer may fall off the roof and take a side off a shrub—accidents happen—but that you will pay him a bonus—say $100 for a substantial job, such as the replacement of a roof—if the job is completed without any such incidental damage. In short, make preservation of the plantings his priority as well as yours.

If the job involves bringing in any sort of heavy equipment, such as a backhoe, mark with plastic tape the paths the equipment operator must use. The wheels of such a machine compress any soil they pass over, and this not only harms the lawn but kills tree roots. Since a tree's roots extend far beyond the reach of its branches, the machine can seriously injure a tree without even driving through the area it shades.

If you have any large and valuable trees in your yard, you should call in a qualified arborist before you close the deal with the contractor. (The American Association of Consulting Arborists in Rockville, Maryland, can refer you to someone in your area.*) Ask the arborist to assess the dollar value of your trees and outline a route for the equipment that will cause the least

* American Association of Consulting Arborists, 15245 Shady Grove Road, Suite 130, Rockville, MD 20850; (301) 947-0483.

harm. Use this as the basis for your discussions with the contractor. And before the contractor begins work, tie a sheath of boards around the base of every tree in the general construction zone. These will serve as a last line of defense if the machine operator has a few beers for lunch and comes back feeling frisky.

So, you think this behavior is paranoid? Consider: how long did it take you to create your garden, and how much time, money, and grief will it take you to reconstruct it if it is destroyed? And how are you going to feel if this happens unnecessarily?

Mark admitted that for many builders, plants are invisible. It is your job to open the builder's eyes.

are all these insects hiding in a rain forest somewhere—the apple tree in your backyard may host 500 different species.

Anything you can devise that will kill all 500 kinds of bug in your 'Golden Delicious' tree might well kill you—or at least it will cut a broad swath through neighborhood wildlife and pets and perhaps show up as cancer in your children. And without doubt, the bugs would recover from the poisoning more quickly than would any of the other victims.

A couple of entomologists (bug experts) once calculated that a particular suburban tulip tree was hosting a flock of 30 million aphids. So let's say you spray that tree and kill virtually all the aphids—no more than one of the 30 million survives. This is an unrealizable goal; even with something horrible like DDT you would not kill such a large percentage of the pests, but let's say you did. That single survivor is bound to be a fertile female—because by the time you can see aphids on your plants, the population consists *entirely* of breeding females. These female aphids don't need to mate to bear young, which they may do daily, and—depending on the species of aphid involved—they may give birth to as many as 100 offspring at a time.

Within a few days, these new aphids mature and start giving birth too. The famous nineteenth-century naturalist Thomas Huxley estimated that if no predators molested them the descendants of a single aphid could, by the end of one summer, equal in weight all the inhabitants of China. Even a century ago, that was a lot of avoirdupois.

The fact that the aphids in your garden don't accomplish this suggests a great truth: bugs, if left alone, will regulate themselves pretty well. Besides, despite their numbers, bugs rarely wreak truly devastating damage on an ornamental garden. Bugs are selective; a given species tends to feed on just a handful of plant species. So an invading swarm of beetles or caterpillars may strip the leaves from a particular tree or shrub—but usually the leaves will grow back, and meanwhile the bugs will have moved on. Anyway, if you have been following our advice, there will be lots of other things going on in the garden so you will hardly miss the casualty. A swarm may wipe out all your petunias; but we'll tell you how to make sure that doesn't leave the garden looking bare.

Your goal as a gardener should be not to control bugs but to learn to live with them. But first we want to describe the pests that you can control, and that you must control, if you want to have any garden at all.

These pests are, unfortunately, the more cuddly ones, which puts many gardeners (Marty, for instance) in a quandary. Marty will grind a beetle under his heel without a qualm; but suggest to him that he ought to get confrontational with a deer, and he freaks out. Yet the beetle is really doing Marty no significant harm, while the deer (a Bambi-rat, as Tom calls them) will gobble up a whole garden, from yew bushes to begonias, without even pausing to clear its palate between courses.

The deer will keep coming back, too, to graze on the re-emerging growth, and so make sure that nothing survives. Wildlife biologists tell us that the exploding deer populations are actually wiping out whole state forests in this fashion. Those cute little critters are the horticultural equivalent of Attila the Hun—and if you don't eliminate them, you can't have a garden or even much of a yard.

Besides, what the deer don't eat in an unprotected garden, the other critters soon will. Woodchucks, rabbits, mice, gophers, and voles are equally voracious, and though their smaller size means that they eat less, it also allows them to penetrate into tight corners and extract the odd bits of greenery that the deer have missed.

Tom's instinctive response to this challenge is the ecologically correct one: he recognizes that rabbits (for example) are higher on the food chain than petunias. So if a rabbit wants to eat Tom's petunias, that's only natural and right. But gardeners are even higher on the chain than rabbits—and if you don't believe us, you should reread Beatrix Potter's classic, *Peter Rabbit*, and pay more attention to what Mr. McGregor did to Peter's father.*

Over the years Tom has eaten a lot of bunny stew. In fact, he once sent his collection of rabbit recipes around to the gardening magazines, with the intention of publishing them as a service to his fellow gardeners. "Peter Rabbit Had It Coming" was the title Tom suggested.

Marty, unfortunately, is just the type of editor who rejected Tom's article. Marty has pointed out that Gandhi never owned an air rifle. (But, as Tom replied, Gandhi had the advantage of living in a place filled with tigers, who did his dirty work for him.) So Marty has insisted that Tom recommend only nonlethal devices, and to Tom's suggestions he has added several of his own.

Tom and Marty's Eight Favorite Devices for Discouraging Pests

1. Mothballs. Don't you hate the way your sweaters smell when you take them out of storage in the fall? Critters hate that smell too. In fact, they hate it worse than you do, since as a rule they have far more sensitive noses. That's why a modest sprinkling of mothballs will ruin the appetite of almost any pest, other than deer and groundhogs.

Tom uses mothballs where he needs a powerful deterrent—when, for instance, he wants to stop an armadillo in its tracks. (Actually, a pickup truck's differential is the best tool for that.) He uses moth crystals when the pest is smaller; just a crystal or two dropped on top of each bulb you plant will protect them from squirrels and mice (or at the very least, you'll have fresher-smelling mice). Tom also uses moth crystals when the area he hopes to protect is highly visible, such as the flower bed beside the front door.

Mothballs and crystals are only a temporary solution, since they melt away in a period of days (in the case of crystals) or weeks (in

---

* The text is vague enough that a child might miss the significance: " 'Now, my dears,' said old Mrs. Rabbit one morning, 'you may go into the fields or down the lane, but don't go into Mr. McGregor's garden: your father had an accident there; he was put into a pie by Mrs. McGregor.' "

the case of balls). But by that time, typically, the pest has moved on, and having found other victims, generally it won't return.

A *word of caution:* mothballs won't harm you or your pets or even the wildlife when used in a well-ventilated place (and as long as you don't eat them), but they are toxic. That's why they keep moths out of your woolens and critters out of your flower beds. Use them with caution around small children. Don't put mothballs or moth crystals where they can wash down into a storm drain or waterway. And apply them in a sprinkle, not a mulch.

2. A roll of 4-foot-high chicken wire. For those, like Marty, who object to violence, a fence may be the only practical way of protecting a garden against rabbits and woodchucks. Chicken wire is cheap ($49.95 for a 75-foot roll at Marty's local hardware store), and it's easy to erect. You can buy steel fence posts, or if you are cheap like Marty, you can cut saplings from the brushy area at the edge of the woods across the street, and use those as posts.

You have to bury the bottom of the chicken wire several inches deep in the ground to keep the varmints from squeezing under the fence—and bend the bottom of the wire outward to create a sort of underground shelf, so that when the woodchuck tries to tunnel under the base of the fence, she runs into a barrier. If the woodchuck is a climber (and we've heard stories of woodchucks scaling 8-foot cyclone fences), leave the top foot of the wire loose—don't fasten it to the posts. That way, when the woodchuck gets up near the fence's top, the wire flops outward and the woodchuck falls off and lands on her back—outside the garden.

For this to work, you have to put the posts on the inside of the wire. If you put the posts on the outside of the fence, the wire will flop inward, flipping the woodchuck into the garden. It'll keep her there, too, until she gets hungry enough to tunnel out.

A chicken-wire fence is quick and easy to erect. Of course, it's also ugly. You can hide most of it by planting a row of morning glories or other fast-growing vines at its base, but it will still have a low-rent kind of look to it. Marty has stretched chicken wire around his vegetable garden, his strawberry bed, and the blueberries, so that his backyard looks like a prison farm now. But if you can't tolerate bloodshed, you'll have only one other option:

3. Electric fencing. Marty insists that this is cruel; Tom gives the pests more credit. Tom believes a rabbit will quickly learn not to touch a hot wire—he learned from just a single jolt, and he was a teenager at the time. Besides, a brief jolt is all the pest (human or otherwise) gets, if you have installed a modern, Underwriters Laboratories–approved fence. These are equipped with "low impedance" controllers that deliver current along the wire in pulses that last only a few ten-thousandths of a second; most of the time, actually, the fence wires are not live. That means that the intruder gets a shock but has time to recoil before getting another. And while the shock is a stinging one, it is not sufficient to injure either animal, child, or forgetful gardener.

A two-strand fence, with one wire set 4 inches above the ground and another wire set 4 inches above that should work fine for raccoons, groundhogs, and rabbits. Where deer are a problem, stretch a third strand at 24 to 30 inches above the ground.

Because the electric fences are designed to ward off rather than physically restrain, they can be relatively flimsy. This makes them easy and inexpensive to erect. Fiberglass posts just ⅜ of an inch in diameter are sufficient to support the wires, and these can usually be pushed into the ground rather than driven. Typically, a two-strand fence is cheaper to install than a similar length of chicken wire, with its more substantial, sledge hammer–driven posts.

Nor are electric fences dangerous—*if* the proper equipment is used. Though the necessary materials are available at local agricultural supply stores and garden centers, beginners would probably do best to buy a kit from the suppliers listed on page 221. Those who distrust their own abilities as electricians should stick to battery-powered fences; these can be equipped with rechargeable batteries and solar-powered chargers, so that the batteries won't need continual changing.

The major disadvantage of an electric fence is that it requires fairly conscientious maintenance. If weeds are allowed to grow up around the lower wires, they will draw off current, reducing or even eliminating altogether the fence's ability to shock. To keep the fence working properly, it is best to mow a swath underneath it once a week.

4. Peanut butter. This can be either a lethal weapon or a wonderful educational tool. For some reason, a wide range of mammalian

pests (small children included) find peanut butter irresistible, so it is the bait of choice for every kind of trap from Havahart to mouse traps.

Even deer love peanut butter. Roger Swain, the host of Public Television's *Victory Garden,* swore to us that if you anoint with peanut butter an electrified wire stretched three feet above the ground (turn off the current for the duration of the anointing process), any passing deer will have to stop for a taste. And that particular deer will never dine chez vous again.

A general word on fences: barriers work much better if they are erected before the animals know that a feast lies on the other side. A modest fence erected in early spring before the garden greens up will often divert most or all of the four-footed pests. Once they have gotten in the habit of feeding in your garden, however, the pests will go to considerable effort to burrow under, climb over, or push through any barrier. So get your fences in early.

5. Your trowel. Confuse the pests. Don't rototill up a bed and put all the petunias together in one spot. That makes them a big target that is easier for a critter to find. And once the critter finds the bed, it has all of your petunias at its mercy. So instead of setting plants out in masses, use your trowel to pop them in here and there. Tuck a petunia in behind a marigold (rabbits hate marigolds) and hide the parsley in among the roses. Go for diversity: plant a lot of different species and mix them all up together. Gertrude Jekyll wouldn't approve, but is she going to chase the rabbits out of your garden?

Mixing up the plants also serves to protect them against epidemics of diseases. The rots and rusts and wilts and dieback germs are, like bugs, fairly specific in what they attack. That means the petunia disease probably won't spread to the marigold, and will likely never find the other petunias, if you've spread them around. If you've put them all together, though, and one falls sick, you can kiss the others good-bye, too.

6. A drip irrigation system. In the last chapter, we told you about how reducing your irrigation reduces the need for weeding. But keeping the garden as a whole less lush and giving individual plants no more water than they need will make your landscape less appealing to critters. Critters like soft, juicy greenery, not the sturdy

tough stuff they will find in a water-conserving yard. Cut back on your irrigation, and the rabbits, woodchucks, deer, and other herbivores will move over to the neighbor's yard.

In the long run, the reduction in irrigation should come as a result of planting mainly species that are well adapted to the local climate and don't need extra water. Most gardeners will find, though, that raising decent vegetables requires regular watering in the vegetable garden. And there are always some beloved trees, flowers, or shrubs that you have to include in your garden, even though they do need more moisture than they will get naturally in your area. To accommodate plants of this sort, install a drip irrigation system.

These are available in kit form at most garden centers and are easy to assemble. There are a variety of systems available; any one of them will reduce your irrigation by at least half. This is because drip irrigation delivers water directly to the soil at the base of the targeted plants, instead of blanketing the whole area. In addition, a drip irrigation system delivers water so slowly that all of it soaks into the soil, in contrast to conventional sprinklers, which apply the water so quickly that much of it runs off across the surface of the soil and is wasted.

Reducing your irrigation will also discourage insect pests, especially those, such as Japanese beetles, who spend part of their life underground. Initially, Japanese beetles home in on the well-irrigated yard as a source of salads, but they also favor such an environment because the soil is moist and soft—a perfect place to lay their eggs and raise a brood of root-gnawing grubs. Frustrate them by refusing to water your lawn in summertime (when the beetles are getting romantic).

Your turf may turn a bit brown at the edges, but unless you live in the desert (in which case no reasonable person would have a lawn), the grass will green up with the return of cool, moist weather in the fall. Best of all, you'll hardly have to mow from July until September.

Tom and Marty water their grass only when they are reseeding a bare patch, and even then they water just the area that has been seeded. Their lawns are perfectly adequate—green (except in midsummer) and reasonably thick. Tom's lawn is also practically weed-free—he eats the weeds as fast as they can sprout. Tom and Marty's lawns never suffer significantly from diseases or insects.

Which isn't the case with many of their neighbors' lawns. They sprinkle religiously all summer long. That means they have to douse their properties with toxic chemicals in the spring to keep the Japanese beetle grubs in check. That's how they spend their twenty minutes a day: attracting pests and then struggling to kill them.

7. The compost bin. We've already described how to build a 20-minute composting bin and provided a 20-minute operating manual, so there's no need to get into the how-tos here. But we do want to point out the role it can play in pest discouragement.

We have nothing against chemicals per se. (In fact, both of us found several we liked a lot back in our reckless youth, but that's another story.) We have learned, though, that chemical fertilizers, when used at the rate recommended on the product labels, overstimulate the plants. The plants grow fast, soft, luxuriant—and become irresistible targets.

Tom and Marty both use some synthetic fertilizers, but only when the plants need a special boost. After setting out flower seedlings in the spring, for instance, Marty will water the young plants with a soluble fertilizer—the blue crystals you mix with water. Marty mixes the fertilizer solution at half the strength recommended by the manufacturer. He's looking to give the seedlings a boost, not a kick.

Tom scatters a few cups of 5-10-5 over his front-yard garden in springtime, when the flowers and ornamental grasses are breaking dormancy and trying to repair the damage caused by winter. For the most part, though, he, like Marty, relies on compost to nourish his plants. They both mix lots of compost into the soil before planting and spread it over the soil around established perennial flowers and shrubs. Tom even uses it to fertilize his lawn.

The reason Tom and Marty prefer compost over synthetic fertilizers is that they have found that it promotes a compact, hardier growth in their plants. They have noticed that their compost-nourished plants generally seem far less attractive to pests than do the plants fed with bagged fertilizers, like Tom's roses. Tom demands a lot from his roses: he cuts them back hard in the spring and expects a parade of flowers all summer long. That's not natural, and Tom figures the rosebushes need extra food.

But he has noticed that they are the plants that attract aphids, Japanese beetles, thrips, and other pests. Tom loves roses so much that he is willing to spray them. But the rest of the plants get compost. So do Marty's.

8. A soup hound. If the critters are really bad in your neighborhood, you should go to the pound and get a dog. Get a fast, street-hardened mongrel—one of those "Heinz 57 Varieties" types where the ears don't match and the tail curls funny. A mutt of this type is far smarter than most purebreds (except, of course, for Marty's ferocious miniature beagle, Sam). A soup hound will typically suffer from fewer health problems, and it knows how to defend its turf (and your turf becomes its turf from the moment you bring it home).

A soup hound will not only chase the wildlife out of the garden, it will keep the neighbors' pets at bay. And if you apply mothballs judiciously, it won't mess in your flower beds. Ever notice how dogs always sniff before they unload?

A Pair of Homemade Sprays

There are occasionally times when bugs do become a serious annoyance to the 20-minute gardener. There may be some particularly bug-attractive plant (such as Marty's hybrid tea roses) that you *must* have, even though it seems to be a magnet for hungry insects. To maintain such a plant you will have to spray, at least occasionally. That's the time, Marty says, to get out the insecticidal soap.

The secret is that virtually any soap is insecticidal. You don't have to drive down to the garden center and buy the premixed stuff. A couple of cups of that will set you back $7, and it won't work any better than the liquid soap you use to wash the dishes. Don't use detergents—what you want is soap. Mix 1 to 3 teaspoons of soap with a gallon of water, and you are ready to go.

Don't spray the plants when the temperature is above 85°F or when the plants are dehydrated; if the foliage is wilted, water the plants thoroughly the night before you spray. If you do spray a heat- or drought-stressed plant, you are liable to burn its foliage and do more harm than good. Finally, resist the impulse to mix up an extra-strong batch for an extra-bad infestation. Marty did that, and the rosebush didn't survive.

A soap spray applied to both the top and bottom of the leaves and to the stems will kill a broad range of insects, from aphids to whiteflies, spider mites, and thrips. The good news is that the soap spray has no residual effect—that is, it leaves no toxic residue on the plant or surrounding soil. That's good for wildlife; soap sprays won't harm birds, fish, even earthworms.

But because soap sprays have no residual effect, and because they won't kill all the insects, you'll have to reapply them as often as once every two or three days for a period of two weeks to really discourage the pests. Part of the problem is that the soap is an indiscriminate killer of insects. It kills many predators as well as herbivores, so when the herbivores reinfest the plant (as they will) there will be no predators there to control their numbers. Soap sprays are a useful, environmentally friendly tool, but they are a blunt-edged instrument.

Marty has also found that an oil spray is another effective means of protecting a special plant. Properly applied, oils poison adult insects and smother the eggs—that makes them especially effective killers. Again, you should not spray them onto heat- or drought-stressed plants; water the night before you spray, and spray only when the air temperature is below 85°F.

You can buy oil sprays at the garden center, but Marty makes his own by mixing a cup of vegetable oil (he prefers olive oil, first virgin cold-press, though Tom finds corn oil to be equally effective) with a tablespoon of liquid soap. Marty shakes this up in a gallon of water and pours it right into the sprayer.

Oil sprays are lethal to aphids, mites, scales, mealybugs, and some caterpillars. Because they contain nothing toxic to humans, you can, of course, use this spray on your vegetable crops, too.

Bug Appreciation

A generation ago, gardening books advocated a clean sweep of garden bugs. "Kill 'em all and let God sort 'em out" was the rule. Nowadays gardening books distinguish between "good bugs" and "bad bugs." Good bugs, of course, are the predators that eat the bugs that eat your plants. After making this distinction, the writers include instructions on how to maintain big populations of good bugs in your garden; the problem, of course, is that as soon as the predators eat all the herbivores, the predators move out—and then the herbivores move back in.

Tom doesn't distinguish between *good* and *bad*. Tom stopped doing that two years ago, after his wife, Suzanne, came home with the *Audubon Society Field Guide to North American Insects and Spiders*. This proved to be a fascinating book, and it freed Tom from most pest-control chores. It did this by turning virtually every bug into an asset.

Attracting Predatory Insects

Even if we won't take a stand on good versus bad bugs, we do enjoy cheering on the predatory insects as they prey on the plant-eating ones. To keep the predatory team strong, we've learned a few tricks that make our yards more attractive to the predators.

Many of the predatory insects are insectivores as larvae but are nectar or pollen eaters once they change into their adult forms. To attract the adults (so that they will fill your yard with larvae) grow plants that produce their flowers in umbels— broad, parasol-like clusters. Such plants include all the members of the carrot family, from Queen Anne's lace to parsley, dill, and fennel. Daisy-like flowers, which are known botanically as "composites," and their relatives the goldenrods are good for attracting predatory wasps and flies. Nasturtiums, sage, buckwheat, strawberries, and buttercups are also attractive to many of the predators.

Mulching around your flowers with shredded leaves or bark not only benefits the plants, it provides a refuge and breeding place for ladybird beetles. You should also provide predatory insects with a source of water—a birdbath filled with gravel and water serves as a convenient drinking place. Of course, if you have followed our advice (see page 153) and decorated your terrace with tubs of water lilies, the lily pads will furnish an ideal perch on which predatory insects can land to get a drink. With all the landings and takeoffs, the tubs by Marty's vegetable garden look like O'Hare airport on a busy day.

Tom's conversion came within a week of two of acquiring the field guide. It began with his first find: a hover fly on one of his son Matthew's marigold flowers. This bug was *good*, according to Tom's gardening books, because although the fly looked something like a yellow jacket wasp (except smaller), this insect is a plant pollinator as an adult, and while a larva is a major predator of aphids.

A couple of evenings later, Tom saw something he thought was a hummingbird come in to hover by the bee balm flowers. Then he realized it was actually a moth; the field guide told him it was a hummingbird moth, a type of sphinx moth. The gardening books called this a *bad* bug, because the caterpillars of the hummingbird moth feed on plants of the honeysuckle family. Fortunately, Tom grows no honeysuckles. He figured the caterpillars were probably eating the Japanese honeysuckle that winds through the woods across the street.

When Tom found a huge, horned, green caterpillar on his tomato plants, he knew it had to be *bad*. This bug was eating its way through the tomato leaves like some kind of insect bulimic. Tom read in his gardening books that he should kill this insect by spraying it with a caterpillar-eating bacteria, *Bacillus thuringiensis*. Or he could plant daisies, goldenrod, parsley, and black-eyed Susans to attract braconid wasps (*good* bugs), which lay their eggs on the hornworm—the wasp larvae eat the hornworms alive.

But the field guide warned that if Tom did these things, he would never get to see the huge gray-brown sphinx moth with the four-inch wingspan, into which the hornworm would metamorphose. That would be really *bad*, because by now, sitting on the stoop with a glass of wine to watch the sphinx moths had become Tom's favorite part of the evening. He began to wonder if he should root out his daisies and parsley to discourage braconid wasps (but weren't they *good*?) and protect the hornworms. Eventually, a glass of wine later, Tom decided to let nature take its course.

Quite a course it has been. Armed with hand lenses, Tom, Suzanne, and Matthew have marveled at the lurid colors of the scarlet-and-green leafhoppers that were sucking juice from the garden plants—and the plants didn't suffer noticeably. How did those huge grapevine beetles know that Tom had planted a grapevine? From nowhere they appeared as soon as the first shoots started climbing the arbor.

Things got a little ugly when Suzanne found black-and-yellow-striped monarch caterpillars on the milkweeds springing up in Tom's asparagus patch. She wouldn't let him weed. Eventually, she agreed that he could pull out any milkweeds that weren't supporting caterpillars, and she even transferred some of the caterpillars out of the garden and onto milkweeds nearby. She also brought one of the gold-trimmed blue-green chrysalises into the house and hung it up in a mason jar so that Tom and Matthew could watch the butterfly emerge. When they opened the jar in the garden, the butterfly flew away. Tom hopes it will migrate back next year. Matthew likes to watch the ant colonies when one attacks another—it's better than Power Rangers. Tom almost likes aphids now, since he knows they will attract the hideous aphid lions—lacewing larvae that suck the juice out of aphids that are sucking the juice out of Tom's roses. Are the aphid lions good or bad? They've got to be good if they are so much fun to watch.

Tom is letting his parsley go to seed—parsley flowers are supposed to attract hover flies—and he's planting goldenrod to attract more parasitic wasps. There is a danger that Tom will become so absorbed in bugs that he will have no time left for gardening. Suzanne has been concerned by his subscription to *The Food Insects Newsletter** ($5 a year from Montana State University in Bozeman). She's lobbying for a milkweed patch. They both agree that they'd like to lay in a big supply of venison sausage. Marty refuses to publish recipes for that, either.

---

* Did you know that Don Chon's restaurant in Mexico City serves a full selection of insect-based dishes, including ant larvae fried with a local relative of Tom's favorite weed, lamb's-quarters? Or that insects supply 30 percent of the protein intake for the Sepik peoples of New Guinea?

2🕐-MINUTE PROJECTS

A Trio of Summer Pleasures

Tom Terrorizes the Neighborhood

Matthew was the one who insisted that the Christopher garden needed a scarecrow. Not that Matthew dislikes birds. He was furious when the mockingbird singlehandedly devoured all the grapes on the arbor—Matthew had counted on eating those grapes himself. But it's only that one fat thief Matthew blames. He wanted the scarecrow because he had learned at the preschool that no well-equipped garden should be without one.

Matthew's father, however, wanted a scarecrow that really works. He did blame the birds—the whole feathered crew—for the loss of his grape crop, and though he has cooled off since, at the time he wanted to chase every last bird out of his side of town.

Tom thought a lot about what would be the most frightening sort of figure to erect in his front yard. He knew that the old standard scarecrow with the checked shirt and straw hat didn't faze birds at all. No, Tom wanted something really appalling. That's when he started really looking at the joggers who ran by his house every evening.

These joggers were students from Suzanne's university. Tom knew from personal experience that they were mostly outstanding young men and women—his wife keeps having them over for dinner, and several have baby-sat for Matthew when Tom and Suzanne wanted to go to the movies or maybe eat a meal in peace and quiet for a change. Those students had always impressed Tom as being very smart. Certainly, if anyone could frighten a crow, they could.

Just look at them, Tom thought, as they ran by with their oddly dyed hair that looked as if it had been styled with a weed whacker. Look at the rings dangling from their noses, eyebrows, lips, even from their panting tongues. I'd be frightened if I were a crow, thought Tom.

Tom ran an ad in the student newspaper, offering to buy used jogging shoes and clothes—he offered "top dollar." He got no replies, and he suspects that was because the students thought he was just a garden-variety pervert. Eventually he had to borrow from Suzanne a sweat suit decorated in university colors and with the university seal. He stuffed it with straw and set it up on a stake in the front yard. Then he stuffed one of Suzanne's old stockings with rags to make a head. He drew a face onto this with an indelible marker and stitched on a handful of big brass curtain rings in appropriate spots (or inappropriate ones, depending on your point of view). When he started to stitch in lengths of yarn to serve as hair, though, Suzanne intervened.

She was coming up for tenure in a year, she reminded Tom, and she didn't want any student demonstrations in her front yard in the meantime. Therefore, Tom was not allowed to use any color of yarn that might suggest his scarecrow was intended to represent one particular group of students. Tom thought long and hard and finally decided to make the hair bright green. That is actually a common hair color at Suzanne's university, but it is always a color of choice.

As a finishing touch, Tom put a baseball cap on the scarecrow's head—and turned the cap around backward, of course.

Tom's scarecrow delighted Matthew, and though it has no effect on the birds, it seems to amuse the joggers. The first evening after Tom set it up, students jogged by, stopped, back-pedaled, grinned, and then went on their way. Like Tom said, they are an outstanding bunch.

Tom has been dreaming about a whole line of scarecrows in this vein. He tried to get Marty to erect a scarecrow in an Armani suit in his front yard, but Marty was too timid. What about scarecrows dressed like yuppies for gentrifiable neighborhoods? Scarecrows dressed like realtors for quiet rural areas? Scarecrows dressed like Oklahomans for Texan front yards, and vice versa? What about really coming clean and dressing up your scarecrow like that next-door neighbor you just can't stand? In the long run, isn't it better to be honest?

Tom thinks that his scarecrows could be the basis for a nationwide catharsis. Who knows, in the end, they might bring back together all sorts of disenchanted groups. It could work. As long as everyone handles it as well as Suzanne's students.

Caterpillar Safari

Several times in the last few years Tom has attended lectures about "butterfly gardening," and he has always come away disappointed. He loves the idea of a garden afloat with live confetti, but the gardening itself, as recommended by the experts, is so passive. Fill your garden with the right kind of plants, they say, and maybe the butterflies will happen by. Sort of like a horticultural cargo cult.

But last summer, thanks to Suzanne, Tom met an activist. Suzanne told Tom that Eric Buddington, one of her students at Wesleyan University, was raising monarch butterflies from eggs—and he claimed this was easy. A phone call later, and Tom and Matthew had a date for an egg-collecting expedition.

A couple of afternoons later (on July 10th), they meet Eric in his lab, where he sits barefooted, poking at the computer keyboard in his lap. Eric explains to Tom what he is doing. Maybe Matthew understands. After Eric logs off, away they go. Tom is imagining a remote glade in the forest; Eric takes them three blocks away to Indian Hill Cemetery.

Indian Hill was the burying ground for the well-to-do of Victorian Middletown, a tree-shaded summit that is positively Gothic with ornate brownstone monuments. Beyond the crypts, though, down by the highway in an undeveloped section, there is a sunny meadow. A flowery tangle of grasses, black-eyed Susans, blue-blossomed knapweeds, yellow wild indigo, and goldenrods, this area supports several patches of milkweed—the monarch caterpillars' only food.

Eric snaps off a milkweed stem topped with purplish blossoms and hands it to Tom; the flowers breathe a sweet, heavy perfume of lilac. What the caterpillars savor in this plant, however, is not the fragrance but the acrid, poisonous sap. The caterpillars can eat this with impunity, and they do, but it fills them with toxins so that even the hungriest bird won't touch them. Milkweed is the monarch caterpillars' secret of survival.

"Here's one," says Eric as he turns over a leaf on a youngish milkweed. He shows Tom a tiny, green-and-gray-striped nipple attached to the leaf's lower surface. It is a monarch butterfly egg. Eric picks the leaf and slips it into a jar.

Would collecting in this fashion hurt the wild population of butterflies? "No," Eric replied, explaining that monarchs run through four to six generations in a single summer and quickly replace any losses. Anyway, the survival rate of caterpillars is about 90 percent in captivity, Eric has found, while it is supposed to be under 1 percent in the wild. Because Eric releases all his butterflies, he is, if anything, assisting in the monarch's propagation.

While Matthew picks flowers to press for his mother, Tom finds and harvests an egg of his own—it shows up clearly against the leaf's mealy underside. That leaf goes in Tom's mason jar. Over the course of the next 20 minutes he finds two more singles, and then a jackpot: a leaf that hosts *two* eggs and a young caterpillar. Eric is impressed—he explains that the caterpillars are fiercely territorial and will actually fight to the death when they meet; indeed, a caterpillar will even destroy any eggs it encounters. For that reason, butterflies almost never lay more than one egg on any given plant.

Tom's satisfied with his bag and Matthew has collected a fair bouquet; they head home. There, as Eric has instructed, Tom uses an X-Acto knife to cut the eggs and small surrounding patches of tissue from the leaves—the leaves curl as they dry and if left entire may trap the caterpillars as they hatch. Tom uses a soft-bristled watercolor brush to move the tiny patches of leaves and eggs into water tumblers, one egg to each tumbler. Then he caps each tumbler with a paper towel secured with a rubber band, and he lines them up in the china cabinet—Eric had told Tom to keep the eggs and caterpillars out of direct sunlight. Tom uses the brush tip to move the young caterpillar into an empty ten-gallon aquarium. He sets the quarter-inch-long creature down on a fresh milkweed leaf and covers the aquarium with a piece of fiberglass screen snugged at the corners with paper clips.

Admittedly, this expedition consumed several 20-minute gardening sessions; Tom and Matthew dawdled for more than an hour in the meadow and it took Tom a half hour more to set up the vivarium in the dining room. But this can hardly be described as hard labor, and over the next week this project twice provided Tom with the excuse to play hooky from household duties. "Quarter-Inch" (as Matthew dubbed the caterpillar) ate a whole milkweed leaf every day, and these had to be green and crisp. Acting on Eric's instructions, Tom had set a handful of leaves stem-down in water in the refrigerator, and this treatment kept them fresh for several days. But by Thursday (and again on Saturday) Tom felt obliged to take Matthew back to the meadow to secure a new supply, even though Tom had observed milkweed growing in several places he passed in his daily routine. (Fortunately for the monarchs, milkweed is a most plentiful wildflower.) Matthew's pressed-flower collection kept growing.

So, too, did Quarter-Inch, who soon became Half-Inch, Inch, and then Two-Inch. In the meantime, two of the eggs hatched. Tom had been checking the water tumblers every morning, since that is when Eric said the hatchings usually occur, and he was prompt in moving the caterpillars to their own milkweed leaves in the aquarium. (Eric had said that a ten-gallon aquarium would accommodate ten caterpillars without fatal encounters.) Still, caring for the caterpillars took no more than five minutes in the morning and five minutes in the evening.

Periodically, as they grew, the caterpillars would climb up onto the walls of the aquarium, hang head down in a J-shaped posture, and shed their skins. Tom took care not to disturb them during this process; Matthew was fascinated by the way they ate their old skins afterward. The caterpillars' colors seemed to intensify with each molt, deepening into bands of vivid yellow, white, and black.

On July 24th, two weeks after Tom had collected him in the cemetery, Three-Inch climbed up the aquarium wall one last time and adopted his molting posture. But this time, when the skin split, it was a chrysalis that emerged, an irregular green-blue capsule that was speckled with glittering gold. By the 30th, the other two caterpillars Tom and Matthew had hatched from eggs had encased themselves in chrysalises, too.

Eric had said that it took about ten days for the caterpillar to transform itself into a butterfly after entering the chrysalis, and sure enough, on August 2nd, Three-Inch's chrysalis started to darken—Tom and Matthew could see the outline of wings through the now semitransparent walls. This, according to Eric, was a sign that the butterfly's emergence was near, and Matthew didn't want to leave for preschool the next morning. Tom moved his computer to the table beside the aquarium. He typed away that morning until about 10 o'clock, when he looked up and saw the chrysalis had shattered. There hung a butterfly, still damp and with wings as limp as a flag on a still day.

Within an hour, though, Three-Inch had fluttered up to the screen atop the aquarium, and Tom rushed out to pick up Matthew. Together they carried the aquarium outdoors and carefully lifted off the lid—the butterfly continued to cling to it until Matthew gave it a gentle shake. Tom waved as it flew off. Matthew shouted good-bye.

Both of the other butterflies emerged and departed within a couple of days. Tom missed the trips to the meadow, but he enjoyed the arguments with Matthew about who it was (Three-Inch-One, Three-Inch-Two, or Three-Inch-Three) that had come back for a visit every time a monarch butterfly fluttered through the garden. Tom has planted an orange-flowered species of milkweed—*Asclepias tuberosa*, sold as "butterfly weed"—in the hope that one of the hatchlings will return to rear a brood in the front yard next year. If they don't, though, Tom and Matthew know where to find them.

Marty's Bulbs of Summer

Dahlias are bulbs you plant in the spring rather than in the fall. There are a number of advantages to this. Primary among them is that if you're like me, you always mean to plant bulbs in the fall, and then one day you wake up and it's Christmas and snowing and you go, "Oops." So God invented spring-planted, summer-flowering bulbs as a kind of horticultural make-up test.

I had a sunny spot in front of the house where I had been growing some mangy rosebushes whose main purpose seemed to be to develop black spots and attract disgusting insects. Dahlias seemed like a good alternative. Heck, a disintegrating corpse would have seemed like a good alternative.

The dahlias took off splendidly and flowered prodigiously all summer. They seemed to exert a hypnotic effect on the bees, who not only came and hovered but landed and stayed for days at a time, crawling around and buzzing drowsily. Hmmmm.

It's hard to know why spring-planted, summer-flowering bulbs aren't more popular. Can it be the public relations campaign from the Dutch government has permanently linked bulb planting with Thanksgiving, so that to grow anything other than tulips seems un-American? Anyway, it's amazing how many seasoned gardeners (or unseasoned ones like me) know nothing about summer-flowering bulbs.

Check them out at your local garden store. There are lots of beautiful kinds besides dahlias, like gladioluses and cannas and the ornamental onions, or alliums. The plants don't require much care, and the flowers last a long time; in short, you get a lot of bang for the buck. Besides, summer-flowering bulbs let you enjoy the first snow of winter without guilt pangs.

What to Do

1. A few weeks before you're ready to put the dahlias outdoors, start them indoors in pots.
2. When they're about three or four inches high and the weather is warm, transfer them into the garden bed.

3. Plant them in a moist and sunny spot.
4. If you live in a northern climate, dig up the dahlia tubers before the first hard frost, dust them off, and store them over the winter in a carton full of straw in a dark, cool place. Next spring, start again.

Chapter 10

The Functionally Literate Gardener

Tom once landed a job reviewing gardening books for one of the country's most prestigious gardening magazines. At first he thought he had died and gone to heaven. Not only was he getting all the gardening books he wanted for free, but he was being paid to read them.

After six months, the books had taken over Tom's garage and were spilling over into the basement (where they were starting to encroach on space he had reserved for his two favorite activities: worm composting and bathtub brewing). By the end of ten months, Tom was climbing over books to get to the coffeepot in the morning. After a year, Tom quit.

He quit not because he had run out of space, but because he realized that he could devote every day of his life to reading another gardening book and still not make a dent in the literature. He decided his time could be better spent weeding than reading.

As Tom had learned, publishing gardening books is now big business. Hundreds of new titles appear every year, earning millions of dollars for publishers, and the rate of publication continually increases. There is a feverish rush to nail down every conceivable aspect of the field.

There are books on perennials. Books on native perennials. Books on native perennial ground covers. Books on native perennial ground covers that flourish in shady sites. Books on native perennial ground covers that flourish in shady sites if you have alkaline soil—and vote Socialist-Worker and live in the Southeast.

Bless 'em all, we say. But we also perceive a problem: if you don't have enough time to garden the conventional way (and you don't, or you wouldn't be reading *this* book), how can you possibly find the time to read all those books that teach you how to do it?

Fortunately, you don't have to.

The 20-minute gardener regards reading gardening books (except for this one, your bible) as being about as useful to your garden as reading an Elmore Leonard novel. It's a nice way to pass a Sunday afternoon, but it's not going to do squat for the roses (unless you compost the book).

Not that the 20-minute gardener thinks he knows everything. He is aware of his limitations and is quick to consult with the experts when necessary. But the 20-minute gardener also knows that there are quicker, easier ways to get the facts than wading through ten thousand pages of verbiage.

The One Other Book You Need

One brisk March afternoon Marty was eager to start work in the garden and was happily engaged in cutting back (butchering) the still-dormant forsythia bush in front of his house when Tom happened to pull into the driveway. Tom looked—then stomped on the accelerator and raced up the driveway with horn blaring and lights flashing; he had to stop Marty before he cut again. Any idiot knows (well, most idiots) that you prune forsythias after they bloom. Forsythias flower in early spring from buds made the previous year; what Marty was doing, by removing branches *before* his bush bloomed, was removing that spring's flowers before they could open.

To prevent a recurrence of this disaster, Tom gave Marty a copy of an old edition of the *McCall's Garden Guide* that he had just picked up at a yard sale for a dollar. Now before Marty prunes, he reads.

To know things like when to prune or when to fertilize does not require a library. The names on the plants in the garden center change from year to year, but that is mostly just a marketing ploy. The basic selection of plants—the ones everyone uses to landscape their yards—don't really change. This year's lilac (the one they named for some tabloid star) may have a slightly different color of flower (or it may not), but 'Oprah' or 'Geraldo' is still a lilac, a near-clone of 'Phil Donahue' (last year's triumph), and it requires the same care that lilacs have always needed.

That means you can still get all the information you need out of the same, fat, dusty, one-volume gardening encyclopedia you have been using for years. As far as we're concerned, the best encyclopedia is the cheapest one, since, for the average gardener's purposes, one is just about as good as another.

That doesn't mean you won't develop preferences. Tom treasures his 1970 vintage copy of *The Wise Gardening Encyclopedia*; his mother bought it for him on the condition that he finally return her 1946 edition. Tom likes his encyclopedia because it is illustrated with murky black-and-white photographs taken by T. H. Everett, his mentor at the New York Botanical Garden. Tom recognizes most of the digging, weeding, and planting gardeners shown in these illustrations. Tom recognizes them even when the illustrations show nothing but a pair of hands—those are hands that used to wallop him when he made a mistake. As he looks at these illustrations, Tom can hear these people—his teachers—shouting advice (and abuse) at him once again. This makes Tom feel young, and it jolts his aging memory into action.

Still, for the soundest gardening advice, Tom recommends that you prowl the tag sales and used-book shops until you find an encyclopedia of even older vintage, something like his mother's broken-backed, coverless 1946 *Wise* (he never should have returned it). Don't look for an untouched first edition; old and shabby is what you want. With garden encyclopedias, shabby is good—it's a sign of wear and suggests that someone actually found the book useful.

But the really important point is the date of publication, which should be before 1950. Encyclopedias of that age were written before gardening was taken over by the chemists, so they offer a much healthier and a more or less "natural" approach to gardening. Garden technology was also relatively primitive then. Those old encyclopedias are pre–weed whacker in date, and the solutions they offer for the average gardening problem are usually refreshingly simple.

Just compare, for example, their treatment of fertilization with that of their modern multivolume counterparts. Tom's mother's *Wise Gardening Encyclopedia* deals with this issue by offering up a paean to manure, 2½ pages of close-set type. "No gardener should spurn a supply of manure however small" it advises; "just as humans cannot keep healthy on a diet wholly of food in tablet form, plants, except in the laboratory, will not thrive indefinitely on chemical fertilizers alone." Thereupon follows a connoisseur's guide that treats of the value of dung from horses bedded on rye straw (the best) versus that of horses bedded on wood shavings, salt hay, and even peat moss.

Even better is the essay on manure in Norman Taylor's *Encyclopedia of Gardening*, which was first published by Houghton Mifflin in 1936 and which many informed reviewers still consider the ultimate in gardening guides. Taylor's discussion of this subject opens on a quaint note: "Not so long ago a school of chiefly feminine gardeners did not admit the word *manure* into polite hort. discussion." That was a *long* time ago, Norman. But what follows this opening statement is advice as sensible today as it ever was.

It must never be forgotten that commercial fertilizers add little permanent value to the soils, and it is exactly this thing which most manures accomplish. Long periods wherein the soil has been treated only with commercial fertilizers, while it may yield good crops, often result in leaving the soil fagged or tired. Such terms may not be in the scientific jargon of the soil scientist, but the fact remains that soil cannot be indefinitely treated as a laboratory to produce crops.

Taylor goes on to advise on the safe and effective use of everything from cow manure to night soil (human manure). Virtually all of the materials he describes (with the exception of bat guano) are being produced in far greater quantities today and have become an enormous disposal problem for farmers and municipalities. Are modern gardeners doing their part?

No, and if you look at the modern encyclopedias you'll see why. Check out the encyclopedia series that Houghton Mifflin is spinning off from Taylor's classic: the Taylor's Guides to Gardening Series (which was up to nineteen volumes the last time we checked) and the accompanying *Taylor's Master Guide to Gardening.* The *Taylor's Guide to Garden Techniques* offers a chapter on chemical formulas but dismisses manure in a couple of lines; the *Master Guide* never mentions manure at all. For shame!

Or compare the treatment of animal invaders. First, from the 1946 *Wise*:

In any such discussion many angles and arguments for and against a particular species necessarily present themselves. The relationship of the animal in question to other living creatures in the garden and to the plant material comes first to mind. Fortunately facts and statistics from scientific works can settle very nicely all such questions and definitely indicate who should be allowed to stay in the garden and who should be snubbed and discouraged.

A balanced treatment elegantly expressed.

Norman Taylor offers frontier justice. You may find his methods of pest control extreme and choose to ignore his advice, but when the rabbits and deer arrive in their devouring hordes, it's nice to know that there is recourse.

What does the *Taylor's Master Guide* say? It avoids any admission that conflict may arise and instead includes a brief plan detailing how you can turn your yard into a giant (but no doubt leafless) feeding station.

Which brings us to Tom's bitterest gripe about modern gardening encyclopedias (besides the excessive cost); these books are produced by marketers, not gardeners. This is evident in the format, which is designed to make you buy all eight dozen volumes (at $18.95 apiece in the case of the Taylor Guides; $60 for the *Master*

Guide), where formerly one would have sufficed. Indeed, despite all the glossy photos and extra bulk, the modern guides of many volumes actually include less useful information than the old-time prototypes.

For whereas Norman Taylor never hesitated to take a stand, the modern editorial panels studiously avoid doing that. Every interest group has money to spend, after all, so why offend any of them? In their feel-good books, ragweed and rabbits have equal rights with flowers and vegetables. This may sound good on paper, but we bet you can guess what the result is in the garden.

Tom would rather argue the issues with his mother's old *Wise*. That crusty book brands the plants it doesn't approve as "obnoxious" and "pernicious"; weeds are quite simply "useless." Tom disagrees with that last statement, but at least when he is reading his gardening encyclopedia he knows right where it stands, and why. That gives him something to react against in forming his own opinions.

Remember: you're a sucker in more than one way if you pay more than a dollar for your garden encyclopedia.

Just the Facts, Ma'am

Much as Tom admires the classic information in his vintage encyclopedias, he knows that they are not equal to answering every query. Their information about pesticides and weed killers, for example, is so outdated as to be positively dangerous. Of course, modern encyclopedias are little better in that respect; recommendations about garden chemicals are continually changing, so that any book becomes outdated before it can emerge from the press.

Additionally, because of their broad scope encyclopedias of any date cannot satisfy questions that deal with regional situations, such as gardening on the red clay soil you may find in Clay County, Georgia. Nor can an encyclopedia supply a really in-depth answer to very specific questions. For help of that kind, though, and for the latest technical information, Tom and Marty know just where to go: the local office of the Cooperative Extension.

This is a marvelous organization that (as the name suggests) represents a cooperative effort between the United States Department of Agriculture and each state's land-grant university. Together, these institutions have put agricultural and horticultural educators in every county of every state. You'll find their number in the county office listings in your telephone book.

Many local Extension offices keep a variety of experts on staff. Typically, Extension personnel can help with soil tests, diagnoses of plant pests and diseases, tips on locally adapted plants, and all sorts of general gardening advice. All of this is done at cost or without charge, and it seems a terrible shame that the overwhelming majority of gardeners never take advantage of this service. Especially since it offers the greatest bargains in gardening literature.

These bargains are the inexpensive, information-packed bulletins that the Cooperative Extensions distribute. These pamphlets are short; they may be no more than a single sheet, though some run to forty or fifty pages. They are plain: folded sheets stapled together and illustrated mainly with graphs and black-and-white photos shot by the agents themselves. But they reflect local experience and the most recent research, they focus on the problems gardeners face in your area, and are they cheap: some bulletins cost as little as thirty-five cents.

When Marty asked for a more detailed evaluation, Tom slipped back into his reviewer mode and ordered a selection of bulletins from three of the most active Cooperative Extensions: the California, New York, and Texas systems. A month or so later the envelopes arrived and Tom sat down for a pleasant afternoon of self-improvement.

He admired the forthright simplicity of the bulletins from Texas A&M University. Simple declarative sentences about *Growing Herbs in Texas*, *Landscaping for Energy Conservation*, and *Slugs and Snails*. It took Tom just eighteen minutes to breeze through the lot, and he was much better equipped to garden in, say, San Antonio afterward.

Had he been living in that lovely city, Tom could have kept the interior of his house eight to ten degrees cooler without air conditioning, just by the way he arranged the trees in his yard. He could have cut his oil consumption by 23 percent in wintertime—which is practically treason in Texas. He learned about twenty-two great herbs—how to grow them, harvest them, and dry them, that would have made his chicken-fried steaks even zestier. He learned more about slug eggs than he wanted to know, but also learned about tracking slugs by their slime trails to the hideouts where these garden outlaws spend their days.

All of this cost him $1.30, plus postage.

California offered slicker graphics and a somewhat more sophisticated attitude. It's "Guide to Homeowners" *Trees for Saving Energy* included a colorful, centerfold plan of a sample landscape with windscreens and "solar-friendly" trees; it pointed out that better gardening could mean a reduced need for power plants and lower energy costs. There was a diagram of special ways to prune both evergreen and deciduous trees to make them a part of this effort.

Soil and Water Management for Home Gardeners was more in the utilitarian mold, a fine basic course in seven pages of text and tables. Where the University of California really scored with Tom, though, was in leaflet 2210, *Do You Want a Home in the Country?*

Tom shouted yes, but then read this thoughtful balancing of the pros and cons. Had he thought about the fact that in the country he would have to get to know his neighbors? And if he planned this as his retirement home, had he thought about the consequences of living at a distance from medical care? This brochure ended up with "If the Country Wins," five pages of information on how to pursue the dream of rural bliss, but by then Tom was surer than ever that he wasn't going to move any farther from the Italian market and the espresso bar. He'd rather make his commute a weekend one, a drive into the country to catch up with his apple trees. Cost: $5.25, plus postage—those slick graphics don't come free.

Tom had saved Cornell University's bulletins for last because he already knew something about them. Having come of age as a gardener in New York, he had spent a good deal of time browsing in the Cornell publications. He still believes they are the best in the country—at least, if you happen to live in the region on which they focus.

Lawn Care Without Pesticides will tell you how, by planting the right turf and then maintaining it the right way, you can free yourself from pesticides and herbicides; *The Types and Uses of Mulch in the Landscape* tells you why a mulch that works in summertime may not benefit your plantings in winter and explains how you can have one that's good for both seasons—and do you know which of the new fabric mulches resist weathering best? *Suggested Practices for Planting and Maintaining Trees and Shrubs* explains why late summer or fall may be a better planting time for trees than spring—and why planting large specimens is not only expensive but even counterproductive (small trees suffer less shock from transplanting and soon overtake the bigger transplants).

Cost: $4.50.

All of these Cooperative Extensions offer videotapes and books as well as bulletins, and Texas offers publications in Spanish, too. Send away for the catalogs of offerings—each state distributes these for free, and you can get all the addresses to which to send a request from your county Extension office. These will put you in touch with information about everything from probating a will to Cambodian dance. Everybody Tom knows is griping about the difficulty of saving for their children's college tuition. Tom plans to buy his son, Matthew, four years' worth of bulletins when the time comes—and boast about his son's Cornell education.

All the News That Fits

Tom and Marty don't want to seem inflexible and reactionary. (Actually, Marty is the only one who worries about this; Tom could care less.) We are willing to admit that there are times when any gardener lusts after novelty. You want advice on what's new and fashionable, what's the happening thing. For this more topical kind of information, you obviously need a more recent publication. Ideally you would like one that focuses on the latest news and is concise, so that you don't waste six weeks of gardening time on your reading.

That sounds like a magazine.

During Tom's teenage years, his parents knew he was going to be something special when, instead of *Playboy*, they found copies of *House & Garden* buried beneath his mattress. Every night Tom would take out the magazine and fantasize about flawless English roses and meadows of wildflowers without a weed. But as he matured, he came to realize that the objects depicted in the magazines he was drooling over had about as much relevance to the real world as did the photographs in the magazines Marty was surreptitiously stashing under *his* bed. (Uhh, *Modern Stamp and Coin*, as I recall—M.A.)

Gardening magazines have been springing up like (fill in your own cliché) lately. While many have informative articles, generally reading gardening magazines is not the most effective way to use your 20 minutes. Magazines seem to broadly divide themselves into two categories. First there are the old-fashioned "how-to" variety, which are constantly giving you projects in articles like "71 Herbs You Can Grow in Shade." These sound terrific, but really, what would you do with seventy-one herbs even if you could grow them?

There is also a new breed of gardening magazine; these are more like home fantasies and are filled with articles such as "Build Your Own Victorian Greenhouse." Unfortunately, such articles only serve to make 20-minute gardeners feel guilty about what we are *not* doing, instead of making us feel good about what we *have* accomplished.

A problem with both types of gardening magazines are the photographs. Tom has been sent out on assignments with famous gardening photographers. These point-and-shoot types were paid almost as much as fashion photographers, and that makes sense because their goal was identical: to snap that rose at exactly the height of the season, when the sun is in the proper position, so those two drops of dew will reflect the Cotswold cottage in the background. Beautiful to look at, but these flowers bear about as much resemblance to ones in a real garden as your family does to the Brady Bunch. If you want to enjoy these photographs as fantasy, fine. Just don't expect *your* roses to look like that.

So where do you turn for topical, up-to-date gardening information? *The 20-Minute Gardener* has identified what it believes is the ultimate source: newsletters.

Why newsletters?

Newsletters have a number of advantages over magazines.

1. They're focused. Newsletters are produced by amateurs, and they generally represent an obsession—with a particular type of plant, or a particular approach to gardening. Finding the newsletter that fits you may take some doing, because there are hundreds of them out there. But once you find the one that matches your enthusiasm you are assured that every paragraph of every issue will be of burning interest.

For example, say you believe, like Tom does, that there hasn't been a good new rose released onto the market in a hundred years. Send $5 to the Heritage Rose Group (c/o Miriam Wilkins, 925 Galvin Drive, El Cerrito, CA 94530) and you'll get a quarterly newsletter that puts you in touch with a nationwide network of like-minded grumps (actually, Tom found the heritage rosarians far too broad-minded).

Of course, you could also go to gardening magazines for information about antique roses. If you were lucky, you'd find one article on the subject in every twenty issues or so. By the time you've assembled a decent file, the roses that are modern now would be antiques.

2. Newsletters are also shorter than magazines; most newsletters are just four to eight pages long. That makes them easier for the busy gardener to digest.

3. Newsletters are un-slick. The few photographs they contain tend to be blurry amateur black-and-white shots as opposed to the semipornographic garden shots in glossy magazines. In other words, newsletters have something to do with real life.

4. Newsletters don't have advertisers, which means they can tell you what works and what doesn't without fear of losing a major account. The only people newsletter editors have to answer to are their readers. They can therefore afford to recommend what's cheap and effective as opposed to what's produced by their advertisers. If you save money, it reflects well on the publication.

5. They're fun. Newsletters are written by people who are fanatical about their particular subject. (Want a wild weekend? Try *The Bamboo Quarterly*'s annual convention in New Iberia, Louisiana.) These publications are driven by love, not by media empires out to start a gardening magazine because their research shows the demographics are hot.

Among the more interesting newsletters we've sampled lately:

• *The New England Farm Bulletin* (PO Box 67, Taunton, MA 02780). A recent issue offered a first-rate piece on bees, in which we learned that bees are the champions of the animal kingdom at holding in waste, which they can do for *months*, until they go off on a "cleansing flight" (the results of which will inevitably land on you or your car). This publication also offers the most thorough guide to state fairs in the New England area as well as useful tables (e.g., the average dates of the last spring frost and the first fall frost for your area) and great classifieds (advertisements for cashmere goats, llamas, and classic tractors).

• *Bob's Newsletter* (PO Box 1841, Santa Rosa, CA 95402) is put out by, well, Bob, four times a year whenever he can manage. Bob prides himself on his political incorrectness, carrying tips and stories that he claims even organic gardening magazines won't go near. It's full of quirky and useful information: an ergonomic study of the least stressful style of spade and an article detailing why so-called pest-free "antique" roses can end up being more trouble than off-the-shelf modern hybrid teas.

• *The Gourd* is published by the American Gourd Society (PO Box 274 TP, Mount Gilead, OH 43338) and is chock-full of growing tips as well as photographs of gourd crafts: everything from gourd drums to gourd birdhouses, gourd fiddles, gourd hats, and gourd handbags. Tom *loved* the photograph of a gourd-clad belly dancer, as well as the shot of an elderly immigrant who stood amid a flock of penguins he had fashioned from gourds whose seed he had brought with him from Greece as a boy. This newsletter is a living slice of Americana. It's also filled with some of the most atrocious puns we've ever seen—my gourdness!

• *Temperate Bamboo Quarterly* (30 Meyers Road, Summertown, TN 38483). Hey, if bamboo is your thing (in other words, you're a bambusero), then seek no further. Besides hardcore information on how to grow bamboo, there are bamboo poems, crafts, events, and a thorough description of the first annual temperate bamboo lovers' conference. Even if bamboo isn't your thing, it's hard not to be impressed by the dedication of the partisans of this amazing plant.

But newsletters are not limited to exotic plants like bamboo. Even the humble marigold has its own newsletter (*Amerigold Newsletter*, c/o Marigold Society of America National Headquarters, PO Box 112, New Britain, PA 18901), in which besides learning about the latest marigold varieties and how best to care for them, we're informed that the U.S. Postal Service has now issued a marigold postage stamp and that Baldwin, New York, has the honor of being designated Marigold City, U.S.A.

Our favorite general-interest newsletters are *The Avant Gardener* and *HortIdeas*. These are both horticultural clipping services. That is, the editors are continually searching the gardening press for interesting items—notes about new methods of pest control, descriptions of must-have new plants, or useful new gardening technologies. They reduce each item to an intriguing paragraph or two and then publish the best dozen or so each month in their newsletter.

A typical item was the note in a recent issue of *The Avant Gardener* (PO Box 489, New York, NY 10028) about the discovery of a novel way of protecting strawberries from hungry birds. Before the plants set fruit, apparently, you must paint a few handfuls of unshelled hazelnuts red and then scatter them throughout your strawberry bed. This attracts birds, and then frustrates them. By the time the real fruit ripens, the birds will be paralyzed by cynicism. Serves them right.

HortIdeas (460 Black Lick Road, Gravel Switch, KY 40328), meanwhile, was reporting on an arid-land-restoration symposium and offering a table of results from an ice storm in Rochester, New York, listing eighty-four different types of shade trees with an indication of how susceptible to breakage each had proven. Tom clipped that table and intends to consult it before he plants any trees at his mother-in-law's near-polar residence in the hills of western Massachusetts.

Skimming these two newsletters takes just minutes a month, but they leave you with the comforting feeling of being entirely up-to-date. And if you want information in depth, all you have to do is read the fine print: both *The Avant Gardener* and *HortIdeas* always include a complete reference with each item they publish, so it's easy to jump back to the original source of information and pursue the subject in detail.

For several years Tom subscribed to *The New York Times* largely because once a week it included a gardening column by

Alan Lacy. Lacy has a genius for searching out the horticulturally unusual and marvelous—and he is a masterful prose stylist as well.

In 1993, Mr. Lacy quit the *Times* to start publishing his own quarterly newsletter, *Alan Lacy's Homeground* (PO Box 271, Linwood, NJ 08221). So now Tom can avoid the depressing experience of informing himself about current events—*Homeground* doesn't bother with them unless they take place in the garden. A recent issue included a wonderful article on peonies, a very useful questioning of how "zones" are assigned to plants, and a contrarian piece about why Mr. Lacy avoids spring perennials. All in all, it's a delightful distillation of useful gardening information from a gardener of the highest spirit.

Newsletters range in price from free to twenty or thirty dollars a year. They can be monthly, quarterly, yearly, or, in the case of Bob, whenever he has time. Most will send you a sample issue at no charge. For a checklist complete with addresses, you can run down to the library and check out Barbara Barton's book *Gardening by Mail* (see page 68).

Gardening Journals

There is yet one more species of garden book, and this is the one that comes with its pages blank—the publisher charges you big bucks, yet you have to supply the words. What a deal.

We believe that the current popularity of this product represents more than the supreme gullibility of certain consumers. The rise in journal keeping is also symptomatic of the unrealistic expectations and ego that some people bring to the humble art of gardening.

In theory, of course, journal keeping serves a useful purpose. You record what you planted where, when things came up (and when they didn't), and track the little triumphs (the first flower) and catastrophes (an unexpected frost) that befall all plants. The ostensible reason for all this is that the next year you take out your trusty, mud-encrusted journal, whip through its pages stained with the soil and sweat of the previous summer's efforts, and use it as a guide for the new year's planting.

But the sad truth is that weather, soil conditions, and virtually everything else vary so drastically from year to year that the fact that the peonies bloomed brilliantly on June 10th this year is not likely to be of much use in planning next year's planting. This year it will probably rain more. Or less. Or since you've pruned back the lilac, the peonies will get more light. Or because you didn't prune the pine, its new growth plunged the peonies into shade.

Marty feels that gardening journals, like sex and the Internet (and especially sex on the Internet) are fascinating for the doer and boring for everyone else (unless you have the talent to produce a literary masterpiece like Katharine White's *Onward and Upward in the Garden*).

As someone who makes his living selling books, Marty admires garden journals as a product, especially the ones you find advertised in upscale catalogs, the leather-bound ones with preworn pages (like prewashed jeans) that often sell for more than the plants and seeds whose experiences they chronicle. He believes that journals, like gardening gloves, clogs, and little pressed-manure frogs, are terrific gifts for people who like the idea of gardening as opposed to the act.

Virtual Gardening

Tom doesn't approve of sex on the Internet either. He worries about those electronic viruses. But he does spend a good deal of time gardening there.

This was not always the case. For many years, Tom found it cheering when electronically literate friends labeled him—the book writer—a dinosaur. After all, dinosaurs ruled the earth for 150 million years, didn't they? But then his fellow dinosaurs began plugging modems into their word processors so that they were accessing rather than researching. Tom began to wonder if he would end up a road kill on that information you-know-what.

So he made an appointment with Alexa Jaffurs, the reference librarian at Wesleyan University's science library. Alexa denied having any special expertise to share with Tom, but he knew different. She's a computer adept who speaks intelligible English and listens to people over the age of twenty-five.

When Tom arrived at Alexa's office she fired up the binary kilowatt-burner and set in motion what she called "a search engine."

She asked it about gardens, and almost immediately an advertisement for Saturn cars popped up on the screen. Tom was impressed, but what came next was even better.

He can describe it only by saying that it was like a three-day drunk in the Library of Congress. Everywhere he turned, Tom tripped over something wonderful, though by the time he figured out what it was, it was gone.

Tom began by stumbling into a catalog of garden-related products with a description of fruit-picker gloves clad in thorn-proof Kevlar. They sounded like they might be lifesavers, in the right circumstances. Then it was on to a guide to the gardens of Ohio; a list of ingredients in "chunky vegetable soup"; an Australian article entitled "Gardens, Villas, and Social Life in Renaissance Florence," complete with a dozen digitized views of the Villa Trebbio; a list of nurseries specializing in irises; a guide to wedding gardens across the United States; an account of a visit by representatives of the Academia Sinica, Taipei, to the Missouri Botanic Garden; the plant database of the University of Warsaw, Poland; and, finally, the home page of a Texas consortium that promotes the construction of gardens for outdoor model railways.

This was all amazing but also overwhelming, because Tom couldn't perceive any real order in the presentation of information. Alexa assured him that there is none. This led Tom to suspect that surfing the Web horticulturally is the antithesis of 20-minute gardening. It may be fascinating, but it yields no tangible results and will eat up all of your time. Not just your leisure time and the time you should be spending with your family, but also the time you should use for earning a living and the time you should allow for feeding and clothing yourself. It's your choice.

Tom did carry away something useful from his hours at Alexa's computer terminal, and that was an introduction to "news groups." He subsequently squandered several weeks exploring these and was able to contact cider makers in England, butterfly gardeners in Pennsylvania, and a woman who had created (well, virtually) a garden designed to attract bats.

Tom sees lots of potential here. The other day he accessed a robotic garden at the University of Southern California and was able to ride around on a mechanical arm deciding which plants would be watered and which would not. That's something entirely beyond the power of page-turning dinosaurs like Marty.

The Best Gardening Book Never Written

Marty scoured the shelves for gardening books that would complement the 20-minute gardener's real-life approach to the subject. He immediately eliminated all of the most modern gardening books, with their full-color glossy photos of impossibly beautiful roses or groups of well-dressed (and obviously well-heeled) folks—with hideously well-behaved children—passing the pesto around on a candlelit table in the rose garden.

Then there's the new breed of "lifestyle" garden memoirs, in which a middle-aged yuppie couple moves to a fancy country address (often commuting by helicopter) and starts canning their own tomato sauce, which gets sold in gourmet stores and makes them instant millionaires. They then offer not-very-subtle comparisons between the life cycles of peonies and the decline of the nation state. Ugh.

Even worse are the eco-memoirs where the reader is made to feel personally responsible for destroying the rain forest because he decided to fertilize the lawn. Let's keep virtue out of gardening books and in fiction, where it belongs.

Marty does feel, however, that there is at least one gardening book that is undoubtedly a classic. It was written over a hundred years ago, has no photographs, pitches no new equipment, and sends readers back to their own common sense more than it recommends any particularly new methods of cultivation.

Walden, by Henry David Thoreau, is an inspiration for all 20-minute gardeners to go against the contemporary grain, with advice such as these chestnuts:

On breaking old habits:
"A single gentle rain makes the grass many shades greener. . . . Like the grass, which confesses the influence of the slightest dew that falls on it, [we should] not spend our time atoning for the neglect of past opportunities, which we were calling our duty. . . . No way of thinking, however old, can be trusted without proof."

On choosing your own design:

"The whole ground of human life seems to some to have been gone over by their predecessors, both the heights and the valleys, and all things to have been cared for. According to Evelyn, 'the wise Solomon prescribed ordinances for the very distances of trees; and the Roman praetors have decided how often you may go into your neighbor's land to gather the acorns which fall on it without trespass, and what share belongs to that neighbor.' "

On why gardening is idiot-proof:

"The soil, it appears, is suited to the seed, for it has sent its radical downward, and it may now send its shoot upward also with confidence."

Why we invented 20-minute gardening:

"As if you could kill time without injuring eternity."

The 20-minute gardener's mantra:

"Simplify, simplify."

2◯-MINUTE PROJECTS

Marty Falls in Love; Tom's Guerrilla Garden

Marty Moon Dances

I'm in love. Of all the plants we researched for the book, this is the one that stole my heart. Actually, it stole my wife's heart too. Moonflower is a vine of the morning glory family. It likes a lot of water and sun and prefers rich, well-drained soil, though my moonflowers were rooted in soil as hard as the desert and they didn't seem to suffer too much. If you have a stone fence or a pillar, set your moonflowers at the base to allow them plenty of opportunity to climb.

For climb they will. Moonflowers take a while to get going; they like consistently warm weather and in the North will stall until summer has settled in. But with warm nights comes a scramble of leaves and twining vines. My moonflowers could climb no higher than the three feet of post I allowed them; Tom's plants, though, easily climbed the five feet of his trellis and seemed to be taking stock of the roof by season's end.

After a month or two of twining and climbing (you'll be wondering whether this plant isn't really an escapee from *The Little Shop of Horrors*), long, thin white buds twisted like a unicorn's horn will appear. By late July or early August, these will unfurl at night into wheels of white with a scent so fragrant yet subtle it makes roses seem like scratch-and-sniffs. By dawn, the blossoms wither, but the next night will bring new blossoms and a new hit of perfume. The display continues well into October. It makes a step outside for a breath of night air a truly memorable experience.

What to Do

1. Order seeds early, and plant around the date of the last spring frost in your area (the beginning of May in Connecticut) in 3-inch containers of potting soil; make sure you nick a hole in the hard seed coats before you plant (see page 18 for Tom's description of how he did this). Set the planted pots in a warm spot (over a radiator is good) and then move them to a sunny windowsill as soon as the seeds germinate.
2. Set the young plants out when the days are warming and the night temperatures aren't dropping below 50°F; that's the last week of May in Connecticut.
3. Keep the soil around the young plants moist and fertilize once a month by watering the plants with ordinary house-plant food.
4. Take lots of nighttime strolls.

Not a Border but a Brawl

Harmony and order are the qualities that most Americans pursue in their gardening. That, Tom has decided, is a mistake. Or at least it is an anachronism, a tradition that derives from another age. For his last 20-minute project, Tom began working on an entirely new kind of garden, one that is much more in keeping with the facts of his life. Traditional gardeners plant "borders"; Tom planted a brawl.

A border is a long ribbon of mannerly shrubs and perennials, a sort of Edwardian garden party where everyone gets along (even if they don't really like each other) and where the monarch (the gardener) reigns unchallenged. In Tom's urban garden, though, it's every plant for himself (unless the plant happens to be female). His plants prefer to settle differences by themselves.

Tom chose these plants because 20 minutes of work a day wouldn't begin to satisfy traditional border flowers. Summer phloxes, delphiniums, and chrysanthemums—the traditional choices—are always in need of staking or deadheading or pinching back. They demand a well-tilled soil and regular feeding with all the right vitamins, and when the aphids move in, those well-bred old-timers simply expire—unless the gardener ex machina (Tom) drops everything and rushes in with the insecticidal soap.

Tom had sworn off that kind off fussing. So he sought out plants that resemble the people who hang out on nearby street corners. These plants belong to a group that traditional gardeners call "garden thugs"—invasive species that take over a garden unless severely repressed. That's exactly what they are doing in Tom's yard now, after two seasons of growth. Already they are jostling each other, the different species all trying to occupy the same space. Let the best plant win, says Tom.

Actually, Tom had strayed from approved practice even before the thugs went into his yard. His European-trained mentors had taught him to begin any garden by double-digging the soil. That is, he was supposed to turn the soil and mix in compost or peat moss to a depth of two lengths of the spade's blade—about twenty inches. Tom used to do that, twenty years ago when his back was younger. But to double-dig the 750-square-foot bed he envisioned was too daunting a prospect in middle age. Besides, at 20 minutes a day, he'd be digging for years.

So Tom didn't dig at all. Instead, in early spring he outlined his new garden bed in the lawn in front of his house (that's his yard's sunniest area—brawlers like sun), marking the edge with wooden stakes and string. That task occupied one 20-minute work session.

The next day, he covered the bed-to-be with newspaper, laying it down half a dozen sheets thick right on top of the turf. Over the next week's worth of 20-minuteses, Tom covered the newspaper with three to four inches of compost and shredded leaves. For two weeks after that he turned to other projects. Then he returned to the new bed to plant. He used a sharp spade for this, planting right through the paper and mulch.

That wouldn't have suited most garden flowers, but it was just fine with the tiger lilies (*Lilium lancifolium*) that a friend gave Tom. Tom's friend had rescued a single bulb from an abandoned homestead some years previously, and this Chinese wildflower had since proliferated out of control. The friend looked distinctly relieved when Tom accepted a sackful.

Transplanted into the unimproved earth, these exotic flowers hardly missed a beat. By July they had covered Tom's new flower bed with a mob of black-spotted orange turbans. In the meantime, Tom had devoted several other 20-minute sessions to planting competitors.

Goldenrod is a notable weed in Tom's area of central Connecticut—Tom ordered half a dozen plants of horticulturally unimproved specimens of stiff goldenrod (*Solidago rigida*) from a prairie-plant nursery in Wisconsin. One evening he planted that. On the next evening, Tom planted prairie grasses he had ordered from the same supplier: big bluestem and prairie dropseed (*Andropogon gerardii* and *Sporobolus heterolepsis*). The wild bergamot (*Monarda fistulosa*) he saved for the following day. The nurseryman had warned that bergamot is a "spreader," and the grasses, Tom knew, used to cover half a million miles of the Midwest.

To these Tom gradually added other brawny species: giant Chinese silver grass (*Miscanthus floridulus*), willow-leaved sunflower (*Helianthus salicifolius*), and a switch grass, *Panicum virgatum* 'Heavy Metal' (the name alone was enough to sell Tom on that). Tom's mother contributed yellow flags (*Iris pseudacorus*—she was overjoyed to see them leave her yard), while his mother-in-law donated some Oriental poppies she had been unable to eradicate even with the help of a goat. A great gardener in Brooklyn (where better to look for Tom's type of plants?) gave Tom roots of Japanese plume poppy (*Macleaya cordata*). She was delighted to find someone who could appreciate this bare-knuckled beauty.

Tom's brawl garden has developed into something like a meadow on steroids—the silver grass and plume poppies have shot up to a height of over eight feet, and the big bluestem topped four in its first season of growth. It is not a refined garden, but it is colorful. It can hold its own against insects and diseases, and is virtually self-sufficient. Tom's main input is to water new plantings occasionally during their first year and to spread more shredded leaves over the garden each fall. In spring, Tom tosses out handfuls of 5-10-5 fertilizer—20 minutes' work takes care of that handily.

There have been casualties. Tom had high hopes for the yellow flags, but they withered in a drought. Tom replaced them with Jerusalem artichokes, which he has been promised will be a glorious and relentless pest. Still in the testing stage is *Aster tataricus*—a friend says that it reaches a height of five to six feet in her garden and that the lavender flowers show up spectacularly in the soft light of late fall. She also promises that once established, it will pop up everywhere.

Tom's only fear at this point is that the worms are undermining him. They keep digesting the shredded leaf mulch so that there are now several inches of loose, black topsoil where once there was only smothered turf and yesterday's news. Tom worries that this may make his brawlers soft and phloxlike. Then he will have to take up the burden of sovereignty once again.

Chapter 11

Gardeners Anonymous

So the roses finally succumbed to the Japanese beetles; the mint ate the basil, and the deer ate the mint. You're sitting outside sipping chardonnay from Pottery Barn glasses on your environmentally correct plantation-grown teak bench feeling depressed, hopelessly inadequate, and duped for having spent twenty bucks on this book, your last best hope.

Our response: Oh, lighten up! It's just *gardening* we're talking about here, not world peace or brain surgery. And fear not! The 20-minute therapists are here with their own accelerated self-help class for the horticulturally impaired. Study these steps and you'll be able to handle anything nature (or anyone and anything else) throws at you.

The 20-Minute Five-Step Program
for Horticultural Self-Help

(Because in 20 minutes, you don't have time for any more.)

Step 1. Gardens Are from Earth;
Gardeners Are from Mars.

Few gardeners ever bother to look up from their beds and take a hint from the local landscape, and this insensitivity is the major cause of horticultural frustration. This truth occurred to us on a recent trip to Denver when we were taken to see a showplace, the garden of the garden columnist for a local newspaper.

We found him out of breath, haggard, rushing around his mini-estate of English-style herbaceous borders, preparing for the arrival of a garden tour. Alas, while meticulous, the borders lacked the lushness they would have had in their native Surrey. Denver, after all, is naturally a dry and rocky place. The garden columnist had only to look up at the horizon and the looming mass of the Front Range to realize that *ascetic* was the way to go here, not lush.

Later we visited the much simpler garden of Steve Olsen, a Denver landscaper who had covered his front yard with mounds of native stone and high mountain plants. We spent our time with *him* drinking margaritas and admiring the flowers, not desperately hunting for weeds.

When a reasonable attempt at growing something fails, you have two choices: you can dig in your heels and try a different fertilizer, more sun, less sun, more chemicals, less chemicals or you can gracefully accept the fact that, for whatever reason, this particular plant does not seem to thrive in your particular environment. So what? It's not like there aren't thousands of others to choose from.

No one ever won an argument with nature.

Step 2. Co-dependent No More.

There must be someone, somewhere, who enjoys catering to a half acre of nagging vegetation, but surely they aren't employed outside the home, nor do they have children, or any desire to have friends or go on vacation or do anything else. They are too busy.

Plants are like children: if you give them everything they want and never make them work for it, they become little monsters and, eventually, big monsters. Too much fertilizer, too frequent watering, overprotective behavior with the bug sprayer, and the plants never develop the ability to stand on their own. They just make greater demands on you. That's why the 20-minute gardener uses his brain rather than poisons to control weeds and pests.

Step 3. I'm Okay, You're Not.

Your problem may be that you are letting other people define success for you. Short of a lawsuit, who really cares what the neighbors think? When Tom was a young, freshly minted horticulturist, he strongly disapproved of those old-timers who clipped the shrubs in front of their house into perfect cones, gumdrops, and cubes. He used to lecture these veteran gardeners on the natural beauty of the plants, which they were violating. They would blow him a Bronx cheer, which, given that Tom really was in the Bronx, was a remarkably mild reaction.

Since then, Tom has absorbed the traditional wisdom of those old-time Bronxites. "Yuh muddah," he replies when some passing Yankee remarks that he doesn't care for the ornamental hay field Tom is creating in his Connecticut front yard. And after ten years of therapy and watching countless crows chomp on his $25-a-bag organic grass seed, Marty has learned to say, "No, I really like pachysandra," with great conviction.

The most successful garden Tom can recall was one in the Big Thicket of east Texas, which some genius had created entirely out of old football helmets. The gardener had spray-painted them gold and hung them upside down from the porch roof, trees, and fence to serve as repositories of brilliant flowers. It was as Texan (and as perfect) as a chicken-fried steak and took maybe 10 minutes a day of care.

The 20-minute gardener can go with Tom's exotic connoisseur plants or Marty's basic-as-apple-pie group. Or go with both. And the neighbors—well, they can always move.

Step 4. Gardeners Who Work like the Dogs.

As a lifelong type A, Marty knows it is possible to turn any hobby into a stomach-churning test of self-worth. That's why he no longer bicycles or runs—he can't keep up with the fashion requirements for the sports. And Tom knows that he can use his horticulturist voodoo to devastating effect. He could put his neighbors' foundation plantings to shame with a collection of the insectivorous Korean rhododendrons he has been studying. But to do this would cost him a second mortgage and countless hours of hand-feeding with flies.

One of the greatest values of 20-minute gardening is that you *can't* accomplish anything that will make you famous or rich in that interval of time. You can, however, attain realistic goals in 20 minutes a day, and with only a reasonable investment of effort. And you can actually have fun in the process.

Remember that sensible delegating is at the heart of the 20-minute gardener's arsenal. Making other people do the hard work frees Tom to have a good time with his five-year-old son, who would rather play catch on the grass than fertilize it. And it enables Marty to stop and smell the roses on his way in from the 6:45 express—even if the beetles have chewed off some of the leaves.

Step 5. Follow Your Bliss.

If there's one inviolable rule of 20-minute gardening, it's this: if you're not having fun, then you're doing something wrong. We've tried to break down some of the most nagging chores into do-able steps, and then we've tried to do away with most of those steps, too, whenever possible (or at least give them to someone else to do). But the very last step in any gardening project can be done only by you—and that's giving yourself permission to relax and enjoy.

Your garden is not a vehicle for impressing people or a series of time-consuming meaningless chores in a life that's already full of meaningless chores. Gardening is something you undertook because you enjoyed it. Remember? So go ahead and enjoy. If you don't accomplish everything you want to, or even everything you should, so what. There's always next year.

20-Minute Self-Actualization

"Is the pain of this self-analysis worth it? And if I do what Tom and Marty tell me to do, will I be expelled from the American Horticultural Society? Will they terminate my subscription to *House Beautiful*?"

Even after our foolproof five-step program you are still having misgivings. No wonder everyone else has left you to your fate. But the 20-minute therapists don't give up. Instead, we are going to switch gears. We have tried reasoned argument; now we are going to inspire with a case study.

What follows is a brief account of the finest 20-minute gardener we know. This man has more fun than any other gardener we have ever met. We can't take credit for that; his achievements are wholly his own. Still, we offer this man as an example because he epitomizes what a gardener can achieve through a spiritual quest, and with a healthy disregard for doing what he is told.

We first met Felder Rushing at a gardener's workshop in New York City. There was the roomful of café society Gertrude Jekyllites, and there was Felder—showing them how to make petunia planters out of old auto tires. With his deliberate drawl he was clearly far from home—he's a seventh-generation Mississippian—but he was managing just fine. After the workshop, he said, he was taking his pickup truck down to the Cross Bronx Expressway. It's bumper-to-bumper stripped cars down there; man, the tires that were there for the picking!

"I don't need 'em," he explained, "but it's an opportunity."

A brief conversation persuaded us that Felder was a natural. Independent of any study or discussion (his degrees are in traditional horticulture, the antithesis of 20-minute gardening, and he's a county agent who's supposed to spend his time telling you how to poison chinch bugs), Felder had arrived at all the conclusions of 20-minute gardening. It was a little like meeting the young Mozart: you go in thinking *you* are the expert but then realize you have nothing to teach. Instead, we scheduled a pilgrimage down to Felder's garden in Jackson.

The heart of this, the front yard, measures just about 40 × 60 feet; the backyard is where Felder has his greenhouse and where he stores the yard art made from old tricycles, tractor parts, rusty tools, and other debris. There's also a 15-foot-wide disk of turf back there that Felder installed because his wife, Terrell, likes to mow.

The garden is far more extensive than mere size might suggest, however. There is a native plant garden, a butterfly garden, a fragrance garden, a reptile garden, even a poisonous plant garden. It's important to educate the kids (Ira, age ten, and Zoe, age six), Felder explained.

Actually, the garden is as much theirs as Felder's or Terrell's, for Ira and Zoe both helped plan and build it. They helped paint the front steps—one yellow, one red, and one green. They use the rope that hangs outside the front door to swing down to the garden's lower level. And Ira was the one who rescued his mother's red high-heeled shoe from the trash and hung it up with the string of red-painted Budweiser cans that are a memento of the party which installed the picket fence. Felder cut the pickets to look like iris leaves and alternated them with lengths of rebar topped with brown and green bottles. The bottles ensure privacy, Felder explains: the neighbors never see past them.

It's a yard jammed not only with play but also with plants; Felder collects what he calls "passalongs," the plants rural southerners have grown for generations. These never appear in nursery catalogs; instead, gardeners pass cuttings or seeds along from one to another.

Felder's garden is rich in these and many other things, so that singling out a few high points is difficult. There is the giant blossom made of an old iron wheel that is wreathed in leaves made of old shovels. There's the pterodactyl fashioned from old leaf rakes and trowel blades. There are the purple gomphrenas—bachelor's buttons they call them in the South—sprouting from an old leather boot. There's the pond that's fed from a rusty farm pump where the duck decoy swims, the pink flamingo lurks, and the toads croak loud. There's the mosaic walk Felder poured for the mailman, letting Ira and Zoe press marbles, strings of beads, and bits of broken tile into the wet concrete. Our favorite, though, was the clump of maroon-colored stalks that a famous plantsmen identified as a magnificent specimen of oh-so-fashionable Japanese blood grass. Shucks, said Felder; that's just a wild sedge that Ira took after with the spray paint.

Felder has schemes for painting whole gardens gold for Christmas. He led the movement to plant a dinosaur garden of primitive plants at the natural history museum when an exhibit of life-sized mechanical dinosaurs stopped there. When the state's Department of Transportation planted California poppies as "wildflowers" along the Mississippi highways, he organized the group that harvested seeds of coreopsis (*Coreopsis tinctoria*), the official state wildflower, from abandoned fields and scattered it from the windows of their cars. He says, "The rules stink, but there are some awful good guidelines out there." Such as?

"I don't wear earrings, so why can't I hang bottles in my trees?"

"I don't wear mascara, so why can't I paint my grasses?"

"I picked up a lot of things from vernacular gardens: you know, the poor folks, the busy folks. When they get home they plant what they like and let it go."

"Instead of problem solving, that low-level cognitive stuff—you ought to be doing this, you ought to be doing that, here's how you fight all the symptoms of bad gardening practice—choose really good plants out of the hundreds of plants that do well here and get them established through their first summer. Then you can just sit back and drink a beer instead of gardening. All that gardening stuff, who's got time for it anymore?"

And most important:

"As long as you are looking for opportunities to poke fun at yourself, you'll always have fresh material."

Epilogue

It was a crisp fall day and Marty decided to drop in on Tom and see if he could sponge a few bottles of home-brewed cider. But when Marty pulled into Tom's driveway, what was that? There was a cement mixer pouring large quantities of the thick gray stuff over the surface of Tom's backyard. Tom, Panama hat on head, was directing the desecration. Marty shrieked.

"Have you lost your mind?"

"What's the problem?" replied Tom, with a calm that made Marty suspect he was too late to taste the cider.

"What on earth are you doing? Remember when I was threatening to pave *my* yard? How you talked me out of it with all that 20-minute stuff about bringing it under control and having fun? And it worked. You should see the papyrus in my garden now, I could film *The Ten Commandments* there.

"I can't believe that you, Mr. 20-Minute Gardener, are actually paving over your garden. Why don't you just plant some of that nicotiana around the edge? A real pond would look attractive, and it doesn't take much time. Or maybe some of those trees from Brooklyn you love so much."

"Marty," said Tom, "who's paving over the garden?"

"What's the cement mixer doing, then?"

"I decided it's too much work taking care of all this greenery, and we wanted a spot where we could have dinner outside and maybe set out some pots of herbs. So I decided to experiment with what we horticulturists call *hardscape*."

"Give me a break, Tom. When I left the city, I swore that I'd never add one bit of concrete to the world. That I would leave it as natural as I found it."

"So you planted papyrus in Westport. Listen, natural is nice, but who's to say that pavement isn't natural? I remember a great desert garden I visited once in Tucson. Gravel and rock are the natural surfaces in the desert, and the lady had turned her garden into a patchwork of different pavements and rock-edged pools with just a plant here and there. It was spectacular, practical, and perfect for the site.

"And the guy in Santa Barbara who lived in his garden. What could be more natural than that? He had an old claw-footed tub set over the barbecue pit so he could take hot baths after supper. There was a phone right there, sitting on a rock.

"Did I ever tell you about the wildlife garden specialist in New Jersey who built a feeding station for vultures in his backyard? He was always looking for roadkills—"

"That's enough." Marty shuddered. Tom looked at him with concern and invited him in; there *was* a bottle left, after all.

"Hardscape, huh?" Marty muttered.

"Pavement-free zone," Tom shot back as he pulled the cork.

"So maybe we have different ideas about what a garden ought to be."

"Maybe we do."

That's 20-minute gardening.

Sources

(Note: where there is a fee charged for a catalog, that sum is typically applied against the cost of the first order.)

Chapter 5: The 20-Minute Toolshed

A. M. Leonard, Inc.
PO Box 816
241 Fox Drive
Piqua, OH 45356
telephone 513-773-2694
catalog free

The Walt Nicke Company
PO Box 433
Topsfield, MA 01983
telephone 508-887-3388
catalog free

Lehman Hardware & Appliances, Inc.
PO Box 41
1 Lehman Circle
Kidron, OH 44636
telephone 330-857-5757
catalog $3

Chapter 6: Tom's Guide to Connoisseur Plants

Japanese pagoda tree (Sophora japonica)
Carroll Gardens
444 East Main Street
Westminster, MD 21157
telephone 410-848-5422
catalog $3

Cedar of Lebanon (Cedrus libani)
Forestfarm
990 Tetherow Road
Williams, OR 97544
telephone 541-846-7269
catalog $4

Sourwood tree (Oxydendrum arboreum)
Greer Gardens
1280 Goodpasture Island Road
Eugene, OR 97401
telephone 541-686-8266
catalog $3

see also Carroll Gardens, above

American persimmon tree (Diospyros virginiana)
Bear Creek Nursery
PO Box 411
Northport, WA 99157
catalog free

Tree of heaven (Ailanthus altissima)
see Forestfarm, above

Wintersweet (Chimonanthus praecox)
Wayside Gardens
1 Garden Lane
Hodges, SC 29695
telephone 800-845-1124
catalog free

see also Greer Gardens, above

Rose-gold pussy willow (Salix gracilistyla)
Carroll Gardens, Forestfarm, and Wayside Gardens (see above) all list the cultivar 'melanostachys' in their catalogs.

Graveyard roses
If you are too lazy to root cuttings yourself, you will find a good selection of "found" roses adapted to Southern climates and soils at The Antique Rose Emporium (Route 5, Box 143, Brenham, TX 77833, telephone 409-836-9051, catalog $5). Heritage Rose Gardens (40350 Wilderness Road, Branscomb, CA 95417, catalog $1.50) lists a wide variety of old-fashioned roses, including many originally collected in various sites around California. Lowe's Own Root Roses (6 Sheffield Road, Nashua, NH 03062, telephone 603-888-2214, catalog $2) maintains an outstanding selection of antique roses, including some that the proprietor Malcolm Lowe originally found in the course of his expeditions.

Japanese stewartia (Stewartia pseudocamellia)
Carroll Gardens, Forestfarm, Greer Gardens, and Wayside Gardens all offer this plant.

Hardy orange (Poncirus trifoliata)
Woodlander's, Inc.
1128 Colleton Avenue
Aiken, SC 29801
telephone 803-648-7522
catalog $2 for a two-year subscription

see also Carroll Gardens and Greer Gardens, above

Scarlet runner beans (Phaseolus coccineus)

J. L. Hudson Seedsman
PO Box 1058
Redwood City, CA 94064
catalog $1

Stokes Seeds, Inc.
Box 548
Buffalo, NY 14240
telephone 716-695-6980
catalog free

Okra (Abelmoschus esculentus *'Burgundy'*)
Johnny's Selected Seeds
Foss Hill Road
Albion, ME 04910
telephone 207-437-9294
catalog free

Sunflowers (Helianthus *spp.*)
Willow-leaved sunflower (Helianthus salicifolius)
Kurt Bluemel, Inc.
2740 Greene Lane
Baldwin, MD 21013
catalog $3

Jerusalem artichoke (Helianthus tuberosus)
W. Atlee Burpee & Co.
300 Park Avenue
Warminster, PA 18974
telephone 800-888-1447
catalog free

English lavender (Lavandula angustifolia), *French lavender*
(Lavandula dentata), *Spanish lavender* (Lavandula stoechas)
Logee's Greenhouses
141 North Street
Danielson, CT 06239
telephone 860-774-8038
catalog $3

Woodruff (Galium odoratum)
see Logee's Greenhouses, above

Garden cress (Lepidium sativum *var.* crispum)
The Cook's Garden
PO Box 535
Londonderry, VT 05148
telephone 802-824-3400
catalog free

Chapter 7: Marty's Top Ten Garden Plants

Blueberries (Vaccinium *spp.*) *for the North*

Henry Field's Seed &
Nursery Co.
415 North Burnett Street
Shenandoah, IA 51602
telephone 605-665-4491
catalog free

J. E. Miller Nurseries, Inc.
5060 West Lake Road
Canandaigua, NY 14424
telephone 800-836-9630
catalog free

see also Forestfarm, above

Blueberries for the South
Edible Landscaping
PO Box 77
Afton, VA 22920
telephone 804-361-9134
catalog free

Strawberries (Fragaria)
see W. Atlee Burpee, Henry Field's Seed & Nursery Co., and J. E. Miller Nurseries, Inc., above

Crown daisy (Chrysanthemum coronarium)
Thompson & Morgan
PO Box 1308
Jackson, NJ 08527
telephone 800-274-7333
catalog free

English daisy (Bellis perennis)
see Thompson & Morgan, above

Feverfew (Tanacetum parthenium)
Nichols Garden Nursery, Inc.
1190 N. Pacific Highway
Albany, OR 97321
telephone 541-928-9280
catalog free

see Thompson & Morgan, above

Marguerite daisy (Argyranthemum frutescens)
see Logee's Greenhouses, above

Oxeye daisy (Leucanthemum vulgare)
see J. L. Hudson Seedsman, above

Painted daisy (Tanacetum coccineum)

Bluestone Perennials	Milaeger's Gardens
7211 Middle Ridge Road	4838 Douglas Avenue
Madison, OH 44057	Racine, WI 53402
telephone 216-428-7535	telephone 414-639-2371
catalog free	catalog $1

African daisy (Arctotis venusta)
see Thompson & Morgan, above

'Heritage' river birch (Betula nigra *'Heritage'*)
see Carroll Gardens, above

Daffodils (Narcissus)
The Daffodil Mart
7463 Heath Trail
Gloucester, VA 23061
telephone 804-693-3966
catalog free

Herbs
see Nichols Garden Nursery, above

Ferns
Fancy Fronds
1911-4th Avenue West
Seattle, WA 98119
telephone 360-793-1472
catalog $1

Hostas
Klehm Nursery
4210 N. Duncan Road
Champaign, IL 61821
telephone 800-553-3715
catalog $4

Chapter 9: Peter Rabbit Had It Coming

Electric fences
Deer Busters
9735-A Bethel Road
Frederick, MD 21702
telephone 800-248-3337
catalog free

Drip irrigation kits and equipment

Gardener's Supply Company	Dripworks
128 Intervale Road	380 Maple Street
Burlington, VT 05401	Willits, CA 95490
telephone 800-234-6630	telephone 800-522-3747
catalog free	catalog free

20-Minute Projects

Night-blooming plants
Pinetree Garden Seeds
Box 300
New Gloucester, ME 04260
telephone 207-926-3400
catalog free

Tillandsias
Holladay Jungle
PO Box 5727
1602 E. Fountain Way
Fresno, CA 93755
telephone 209-229-9858
price list free

Composters
SolarCone, Inc.
PO Box 67
Seward, IL 61077
telephone 800-80-SOLAR

Coleus
Color Farm Growers
2710 Thornhill Road
Auburndale, FL 33823
telephone 941-967-9895
price list free

Stokes Seeds (see above) offers seed of twenty-five cultivars

Nicotiana
see Pinetree Garden Seeds, above

Water plants
Lilypons Water Gardens
PO Box 10
Buckeystown, MD 21717
telephone 301-874-5133
catalog free

Window box herbs
Well-Sweep Herb Farm
205 Mt. Bethel Road
Port Murray, NJ 07865
telephone 908-852-5390
catalog $2

see also Nichols Garden Nursery,
above

Dutch Bulbs
Dutch Gardens, Inc.
PO Box 200
Adelphia, NJ 07710
telephone 800-818-3861
catalog free

see also The Daffodil Mart, above

Seed Mats
Smith & Hawken
2 Arbor Lane
PO Box 6900
Florence, KY 41022
telephone 800-776-3336
catalog free

William Tricker, Inc.
7125 Tanglewood Drive
Independence, OH 44131
telephone 216-524-3491
catalog $2

Summer-blooming bulbs
Cruickshank's Inc.
1015 Mount Pleasant Road
Toronto, ON, Canada M4P 2M1
telephone 800-665-5605
catalog $3

McClure & Zimmerman
PO Box 368
108 W. Winnebago
Friesland, WI 53935
telephone 414-326-4220
catalog free

see also Dutch Gardens, above

The Waushara Gardens
N5491 5th Drive
Plainfield, WI 54966
telephone 715-335-4462
catalog $1

Moonflowers
see Pinetree Garden Seeds, above

Garden thugs
tiger lily (*Lilium lancifolium*)
Jacques Amand
PO Box 59001
Potomac, MD 20859
telephone 800-452-5414
catalog $2

(*Lilium lancifolium* is listed as *Lilium tigrinum* here)

stiff goldenrod (*Solidago rigida*), big bluestem (*Andropogon gerardii*), prairie dropseed (*Sporobolus heterolepsis*), wild bergamot (*Monarda fistulosa*)
Prairie Nursery
PO Box 306
Westfield, WI 53964
telephone 608-296-3679
catalog $3 for a two-year subscription

giant Chinese silver grass (*Miscanthus floridulus*), willow-leaved sunflower (*Helianthus salicifolius*), switch grass (*Panicum virgatum* 'Heavy Metal')
see Kurt Bluemel, above

yellow flag (*Iris pseudacorus*)
see Carroll Gardens, above

oriental poppies (*Papaver orientalis*)
see Bluestone Perennials and Wayside Gardens, above

Japanese plume poppy (*Macleaya cordata*)
see Carroll Gardens, above

Tartarian Aster (*Aster tataricus*)
see Carroll Gardens, above

Acknowledgments

We owe a large measure of thanks to our families, in particular to our wives, Judy and Suzanne, who remained supportive (within reason) through our sometimes strange horticultural experiments, and in many cases contributed the effort (20 minutes daily) that made them work. Tom wants also to thank his son, Matthew, who took a personal interest in the 20-minute projects, transforming them in ways no adult could have imagined. Marty thanks his Daniel and Madeleine for their priceless insights into the arcane labor habits of teenagers.

In addition, we wish to thank once again the astonishing librarians of the New York Botanical Garden, who serve up the most amazing research materials in the most matter-of-fact way. Dora Galitzki, in particular, the Botanical Garden's plant information specialist, demonstrated a superhuman patience in answering our telephone calls, and mixed advice with information in the most tactful way.

Thanks to Sal Gilbertie for his insights into the psyche of horticultural shoppers, and to Judy Glattstein for showing us how to look at old gardens with a fresh eye.

Jane Herold and Ruth Lively both contributed invaluable female perspectives on what was threatening to become too male a manuscript. And how can we adequately express our gratitude to Felder Rushing, who initiated us into the garden mysteries of the Mississippi Delta, and drove his pickup truck all the way from Jackson to Connecticut to personally deliver an antique cast-iron plantation bell?

And finally thanks to Ann Godoff for helping us cut to the chase and for being there at the finish line.

ABOUT THE AUTHORS

TOM CHRISTOPHER is a professional horticulturist. His first book, *In Search of Lost Roses*, won the 1990 Quill and Trowel Award of Excellence of the Garden Writers Association of America. He has written for publications such as *The New York Times* and *Martha Stewart Living*, given programs at botanic gardens, arboreta, and museums all over the United States, and has been featured on National Public Radio. He lives in Middletown, Connecticut.

MARTY ASHER is editor in chief of Vintage Books. He is the author of a novel, *Shelter* (Arbor House), and *57 Reasons Not to Have a Nuclear War* (Warner Books). His humor pieces have appeared on *The New York Times* op-ed page and in *Newsday*. He lives in Westport, Connecticut.

ABOUT THE TYPE

This book was set in Sabon, a typeface designed by the well-known German typographer Jan Tschichold (1902–74). Sabon's design is based on the original letterforms of Claude Garamond and was created specifically to be used for three sources: foundry type for hand composition, Linotype, and Monotype. Tschichold named his typeface for the famous Frankfurt typefounder Jacques Sabon, who died in 1580.